WHERE
DEAD VOICES
GATHER

ALSO BY NICK TOSCHES

Country

Hellfire

Unsung Heroes of Rock 'n' Roll

Power on Earth

Cut Numbers

Dino

Trinities

Chaldea

The Nick Tosches Reader

The Devil and Sonny Liston

WHERE

DEAD VOICES

GATHER

NICK TOSCHES

LITTLE, BROWN AND COMPANY
BOSTON   NEW YORK   LONDON

First Edition

Library of Congress Cataloging-in-Publication Data
Tosches, Nick.
Where dead voices gather / Nick Tosches — 1st ed.
p.   cm.
Includes index.
ISBN 0-316-89507-5
1. Miller, Emmett, 1900–1962.   2. Singers — United States —
Biography.   3. Blackface entertainers — United States —
Biography.   I. Title.

ML420.M509 T68 2001
782.42164'092 — dc21
[B]   2001018608

10 9 8 7 6 5 4 3 2 1

Designed by Paula Russell Szafranski

Q-FF

Printed in the United States of America

Mashed Potatoes started long time ago.

—Dee Dee Sharp

In the beginning was the Word.

—John 1:1

Alternative music sucks. Blows dead dogs. I hate alternative music. I hate alternative people. They can all kiss my ass. Let's go have a big steak and fuck without a rubber and do some heroin afterward.

—James "Iggy Pop" Osterberg

WHERE
DEAD VOICES
GATHER

Many years ago, I wrote a book called *Country*. Two of the chapters closest to its heart were devoted to the mystery of Emmett Miller, whose startling and mesmerizing music seemed to be a Rosetta Stone to the understanding of the mixed and mongrel bloodlines of country and blues, of jazz and pop, of all that we know as American music.

The alchemy of Emmett Miller's music is as startling today as it was when he wrought it. Definable neither as country nor as blues, as jazz nor as pop, as black nor as white, but as both culmination and transcendence of these bloodlines and more, that alchemy, that music, stands as one of the most wondrous emanations, a birth-cry really, of the many-faced and one-souled chimera of all that has come to be called American music. The very concept of him — a white man in blackface, a hillbilly singer and a jazz singer both, a son of the deep South and a roué of Broadway — is at once unique, mythic, and a perfect representation of the schizophrenic heart of what this country, with a straight face, calls its culture.

I first became intrigued by the elusive figure of Emmett Miller in 1974. I may have been vaguely aware of him before then, but it was *I Love Dixie Blues,* the album Merle Haggard dedicated in part to Miller's music, that truly whetted my curiosity. In the bargain bin of a record store on Eighth Street in New York, I found a copy of an album whose stark and drab cover was ugly even by bootleg standards: title misspelled in plain black lettering on plain yellow stock. But this cover belied not only the beautiful disc of clear green vinyl that lay within, but more so the wonder of what that green vinyl held. Issued by the Old Masters label in 1969, *Emmet Miller Acc. by His Georgia Crackers* had been the first in a series of limited-edition pressings for jazz collectors; the spelling of Miller's name was obviously not as important as the fact that these recordings featured rare performances by Tommy and Jimmy Dorsey, Eddie Lang, and Gene Krupa. Subsequently reissued on common black vinyl but with Miller's name spelled right, in black on white, this album remained the sole available collection of Miller's work for more than a quarter of a century, superseded only in 1996 by *Emmett Miller: The Minstrel Man from Georgia,* a Columbia/Legacy CD that included six recordings more than the earlier album.

When I heard Miller's actual voice, forthshining from the coruscations of those slow-spinning emerald grooves, I was astounded, and my search for information on him began in earnest. What little I found was included three years later in *Country.* "It is not known exactly when Emmett Miller was born or when he died," I wrote. "Nor is it known where he came from or where he went. We don't even know what he looked like, really."

For a long time, these statements remained true. In November of 1988, eleven years to the month after the publication of *Country,* another book — bigger and more lavish, but with a similar title — brought forth the first published photograph of Miller. The book was *Country: The Music and the Musicians,* produced by the Country Music Foundation and Abbeville Press. I wrote the chapter on honky-tonk, in which I devoted two paragraphs to Miller's influence on Hank Williams; and it was in this context that the photograph of Miller, middle-aged and in blackface, appeared as an illustration. Five years later, Abbeville published a parallel volume called *Nothing But the Blues: The Music and the Musicians,* in which a second picture of Miller, also in blackface, accompanied four paragraphs on him, as an influence on Jimmie Rodgers, in a chapter by Charles Wolfe on white country blues. But beyond these curious masked images, the mystery of Emmett Miller remained largely unsolved, and the words I'd written long ago remained largely true.

In 1994, in a *Journal of Country Music* article called "The Strange and Hermetical Case of Emmett Miller," I set forth all that had been discovered regarding Miller since the writing of *Country.* And yet, even then, it could not be said with certainty exactly when or where he was born, or exactly when or where he died, or even whether Emmett Miller was really his name. The paragraphs on Miller in *Nothing But the Blues* stated with an air of certitude that "Miller was born in Macon, Georgia, in 1903." This assertion would be repeated by Wolfe a few years later in the notes to the *Minstrel Man from Georgia* CD: "Emmett Miller, we now know, was from Macon, Georgia, born there in 1903. His parents were longtime residents of the area, and owned a nearby farm." But no evidence for these "facts" was offered, and I chose to doubt them. As it turned out, I was right to doubt: Emmett Miller was not born in 1903, and drinking milk was probably the closest his family came to owning a farm.

But for all my sensible doubting and senseless searching, the mystery of Emmett Miller, after twenty years, remained unsolved. And who cared? Indeed, when I stopped to think of it, I wondered what end this search could serve, except, as it did, to distract me from more meaningful and lucrative pursuits. Unfinished poems, an unfinished novel, magazine assignments were pushed aside, and for what? To follow a ghost? This distraction from more meaningful and lucrative pursuits had, for me, a strong, perhaps pathological appeal; but that did not explain it, for there are other far more enjoyable distractions. Ultimately I did not and could not, I do not and cannot, explain it. I can say that the search, the mystery, was twofold. Who was this guy — when was he born, when did he die? And what was the source of his music, vanished in the undocumented darkness and the lost and unknown recordings of an unexplored subculture? Whether seen as detective work or archeology, as serious investigation or deranged folly, the case of Emmett Miller was not without its gratifications, its thrills and satisfactions of discovery and of learning.

As for its being without meaning, it now has occurred to me, in the few sentences since my mention of more meaningful and lucrative pursuits, that, after all is said and done, meaning is the biggest sucker's-racket of all; and any regard for it, no matter how fleeting, befits a middle-aged fool like me. So meaning be damned; on with these words.

In the spring of 1996, as was I revising and expanding the *Journal* article to appear as the appendix to the reprint of *Country* published by Da Capo Press, I received a call from my friend and intrepid cohort Bret Wood.

Earlier Bret had found, amid handwritten records of the Thirteenth Census of the United States (1910), evidence of a thirteen-year-old white male named Emmett Miller living with his family in the town of Barnesville, in Pike County, Georgia, about midway between Atlanta and Macon.

For years I had been unsure that Emmett Miller was the real name of the person whose identity I sought. Poring through the "Minstrelsy" columns of issues of *Billboard* from the 1920s, on reel after reel of microfilm, I had come across many obscure performers named Emmett. Too many. I suspected that the name of Emmett had been taken commonly by minstrels to evoke the name of Daniel Decatur Emmett, the most celebrated of the old-time minstrels. I thought this might help to explain why no biographical facts had been unearthed regarding the birth, death, or offstage life of Emmett Miller. At the same time, removing the possible baffle of his first name left only a surname so common that his true identity might never be found.

But here was an actual Emmett Miller. The Barnesville census was enumerated on April 27, 1910; the thirteen-year-old Emmett Miller was listed as the son of one Walter Moore. Why his surname, like that of his four siblings, was different from his father's was a perplexing detail; but any detail, no matter how perplexing, was welcome amid the vaster perplexing vagueness of the search for Emmett Miller. For all my doubts regarding the accepted "facts" of Emmett Miller's origin, I shared the assumption, based on a 1928 published reference to him as "the young man from Macon," that Macon was indeed his hometown. But I figured now that Miller might have named that nearby and well-known town as such instead of small, little-known Barnesville. The census record would fix his year of birth at 1896 or 1897. There seemed to be no other documentation of an Emmett Miller that presented itself as a possibility. A thirty-year-old mulatto house-mover boarding in Macon was found in the census of 1920: an unlikely candidate. While Bret drew no conclusions, I rashly did, and offered them just as rashly in the letters section of the *Journal of Country Music,* Vol. 17, No. 3. This proposed evidence, I dare say, met with no little acceptance by the esteemed and eminent community of Millerologists at large; and I felt that a search of nearly twenty years was nearing its end.

But alas, as they say in the funnybooks, alas.

Then, on April 4, 1996, in the state archives at Atlanta, Bret found the document that would at long last truly serve as the key to the mystery of Emmett Miller.

There would be no record of Emmett Miller's birth. We knew that much. Birth certificates, registrations of birth, were not legally required in Georgia until 1919. Until that time, they were rare, especially for children born at home, as most were. Though access to existing birth records in Georgia is restricted to the persons whose records they are, a worker at the Bibb County Health Department in Macon was both able and kind to confirm that there was, as expected, no birth certificate in the name of Emmett Miller. The offices of the health department are located on Hemlock Street: an irony here compounded, for it was through Emmett Miller's death, and not his birth, that the story of his life opened to me.

The revelatory document that Bret found in the state capital was a certificate of death, Georgia State File No. 9378: a record of finality that might serve as well, I hoped, to seal and lay to rest an obsession.

There was time to incorporate only the barest elements of this discovery into the *Country* appendix. That done, Bret and I arranged to travel to Macon, to where the clues of this document beckoned. "Emmett Miller: The Final Chapter," an account based on what we gathered, the missing pieces of the life of Emmett Miller, was written for the *Journal of Country Music*. Though I was the author of that account, it could not have been written without the work of Bret Wood, for whose inspired research skills I here express my profound respect, and for whose selfless dedication to this loss-intensive project, my profounder gratitude.

The article proved to be far from a final chapter. Even as I readied it for publication, I knew that there was more to be discovered, that further exploration lay before me. What follows, these years later, is a synthesis — a bringing to harmony, a bringing to culmination — of all that I have written regarding Emmett Miller, and of all that I have learned regarding Emmett Miller. Above all, it is a bringing to an end of a mystery — and the bringing to light, however dim, of a far bigger mystery, and the journey to solve that bigger mystery in turn: through kerosene lamp and light of neon and no light at all, through palimpsest and shards, the echoic whisperings of ghosts, howls from hidden vanished places, loud electric crackling rhythms and cries of seers and fools, all-telling breezes, no-telling winds.

Emmett Miller came out of the minstrelsy tradition. Yes, out of that tradition so named, since at least the thirteenth century, in its archaic and poetic sense of making music and song, the art of the minstrels, a word from the Old French, from the age of those minstrels whose music filled the castles and the air and the poetry of the age of Dante. But more so out of that particularly American tradition like-named since the 1840s. Strange, perhaps, even to call it a tradition, since it flourished for little more than eighty years, the mere span of a fortunate human life. But in a culture whose own age is barely thrice that, American minstrelsy, the longest-lived emanation of that culture, had by its autumn become a tradition indeed.

That tradition, which dominated American music and show business from the middle of the nineteenth century until after the turn of the twentieth, was — simply, bizarrely, inexplicably — a form of stage entertainment in which men blackened their faces, burlesqued the demeanor and behavior of Southern blacks, and performed what were presented as the songs and music of those blacks. At first confined to small performances in Manhattan, minstrelsy shows grew into immense touring troupes that were the most popular mass medium of an age before phonograph recordings, flickering images, and electrical broadcasts removed the element of geography from the commerce of entertainment. And in that later age, some of the earliest stars of those recordings, flickering images, and electrical broadcasts — Al Jolson foremost among them — were born of blackface minstrelsy.

It was a tradition whose documented roots can be dated to the performance of Lewis Hallam, blacked-up as Mungo, in Charles Dibdin's comic opera *The Padlock* at the John Street Theatre, New York City, on May 29, 1769. Thirty years later, on December 30, 1799, at the Federal Street Theatre, Boston, the German-born Gottlieb Graupner sang "The Gay Negro Boy" in black caricature in Aphra Behn's *Oroonoko*. It was a tradition that was born in the North and died in the South.

The first celebrated blackface singers rose to fame in the late 1820s and early 1830s. George Washington Dixon was said to be known as early as 1827 for his Albany performances of "The Coal Black Rose" and "My Long-Tail Blue," which he brought to the Lafayette Theatre in New York on July 19, 1828. (The "long-tail blue" was the swallowtail jacket emblematic of the wardrobe of urban black dandies — zip coons — of the early nineteenth century. Dixon's "Zip Coon" celebrated such a dandy in 1834, and the engraving on the cover of the sheet music portrayed a zip coon in just such a jacket.) Dixon is believed to have been jailed frequently for slanderous writings and acts of civil disturbance, and it was written of him that he "later became notorious as a filibuster during the Yucatan disturbances, and died in New Orleans in 1861." Thomas Dartmouth (Daddy) Rice (1808–60) was known by 1831 for his song-and-dance routine "Jim Crow."

In the Petersburg, Virginia, *Farmer's Register* of April 1, 1838, William B. Smith published an account of his experiences at a "beer dance" held by slaves on a neighboring plantation. He described their dancing, recorded bits of their song and speech, and concluded with the observation that "Virginia slaves were the happiest of the human race."

Not quite five years later, on February 6, 1843, the Virginia Minstrels, the first regularly organized blackface group, made their debut at the Bowery Amphitheatre in New York. Bills for the show that Monday evening announced "the novel, grotesque, original and surpassingly melodious Ethiopian Band entitled THE VIRGINIA MINSTRELS"; and it was not long before all blackface performers came to be called minstrels.

It was with the Virginia Minstrels and their successors that blackface minstrelsy became the heart of nineteenth-century show business, the first emanation of a pervasive and purely American mass culture; though, like most subsequent emanations of American culture, its vogue soon spread abroad to England.

Collections of minstrelsy date to the publication in 1843 in Boston of *The Celebrated Negro Melodies, as Sung by the Virginia Minstrels,* arranged by Thomas Comer (1790–1862), a popular Boston music-man who also published in that year his arrangement of "The Tiger Quick Step." The first serious survey of the subject, Allston T. Brown's *Early History of Negro Minstrelsy,* came in 1874. Brown (1836–1918), who worked as a theatrical agent and journalist in New York from 1860 until his death, was the author of the 1870 *History of the American Stage,* which he would later expand into the three-volume *History of the American Stage from the First Performance in 1732 to 1901.* (In the same year that Brown's *Early History of American Minstrelsy* was published came, from the same publisher, R. M. DeWitt of New York, Charles Day's *Fun in Black.* It was the house of DeWitt that had published Richard Drake's *Revelations of a Slave Smuggler* in 1860.)

Following Brown's 1874 work, the chronicling of minstrelsy began anew in earnest in 1909, with Edward Le Roy Rice's little booklet *1000 Men of Minstrelsy; 1 Woman,* which preceded his full volume, *Monarchs of Minstrelsy, from "Daddy" Rice to Date,* published in 1911. Since then, shelves of books have been written about minstrelsy. In recent years, much of an interpretive nature has been written of this first indigenous American theatrical form, and of blackface as its central element. Michael Rogin, a professor of political science at the University of California, Berkeley, writes in *Blackface, White Noise: Jewish Immigrants in the Hollywood Melting Pot* (1996): "Seen in blackface and from the South, the United States is at once a *Herrenvolk* republic, where racial subordination hides class inequality, and a capitalist society permeated by longing for a lost, pre-industrial, feudal home."

Rogin's study is valuable, interesting, and often astute, but the sort of fatuous nonsense here quoted is typical of the pseudo-intellectual parlor games endemic to such interpretative exercises. As noted and as we shall further see, blackface minstrelsy was born not of the South but of the North, and its vision, though embraced by the South, was of the urban Northeast; and as we shall also see, the popularity of blackface minstrelsy, America's first cultural export, was as great in England as at home. To speak with a straight face of minstrelsy in terms of *Herrenvolk,* the Nazi concept of master-race, or in terms of ancestral feudal memories is to illuminate not so much the subject at hand but rather the essential folly of academic thinking. When the scholar here quoted invokes Jacques Lacan in his analysis of *Jolson Sings Again,* we enter a realm of fantasy beyond that of minstrelsy itself, an *intentio-lectoris* sideshow as vapid and as ridiculous in its pretensions as Sartre's misreadings of Faulkner.

The scholar under scrutiny is not alone. I have books here with titles such as *Inside the Minstrel Mask: Readings in Nineteenth-Century Blackface Minstrelsy* (1996), *Demons of Disorder: Early Blackface Minstrels and Their World* (1997), *Raising Cain: Blackface Performance from Jim Crow to Hip Hop* (1998), and *A Right to Sing the Blues: African Americans, Jews, and American Popular Song* (1999), which attempts to reconcile the Jewish takeover of latter-day blackface minstrelsy — through performers such as Al Jolson and coon-song composers such as Irving Berlin — with the problematic but cherished expiatory notion of a common bond between the black and Jewish "experiences." All these books have value, albeit not always equal to their list prices, but in every case that value is undermined by specious theory and academic gibberish. Eric Lott in *Love and Theft: Blackface Minstrelsy and the American Working Class* (1993), sees minstrelsy as emblematic of "cross-racial desire," as "less a sign of absolute white power and control than of panic, anxiety, terror, and pleasure." The *New York Times* captioned its review of Lott's book "Minstrel Tradition: Not Just a Racist Relic," as if to imply that the blackface caricatures of minstrelsy were somehow more racist than the insidious stereotype of today's popular entertainment; as if to imply the playing of blacks by whites to be more demeaning or momentous an absurdity than the playing of Italians by Jews and WASPs, from *Little Caesar* to *The Godfather,* and every other manner of ethnic fraud upon which our popular culture has to this day been based.

Yes. Minstrelsy was a form of stage entertainment in which men blackened their faces, burlesqued the demeanor and behavior of Southern blacks, and, above all, performed what were presented as the songs and music of those blacks. But it was not so simple as that. Not all minstrels were white: many of those who blackened their faces in burlesque were black. And while the songs and music of minstrelsy were indeed usually far from black in origin, the impact of those songs and that music was profound upon the inchoate and gestative forms of blues and jazz. As for the grotesquerie of minstrelsy, there were many, both black and white, who found it no more offensive than the comedy built upon any exaggerated ethnic stereotyping. As late as 1922, a debate was carried on in earnest in the pages of the *New York Herald* as to whether blacks or whites were better at playing blacks: "Your correspondent who signs himself 'Negro' makes a mistake in taking issue with Herbert S. Renton on the comparative merits of white men and negros as blackface performers." And it must be remembered that minstrelsy was born in the anti-slavery climate of the emancipatory North, in the most sophisticated and cosmopolitan city of America.

If minstrelsy is to be understood, it must be seen neither with myopic simplicity, as a "racist relic" — a phrase no less applicable to the *Times* than to the subject under review — nor as a textbook manifestation of ideology or psychology.

Now that I have ingratiated myself with that arbiter of literary consumerism, let us return to, and dispense with, the question at hand — indeed, with all questions better suited to advertising copy than to a mind freed from the cheap fetters of store-bought, off-the-rack intellect.

Thus: where did minstrelsy come from, and what was it all about? How about: what is the meaning of rock 'n' roll? Hell, it's like the man says: if you've got to ask, you'll never know.

Besides, this is not a book about minstrelsy any more or less than it is a book about rock 'n' roll. Besides, Emmett Miller's was a voice from the death, not the life, of minstrelsy; a voice from Erebus. Besides, this is not really a book about Emmett Miller. It is a book about that Rosetta Stone, a book about that Erebus.

So let us have nothing of the proper thought of fools and mediocrity and misknowing. Let our excavations in the graveyard of data, our journey through the haunted carnival of endless night, be undefiled by thought itself, which, in Miller studies as in life, is the enemy of truth as of the soul.

The leader of the Virginia Minstrels was a twenty-eight-year-old Yankee named Daniel Decatur Emmett (1815–1904), who was said to have first blacked-up at the age of sixteen, in the year of Daddy Rice's "Jim Crow." With him in the Virginia Minstrels were three others: Frank Brower (1823–74); Dick Pelham (1815–76), whose real name was Richard Ward Pell; and Billy Whitlock (1813–78). The group did not last a year; they disbanded following a British tour later in 1843. By then there were the Ethiopian Serenaders, also known as the Boston Minstrels, and the Congo Melodists of British-born James Buckley (1803–72), later known as Buckley's New Orleans Serenaders. In England, where the presence of blacks was all but unknown, the popularity of blackface minstrelsy was immediate and great; and blackface would survive there as a part of popular culture long after it had been suppressed and forsaken in its native America. In a way, England's exposure to American minstrelsy was not without antecedents. Charles Didbin, the author of *The Padlock,* mentioned above, was a British gentleman whose noble-savage blackamoor songs, popular in the taverns and drawing rooms of late-eighteenth-century England, had portrayed blacks as figures both comical and emblematic of a wistful and pitiable innocence, portrayals not unlike those of early minstrelsy.

Christy's Minstrels, the most famous of the New York shows, were active by May of 1844; and there were the Kentucky Minstrels, and the Ring and Parker Minstrels. In an 1846 article called "True American Singing," Walt Whitman professed a liking for a minstrel group called the Harmoneons: "Indeed, their negro singing altogether proves how shiningly golden talent can be spread over a subject generally considered 'low.'"

Whitman (1819–92) was a devotee of minstrelsy, of what he called "nigger songs." He saw Daddy Rice perform often; wrote of minstrel bands, including the Christy Minstrels, for the *Brooklyn Star* and the *Brooklyn Daily Eagle* in 1846–47; considered Stephen Foster's songs to be "our best work so far" in American music. Regard for Foster was shared by Abraham Lincoln (1809–65), who also possessed a fondness for minstrelsy, and by Frederick Douglass (1817–95), who had escaped from slavery in 1838, and who described Foster's songs as expressive of "the finest feelings of human nature."

It should also be noted, however, that Douglass had no such praise for minstrelsy, which he described in 1848 as "sporting over the miseries and misfortunes of an oppressed people." Those so engaged were "contemptible." He named the Virginia Minstrels, the Christy Minstrels, the Ethiopian Serenaders as "the filthy scum of white society, who have stolen from us a complexion denied to them by nature, in which to make money, and pander to the corrupt taste of their white fellow citizens."

Stephen Collins Foster (1826–64), a native of Pittsburgh, was the first American to make a living writing songs. What he knew of the South, he learned through minstrel shows — a job as a bookkeeper for his brother in Cincinnati in 1846 had brought him as far south as he had been — and his vision of the South, beginning with his *Songs of the Sable Harmonists* of 1848, in turn gave minstrelsy, and America, its most popular and abiding songs: "Oh! Susanna" (1847), "Camptown Races" (1850), "The Old Folks at Home" (1851), "Massa's in de Cold, Cold Ground" (1852), "My Old Kentucky Home" (1853), "Jeanie with the Light Brown Hair" (1854), "Old Black Joe" (1860) — roughly a hundred seventy-five of them. Foster's South, the South of minstrelsy, a South dreamt by the North, was a romance embraced by the South itself; for the greatest nostalgia is that for what has never truly been.

Foster published his first composition ("Open Thy Lattice, Love") in 1844 at the age of eighteen. Three years later, "Susanna," which came to be known as "Oh! Susanna," was published "as sung by G. N. Christy," the lead singer of the Christy Minstrels.

Prior to its publication, "Susanna" had been popularized in Pittsburgh by local blackface acts such as the Sable Brothers and the music-hall singer Nelson Kneass. Ironically, given his affection for Foster's music, it was a report of the Sable Brothers' shows at the Eagle Saloon that provoked Frederick Douglass to his denunciation of such performers as "contemptible." As the popularity of "Susanna" spread beyond Pittsburgh, the song was picked up by Christy, who made it a part of his record-breaking New York show.

This was the beginning of an arrangement whereby Foster's songs were commonly published in the name of Edwin P. Christy (1815–62), the founder and interlocutor of Christy's Minstrels, whose performances of Foster's songs in the late 1840s and early 1850s were to a great extent responsible for Foster's success. Foster later wished to renege on this arrangement: his minstrel songs at first had embarrassed him; now he wanted his name associated with their success. He wrote to Christy in May of 1852, addressing him impersonally as "Dear Sir":

"As I once intimated to you, I had the intention of omitting my name on my Ethiopian songs, owing to the prejudice against them by some, which might injure my reputation as a writer in another style of music, but I find that by my efforts I have done a great deal to build up a taste for the Ethiopian songs among refined people by making the words suitable to their taste, instead of the trashy and really offensive words which belong to some songs of that order. Therefore I have concluded to reinstate my name on my songs and to pursue the Ethiopian business without fear or shame and lend all my energies to making the business live, at the same time that I will wish to establish my name as the best Ethiopian song-writer. But I am not encouraged in undertaking this so long as 'The Old Folks at Home' stares me in the face with another's name on it. As it was at my own solicitation that you allowed your name to be placed on the song, I hope that the above reasons will be sufficient explanation for my desire to place my own name on it as author and composer, while at the same time I wish to leave the name of your band on the title page. This is a little matter of pride in myself which it will certainly be to your interest to encourage."

Foster went on in his letter to offer a refund of money already paid him by Christy, as well as his promise of "an opening chorus in my best style, free of charge, and in any other way in my power to advance your interests hereafter."

Christy would have nothing of it. His only response was to scrawl "vacillating skunk" across the back of the letter. His name would appear on the music until the copyright ran out in 1879, years after both of them were dead.

The lead singer of the Christy show in the years 1847–53, the man who sang Foster's songs, was George N. Harrington (1827–68), whom the world knew as George N. Christy. The two other regular members of the little troupe were Christys by birth: E.P.'s two young sons, E. Byron (1838–66) and William Christy (1839–62). William, whose "greatest proficiency was in the delineament of the female character," died in 1862 at the age of twenty-two. E. Byron died four years later at twenty-eight.

As for Stephen Foster and E. P. Christy, those two kindred and inimical purveyors of an idyllic dreamland of mirth, blithe sentiment, and harmony: both succumbed in the end to a darkness within. By the time he retired in 1854, Christy was believed to be half mad. In 1862, the year of his son William's death, he killed himself, leaping from a New York window at the age of forty-seven. Foster, a drunkard, died nearly destitute three years later in a ward of Bellevue Hospital, New York, at the age of thirty-eight. Today "The Old Folks at Home" is recognized as having sold more than twenty million copies in sheet music, and has been reckoned to be one of the ten most-recorded songs of all time. In 1990, a single leaf of early piano music by Foster, "Autumn Waltz," sold at Christie's for $77,000.

In 1864, the year of Foster's death, *Chambers's Encyclopaedia* stated quite accurately that "In most cases the members of the ne-gro minstrel troupes are only negros in name, with face and hands blackened."

There were exceptions, such as William Henry Lane (1825–52), a native of New York who performed as Master Juba. (Written references to black dancing as "juba" date to the 1820s; and William B. Smith's article in the *Farmer's Register* of 1838 refers to the "Juber" dance-song and hand-rhythms of the slaves. The word may be from *giouba,* an African step-dance.) Lane worked in several minstrel shows and on his own; and it is he who appears namelessly as "the greatest dancer known" in Charles Dickens's account of entertainment at Almack's dance hall in the Five Points section of New York, in his *American Notes for General Circulation* of 1842. It was in Dickens's London that Lane a decade later died.

The first black group performance seems to have been a show organized by a white slave-owner, Louis Tabaray, in New Orleans in 1791. By the 1850s there were independent black musical troupes, such as the Lucca Family of Connecticut, one member of which, bass-baritone and cellist John Lucca, Jr., later entered minstrelsy.

Frederick Douglass, who denounced minstrelsy in 1848, was moved to speak on the subject again in June of 1849, when he announced in his newspaper the coming to Rochester of "Gavitt's Original Ethiopian Serenaders, said to be composed entirely of colored people." He deemed it as "something gained, when the colored man in any form can appear before a white audience; and we think that even this company, with industry, application, and a proper cultivation of their taste, may yet be instrumental in removing the prejudice against our race. But they must cease to exaggerate the exaggerations of our enemies; and represent the colored man rather as he is, than as Ethiopian Minstrels usually represent him to be."

By 1856 there were isolated instances of black minstrel shows in the Northeast — "we do not see why the genuine article should not succeed," reflected the *New York Clipper* of one such show in November of 1858 — but it was not until 1865 that the first black minstrel group of significance made its debut: the Georgia Minstrels, a band of ex-slaves organized in Macon, Georgia, by a white man named W. H. Lee. "These are real 'nigs,'" noted a review in the *New York Clipper* of December 23, 1865. By July of 1866 the troupe was taken over by Sam Hague of Utica, New York; and by the end of that year, there were at least three black troupes going by the name of the Georgia Minstrels, the best known of them being Booker and Clayton's Georgia Minstrels. It became not uncommon for black troupes to distinguish themselves from their white counterparts by adopting the designation Georgia Minstrels.

After the Civil War, black men in blackface and black minstrel shows became plentiful. As comedians and singers of coon songs, performers such as Sam Lucas (1840–1916), Billy Kersands (1854–1915) and James A. Bland (1854–1911) enjoyed lucrative careers as blacked-up black men in the post-bellum period.

The idea of blacks in blackface may at first glance seem to invite all manner of philosophical inquiry and intellectual parlor games. But is the willingness of blacks to assume the mask of gross stereotype any more baffling or troubling than the universal tendency to masquerade? White Southerners embrace and cultivate the theatrically defined stereotype of the good old boy. Italian-Americans mimic the words and ways and assume the roles that Hollywood has created for them. The Irish in America would evaporate were it not for the devotion to role-playing that lends them the illusion of actuality. America alone of nations envisioned herself in terms of a dream. Nothing in this country is real, everyone an actor. From long-tail blue to dashiki, from the organ-grinder to the godfather, it is all a masquerade. If the halcyon lark of antebellum plantation life invented by minstrelsy was a sham, it was at least a sham that few took for reality. The same cannot be said of modern cultural shams such as the fantasy of African-American roots perceived in, say, Kwanzaa, a fake holiday invented in America in 1966, and no closer than minstrelsy to the reality of any true African culture. Like the stereotypical posings of rap, the hoax of African-American consciousness, of Kwanzaa Kultur, is an emanation of true black minstrelsy. Though, as always, it is the noble white man — Hallmark and the corporate media — that profits most, it is a minstrelsy perpetrated and embraced by blacks, played not for laughs but in earnest.

Popular culture is the product of who we are only in that it is the product of the lies, pretenses, and falsehoods that define us, and beneath which we hide and often, ultimately, lose the little truth from which we flee. Its meaning, insofar as it has any meaning at all, is essentially pathic. In the case of the black man in blackface, it can at least be said that his motive was forthright, respectable, and pure: that is, money. The same can be true of the professional good old boy, the professional Italian-American, the professional Irishman, as long as they are faking it on stage, selling it to the suckers. It is when they bear the masquerade, the role, offstage — when the stage walk and the stage talk become the street walk and the street talk, when show business becomes the business of life — that they become truly frauds. As far as I can tell, this was not the case generally with blacks who blacked up to make a buck. Offstage they lived apart from stereotype — more than can be said of many of the professional ethnic pretenders of today, be they white or black, singers or actors.

Sam Lucas, who was born to free parents in Ohio, attended Wilberforce University, worked as a barber, and served in the Union army before entering minstrelsy in 1869. He sang many of his own songs, including "De Day I Was Sot Free," "My Dear Old Southern Home," and "Carve Dat Possum," certainly the most carnivorous of coon songs, with its memorable opening couplet:

> *De possum meat am good to eat,*
> *Carve him to de heart.*

Ike Simond (1847–c. 1905), "a banjo player comique" known as Old Slack, recalled in his *Reminiscence and Pocket History of the Colored Profession from 1865 to 1891* that Lucas told him at one point that "he would never black his face again, and as I have met him in nearly every city of the United States since that time I don't think he ever has." Lucas eventually became the first black performer to be cast in a starring moving-picture role, as Tom in the seventh filming of *Uncle Tom's Cabin,* a World Pictures five-reeler of 1914.

Billy Kersands was from New York. He danced, mimicked frogs and cows in his songs (I think of Clarence "Frogman" Henry singing "Ain't Got No Home" in 1956), and capped his sly performances as a babber-lipped buffoon by placing billiard balls or a cup and saucer in his mouth (I think of the guy with the balls in his mouth on the cover of the Rolling Stones' *Exile on Main St.*). He was the master of the Essence, the most famous of minstrelsy dances, born of the Shuffle and progenitor of the Soft Shoe. He led his own troupe, Billy Kersands' Minstrels, and in the 1870s and 1880s was the highest-paid black entertainer of the day, as popular among blacks as among whites. He once told a fellow entertainer: "Son, if they hate me, I'm still whipping them, because I'm making them laugh." Recalling his own minstrel years, W. C. Handy wrote: "It goes without saying that minstrels were a disreputable lot in the eyes of a large section of upper-crust Negroes." They seem disreputable yet — misunderstood, neglected, regarded as an embarrassment — in the eyes of history. Today Kersands, like Lucas, is ignored by the five volumes of the *Encyclopedia of African-American Culture and History* (1966), by the six volumes of *The African American Encyclopedia* (1993).

Not so for the apparently more respectable James A. Bland, one of whose compositions came to be embraced in 1940 as the state song of Virginia. Bland was born to a free family in Flushing, New York, and grew up in Washington, D.C., where his father was an examiner with the U.S. Patent Office, and where James attended Howard University before joining Haverly's Colored Minstrels, in which Lucas and Kersands also worked. He was later a featured member of Sprague's Georgia Minstrels, and became a sort of black Stephen Foster, composing minstrel classics such as "Carry Me Back to Old Virginny" (1878) and "Oh, Dem Golden Slippers" (1879). He ended up in Philadelphia, where, like Stephen Foster before him, he died in poverty.

Bert Williams (1874–1922), an emigrant from Antigua who would become the most famous of black entertainers, entered minstrelsy in 1892, after attending Stanford University. Shepherd Edmonds (1876–1957), from Memphis, and Sylvester Russell (c. 1865–1930), from New Jersey, were two noted black musicians who worked in the 1890s in the Al G. Field Minstrels, the show with which Emmett Miller was associated at the height of his career. Russell went on to become a music and drama editor for *The Freeman*.

From one black troupe alone, the Mississippi-based Rabbit Foot Company, later the Rabbit Foot Minstrels, would emerge the classic big-city blues singers Ma Rainey, Ida Cox, and Bessie Smith, as well as the rhythm-and-blues progenitor Louis Jordan. Blues artist Skip James also worked briefly with the Rabbit Foot organization. W. C. Handy, the so-called father of the blues, was a minstrel musician from 1896 to 1903, punctuated in 1900 by a stint as a college musical director. Country blues singers who worked in blackface included Furry Lewis, Jim Jackson, and Big Joe Williams. Rufus Thomas, whose "Bear Cat" of 1953 became the first hit on Sam

Phillips's little Sun Records label, was a latter-day alumnus of the Rabbit Foot Minstrels. Born in Casey, Mississippi, in 1917, and raised in Memphis, Thomas worked the Rabbit Foot tent show in the thirties. "I was putting that black stuff on my face," he later recalled of those days.

While coon and minstrel recordings, either by blacks or by whites, were primarily sold to the white market, black minstrelsy also had its place in the so-called race market. Perry Bradford was the author of "Crazy Blues." Recorded by Mamie Smith and Her Jazz Hounds in 1920, it was the first bestselling blues record. Bradford was also a member of a group called the Gulf Coast Minstrels, who recorded two of his less-known compositions for Columbia in November 1923: "I Ain't Skeered of Work" and "Darktown Camp Meeting." These recordings by the black Gulf Coast Minstrels, essentially indistinguishable from white blackface minstrelsy routines of the day, were released in January 1924 in the Columbia race series, nestled between releases by King Oliver's Jazz Band and Bessie Smith.

Gus Cannon, an early associate in Memphis of Jim Jackson, recorded at his first session, in the fall of 1927, a version of "My Money Never Runs Out," by the black nineteenth-century coonsong writer Irving Jones. A year later, in the fall of 1928, Bo Chatman, one of the founding members of the Mississippi Sheiks, began his recording career with a piece of minstrelsy called "The Yellow Coon Has No Race." That same season, Chatman fiddled on a recording by the minstrel singer Alec Johnson of the Bert Williams song "Next Week, Sometime." It is in the work of early bluesmen such as Gus Cannon (1885–1979), Papa Charlie Jackson (1885–1938), Jim Jackson (1890–1937), and Bo Chatman (1893–1964) that the interminglings of latter-day minstrelsy, the Tin Pan Alley coon song, the black songster tradition, and the early blues are most pronounced.

It is a common misbelief that minstrelsy drew upon an actual black folk source for its musical inspiration, that it plundered and parlorized the songs of blacks for its repertoire. Writing of minstrelsy in antebellum New York, Luc Sante in his generally wonderful book *Low Life* says that "Black bands played at dances, in concert saloons, and on the street, most often in quartets dominated by fiddle and banjo, and an idea of what songs they played can be gotten from the well-known minstrel tunes, nearly all of which were stolen from them." It is his final phrase that skews the validity of his statement. If an idea of what those black bands in New York were playing can be gotten from minstrelsy, it is only because those bands derived much of their material from minstrelsy, not the other way around.

The Virginia Minstrels of 1843 had centered their first shows on the figure of the ragged plantation black, drawing to some extent from actual black sources. But the nature and format of minstrel shows soon changed. The figure of the black dandy, the Northern zip coon, was introduced and came to dominate the opening part of the show, while the figure of the old-fashioned plantation black was relegated to the second part. With the ascendance of the zip-coon figure came the increasing use of sentimental ballads and the addition to the show of a central interlude part, the olio, dedicated to a variety of musical and comedy acts.

The songs of minstrelsy in its heyday came from Northern composers such as Stephen Foster and his black counterpart James A. Bland, and from the penny-confectionery pens of lesser poetasters; and they were songs that often became as popular among blacks as among whites. Of the great vogue among every social class, both white and black, of "The Old Folks at Home" — the one we have come to know as "Swanee" — the *Albany Register* remarked in 1852 that "there is not a 'live darkey,' young or old, but can whistle, sing, dance, and play it." As the music historian Charles Hamm has said of Foster's impact: "Never before, and rarely since, did any music come so close to being a shared experience for so many Americans." More than a century later, the songs of Stephen Foster still imbued the living spirit of American Music: Ray Charles recorded "Swanee River Rock" for Atlantic in 1957; Jerry Lee Lewis recorded "Old Black Joe" for Sun in 1960; later in the sixties, Ornette Coleman wove shards of the same song into his concert performances.

Martin Delany was a black contemporary of Stephen Foster in Pittsburgh, an apprentice to the doctor whose daughter married Foster. Delany was active in the anti-slavery movement, and an associate of Frederick Douglass, for whose weekly paper he was a correspondent. He was described by Douglass as "the intensest embodiment of black Nationality to be met with outside the valley of the Niger." In 1858 Delaney wrote a novel called *Blake.* In it he appropriated three of Foster's songs, which he placed in the mouths of black characters.

In the four volumes of *Christy and Fox's Complete Melodist and Joke-Book* of 1858, there is not a single song that can be said to be derived from black folk tradition. Inversely, however, the folklorist Newman I. White, in examining the origins of the 680 songs he collected in his *American Negro Folk-Songs* of 1928, considered that 104 of them revealed "traces of the antebellum minstrel song." Such traces are even more plentiful in early blues recordings, both urban and rural.

The songs and music of the minstrel shows, and of their smaller and tawdrier counterparts, the medicine shows, were as important an influence on Southern black music, on what came to be called the blues, as on white Southern music, which came to be called country. Minstrelsy was the common blood, inspiration, and breeding ground of both these inchoate forms.

One example may prove illuminating. "I've Got a Gal for Ev'ry Day in the Week" was a ragtime coon song composed in 1900, with lyrics by the Irish comic Pat Rooney and music by Harry Von Tilzer.

It emerged, metamorphosed, as part of the black songster and blues traditions: recorded as "Gang of Brown Skin Women" by Papa Harvey Hull and Long "Cleve" Reed for Gennett in the spring of 1927, and in early 1928 for Victor as "My Monday Blues" by Jim Jackson, a Mississippi-born veteran of the medicine-show circuit who derived much from minstrelsy — who, simply put, did as every performer, black or white, rural or urban, did: took from where he could. In 1944 the song emerged, metamorphosed once again, as a fast-swinging blast of proto-rock-'n'-roll jive by Big Joe Turner, accompanied by boogie-woogie pianist Pete Johnson. The title of Turner's Decca recording, "I Got a Gal for Every Day in the Week," recalls the 1900 coon-song original, but Turner takes for himself the credit as the song's composer.

Friedrich Nietzsche died the year that Rooney and Von Tilzer put their names to "I've Got a Gal for Ev'ry Day in the Week." It was in his book *Beyond Good and Evil* (1886) that the philosopher had declared: "The Jews are beyond doubt the strongest, toughest, and purest race now living in Europe; they know how to prevail even under the worst conditions, even better than under favorable conditions, by means of virtues that today one would mark as vices." The descendants in America of the Jews whom Nietzsche praised and admired proved him right. Just as Arnold Rothstein (1882–1928) created and ruled the system of organized crime that would prevail through the century, so men such as Von Tilzer, in taking control of Tin Pan Alley and the coon-song industry, came to dominate not only the popular music of the day, but, through their invention and rule of Hollywood, popular culture itself.

And here let us pause a moment to address this matter, or this myth, of race.

In June 2000, Celera Genomics and the thirteen-year-old international consortium of publicly funded research laboratories that had come to be known as the Human Genome Project announced that the human genome had at last been sequenced, revealing for taxonomy the swarming sea of deoxyribonucleic acid — DNA — whose multifarious spiralings store the genetic information in the human cell. While many marveled at the medical and scientific potentialities of this revelation, few perceived the greater revelation, a silent cataclysm of ontology, that had been laid bare in the course of the quest to solve the mysteries of the genome.

In his study "The Human Genome," written in light of the announcement of the sequencing of the chemical core of human life, Geoffrey Carr, the science editor of *The Economist,* looked toward the work of men such as the late molecular evolutionist Allan C. Wilson (1934–91) of the University of California at Berkeley and the geneticist Luigi Luca Cavalli-Sforza of Stanford University. Carr writes of these scientists' groundbreaking research:

"It challenges the assumption that there are significant genetic differences between human races and, indeed, that the idea of 'race' has any biological meaning at all."

In fact, "compared with chimpanzees, humans are, indeed, a single race. One group of 55 chimps in West Africa shows more genetic diversity than the whole of humanity."

While disproving the deep-grained notion of race, genetics can, through certain mitochondrial, matrilineal traits of DNA, illuminate the migratory and mating history of the generations of humanity, which can be corroborated by patrilineal traits in the DNA of Y-chromosomes. Seemingly bizarre traditional beliefs have been confirmed:

"The legends of the Lemba, a southern-African people, claim they are descended from the Jews, a Middle-Eastern people. An analysis of Lemba Y-chromosomes supports this idea; around 50% of those chromosomes carry genetic markers that are common amongst Jewish men, but absent in the Lemba's neighbours in Africa.

"Despite the existence of such genetic markers for particular groups, though, the genes carry a wider, paradoxical, lesson about 'racial' differences — which is that, in the main, there aren't any."

Jews in blackface. Lemba black of face. Melanin and matzoh. "Pork Chop Blues" sang Bessie Brown in 1924, with Coleman Hawkins on tenor sax behind her, the flip side of "Mississippi Delta Blues." The Lemba, they don't eat no pork; don't eat no hippo, either, 'cause it looks like pig.

And yet the idea of race is as strong today as it was in the days of minstrelsy, as it has been throughout all history. Racial pride? The chimpanzees perhaps are entitled to such. We are beneath it.

After the Civil War minstrelsy grew grand and garish. The first transcontinental railroad was completed in 1869, and the expanding web of railways provided fast and easy transportation for bigger and bigger troupes, which came more and more to encompass the wholesale variety of vaudeville.

The decline of minstrelsy had been bemoaned for many years. As early as 1854, looking back upon the brief history of minstrelsy as if it were in its twilight, an anonymous writer in the *New York Musical Review* titled his article "Obituary, Not Eulogistic: Negro Minstrelsy Is Dead." He wrote of a certain lamentable "*bleaching* process."

Four years later, in the introductory "Critique" to *George Christy's Ethiopian Joke Book, No. 3,* dated July 1858, we read that, "Years ago, *Negro* Eccentricities truly and absolutely was the style of performance, and professionals gained notoriety in accordance with the perfectness with which they imitated the droll African race; but now, unfortunately, operatic fandangoes and *improbabilities,* in which, in many cases, the Negro character never did, and in no wise can be made to harmonize, and positions totally incompatible with Negro life, have made sad inroads upon the prerogatives of the Ethiopian stage; and these usurpations threaten to, and will, eventually, overturn the selectness of that peculiar stage, and institute instead a perverted taste — if they be persevered in."

These sentiments, the antebellum precursor of the rock-'n'-roll-is-dead syndrome, likely reflect a great deal of truth: the more popular minstrelsy became, the more it informed popular culture, the more polluted by popular culture it became. Nevertheless, today the golden age of minstrelsy is commonly said to have spanned the years 1843–75; and the age of its decline is set at 1875–95, roughly the years of vaudeville's rise.

In the last years of the nineteenth century and the first years of the twentieth, as vaudeville-era Tin Pan Alley became the primary well of minstrelsy, and as blues and jazz, through the sagacious musical carpetbagging of men such as W. C. Handy and Clarence Williams, became an integral part of Tin Pan Alley, the circle of the uroboros was complete: minstrelsy had flowed into the blues, the blues had influenced Tin Pan Alley, and Tin Pan Alley had become the voice of minstrelsy. The earliest known utterance of the word "jazz" occurs in "Uncle Josh in Society," a 1909 Columbia recording by Cal Stewart (1856–1919), a Virginia-born veteran of nineteenth-century medicine shows and vaudeville.

By then, words such as "hip" and "hep" were well-established elements of the vocabulary of those who would soon be known as cats, cool and otherwise. The origin of "hip," whose currency was common enough for it to have appeared in print by 1904 — the year, coincidentally, that the first opium song, "Willie the Weeper," seems to have originated in vaudeville — may have derived from the classic, age-old pelvic-centered, side-lying opium-smoking position, and may have been used originally as a sign of mutual recognition and reference by those who were in the know of the big sweet smoke. Recorded as a jazz-band instrumental by King Oliver and His Dixie Syncopators in April of 1927, it was through the recording of "Willie the Weeper," three months later, by the intriguing Alabama-born jazz-blues stylist and female impersonator Frankie "Half-Pint" Jaxon, that this song of the "dreamin' habit" came not only to be associated with a fanciful blues tradition, but to reach a new and wider audience as well. (An earlier version of the song, printed in 1926, includes explicit reference to "hop," as well as to "coke" and to "hittin' up the hypo," all of which are absent from Jaxon's version.)

Though "gong," a white slang word for opium pipe, was common hip parlance by 1914, it was not until early 1931 that Cab Calloway (1907–94), the Harlem hierophant of all things hip — and aware no doubt of "Willie the Weeper" — introduced "Minnie the Moocher," a "lowdown hoochie-coocher" who was taught "how to kick the gong around" by a "cokey" named Smoky down in Chinatown. The great success of this recording — copyrighted as "Minnie the Moocher: The Ho De Ho Song" in the names of Cab Calloway and Irving Mills, the lyricist of "Lovesick Blues" — inspired Calloway to follow it some months later, in the fall of 1931, with "Kickin' the Gong Around."

So popular was "Minnie the Moocher" that it became Cab Calloway's signature song through the rest of his career. In 1932, in those less censorial days when the Mosaic commandments of the Production Code Administration were violated with impunity, "Minnie the Moocher" was made into a Max Fleisher Talkatoon, an early, seven-minute, sixteen-millimeter animated sound film featuring Betty Boop and the Calloway orchestra. The 1976 autobiography he co-authored would bear the title *Of Minnie the Moocher & Me;* and he would perform the song, lie-down hip as ever, in the 1980 picture *The Blues Brothers.*

The foregoing is what Quintilian called an *excursus.* Get used to it, or get out.

In his 1941 autobiography, *Father of the Blues,* W. C. Handy wrote that "The Memphis Blues," copyrighted by him in 1912, "was the first of all the many published 'blues,' and it set a new fashion in American popular music and contributed to the rise of jazz, or, if you prefer, swing, and even boogie-woogie." As Handy composed it, "The Memphis Blues" had no lyrics; it was an instrumental piece, and was originally published as such in September 1912. A year later the Theron C. Bennett Co., to whom Handy had assigned rights, published a new version of "The Memphis Blues," with lyrics by George A. Norton, the lyricist of "My Melancholy Baby," another recent song to which Bennett had acquired rights. The cover of the new edition of "The Memphis Blues" described it as "A Southern Rag by W. C. Handy" and as "Geo. A. Norton's Song Founded on W. C. Handy's World Wide 'Blue' Melody."

It was the minstrel troupe of George "Honey Boy" Evans that popularized "The Memphis Blues" in 1913–14, in an arrangement by Edward V. Cupero, the musical director and bandleader of Evans's show. A portrait of Evans in blackface appears beneath the title of the sheet music, along with the statement that the song is "Successfully Featured by Ed. V. Cupero's Band and Orchestra in Geor. Evans' 'Honey Boy' Minstrels." The cover is otherwise dominated by portraits of Cupero in a conducting pose, and of the Evans band standing in uniformed formality.

The first recording of "The Memphis Blues," by the Victor Military Band on July 15 of 1914, used Cupero's arrangement. Another recording, by Prince's Orchestra for Columbia, followed nine days later, on July 24. Both were described in their respective catalogues as "one-step" dance songs, and both sold well. Handy's "Southern rag," as overhauled by the author of "Melancholy Baby," as popularized by a minstrel troupe and recorded by a couple of white New York studio orchestras, became the first of the "blues" hits. To his credit, Handy, the former minstrel, was quick to acknowledge Honey Boy Evans's role in the song's success.

Actually "The Memphis Blues" was not "the first of all the many published 'blues,'" as Handy put it. Artie Matthews's "Baby Seals Blues" was published earlier the same year. And there was another "blues" with lyrics that preceded the revamped "Memphis Blues" of September 1913.

The blackface minstrel Lee Roy "Lasses" White copyrighted his "Nigger Blues" on July 21, 1913. It was recorded in the fall of 1916 by the tenor George O'Connor and by the Victor Military Band. O'Connor was a Washington, D.C., lawyer and "an exclusive Columbia artist" who had achieved some popularity as an "interpreter of humorous dialect songs." His "Nigger Blues" was released as the flip side of Al Jolson's "I'm Saving the Means to Get to New Orleans." The Victor Military Band's instrumental version was sold as a fox-trot. Al Bernard recorded "Nigger Blues" for Edison in 1919. Lasses White himself recorded a version, for Victor in 1935, but sensibilities had changed somewhat by then, and Victor, proud as it may have been of its 1916 fox-trot, predictably and prudently chose not to release it.

That "new fashion in American popular music" that Handy spoke of; "the rise of jazz, or, if you prefer, swing, and even boogie-woogie" — and let's add rock 'n' roll, as Handy himself might have done if he had written, say, fifteen years later — it was not born, that fashion, that rise, of anything pure. The true story of "The Memphis Blues," like the story of Pat Rooney's song and Jim Jackson's song and Big Joe Turner's song, is the story of American music itself: the story of the black stealing from the black, the white from the white, and the one from the other; of Tin Pan Alley songs culled from the air and taken into the pines and the fields, gone feral and misperceived as primitive folk expression; of ancient breezes from those pines and those fields drifting endlessly anew through the rhythms of generations.

By 1913 truly hot jazz was being recorded by James Reese Europe (1881–1919), the black orchestra-leader whose "Down Home Rag" of that year was nothing less than the ragtime-gone-berserk equivalent of John Coltrane's *Ascension*.

The first record release by the Original Dixieland Jazz Band was "Livery Stable Blues," in the spring of 1917. The record was a hit, and the song, whose authorship was claimed by Nick LaRocca, the band's leader and cornet-player, became the object of a copyright case. The following exchange from the trial was reported by the *Chicago Daily News* of October 23, 1917:

"What is this new thing called 'Blues'? And what is this new Rhythm?" asked Judge George A. Carpenter of Alcide "Yellow" Nuñez, the New Orleans clarinetist whose place in the Original Dixieland Jazz Band had been taken by Larry Shields prior to recording.

"Nuttin' new about 'em, jedge. They're part of our life for donkey's years. Jest lately we expose 'em to you public and you all hot and bothered. Some complain, but others dance. We always play 'em natural like the flow of a stream, the lope of a buzzard, the rock and roll of well-oiled wheels on steady rails. We jest layin' easy on the back o' the beat. But you jump ahead o' that beat and twist and jerk like a Ford flivver in a tantrum. Go jump ahead with it, jedge, go with it! It's the world's music now!"

The exchange seems to foreshadow the "Virginian Judge" series of dialect courtroom routines that Walter C. Kelly recorded for Victor in 1925–26. The reporter does indeed seem to be a proponent of the dialect-comedy school of transcription, and there is no telling where the minstrelsy of his imagination overtakes the reality of what Nuñez in fact said. Nevertheless, this courtroom whimsy speaks as well as anything of breezes and thievings and that "new fashion in American popular music," that "rise of jazz, or, if you prefer, swing, and even boogie-woogie," and yes, in one serendipitous metaphor, even rock 'n' roll.

Blackface, white face, false face. "Originality is but high-born stealth." These may be the only words written by Edward Dahlberg that are worth remembering; and who knows where he got them.

Dan Emmett, the founder of the first minstrel troupe, had gone on to join Bryant's Minstrels in 1858. A year later he had introduced the song "Dixie." Though speculation regarding its true origin has been ceaseless, the song was copyrighted in his name as "I Wish I Was in Dixie's Land" in 1860. Attending a minstrel show not long before the election of that year, Abraham Lincoln heard "Dixie" for the first time, and so enraptured was he by it that he hollered out "Let's have it again! Let's have it again!" As the war that followed neared its end, he advocated the song as one that the reunited nation could join in singing. If the founding of the first minstrel troupe had not rendered Dan Emmett the most celebrated and legendary of minstrels, "Dixie" surely did. It became the anthem of the South, and he its blackface Orpheus.

Dan Emmett, the most famous minstrel, the Northerner who gave the South its most enduring song, lived to see the twentieth century. By the time of his death at eighty-nine in 1904 (the year Al Jolson began appearing in blackface), younger minstrels had taken to adopting the name of Emmett in tribute and for cachet. It was a practice that continued well into the decline of minstrelsy, and for a long time I thought that Emmett Miller's true identity might have been irrevocably lost to it. But now I know otherwise.

Lena Christian was born on December 29, 1873, in rural Wilkinson County, Georgia, the fourth child and first daughter of a twenty-five-year-old farm laborer named Doctor F. Christian and his twenty-two-year-old wife, Fannie Crumbly Christian.

The nearest big town was Macon, in Bibb County to the west. There, when she was sixteen or seventeen, Lena Christian found work at the Manchester Manufacturing Company. She lived nearby as a boarder on Manchester Row.

John Pink Miller was from Washington County. He had been born there, in Oconee, on May 14, 1874, one of nine children, to William and Ollie Allen Miller. Like Lena Christian, he had sought work in Macon; like her, he had found it, at the Bibb Manufacturing Company; and like her, he boarded near the factory where he worked.

On February 9, 1892 — she was eighteen, he was seventeen — they were married. The ceremony was performed by Rev. Lewis B. Payne, the Methodist-Episcopalian minister who was superintendent of the South Georgia Orphans' Home, located out near Forsyth Road, about a mile from town.

John Pink — or simply Pink, as many knew him — was a mill hand and laborer. He changed jobs frequently: after Bibb he worked at the Macon Knitting Company on Hawthorne Street; at Manchester Manufacturing, where Lena had worked; at Payne C. Mills; and elsewhere. Macon was growing. By 1910, when the city's population was reckoned at 40,655, John Miller managed to get a job as a streetcar motorman. His brother-in-law Joseph Simmone, his sister Emma's husband, worked as a streetcar director in East Macon, and John may have come to the job through him. By 1911 John Pink Miller joined the city fire department, where he would work as a chauffeur for twenty-one years.

Lena by then had borne him five children, but only two of them had survived. There was a daughter, Nora Belle, born on August 2, 1903. They called her Mattie, after a younger sister of Lena. And there was Mattie's big brother.

Emmett Dewey Miller was born in Macon on Friday, February 2, 1900.

This may not be the equivalent, perhaps, of a precise dating of the Magdalen Papyrus; but hey, pallie, after twenty years' searching, it is no matter of mean potatoes, either. That I share this coveted revelation so selflessly, openly, and without gain attests surely that I am the Christian I hold myself to be. So take it, and may it serve you well. All I ask — and it is nothing — is that you do not take credit where credit is not due. A gift such as this belongs to the world. May scholars everywhere, and seekers after every knowledge, look to me and by my example learn. Pull down thy vanity, thy greed and vainglory, pull down.

On now to other paragraphs, other revelations. For many lie before us.

The Millers boarded at a succession of homes: from Roff Home Avenue, in the Vineville area, where they lived in 1896, when John worked at Macon Knitting, to Oak Haven Avenue, where they lived in 1898, when John worked at Manchester; back to the Vineville district, where they boarded in 1900 at the home of R. L. Williams, where Emmett was likely born, close to the Central of Georgia railroad. In 1902 they were at 226 Roff Home Avenue; and by 1905 they moved to 772 Oglethorpe Street. In 1910 they were renting at 1010 Oglethorpe; by then John Pink's widowed mother, fifty-nine-year-old Ollie, was living with them. Nineteen twelve found them at 1004 Oglethorpe. From there they moved to 131 Ross Street. In 1915 they were at 914 Elm Street; in 1917, back on Oglethorpe, number 1109.

Emmett was raised in the Methodist church. Both his parents became members of the Second Street Methodist congregation.

And both his parents could read and write; and they saw to it that Emmett and Nora Belle got their learning. Emmett started school in 1905. He attended elementary classes at Alexander School Number 2 on College Street. He entered the fourth grade there on September 23, 1909, graduated from it in June 1910. He suffered the fifth grade twice, entered it at the age of ten and finally went on to the sixth grade when he was twelve. On June 10, 1914, he graduated from the seventh and last grade of Alexander School Number 2 and was promoted to Lanier Junior High School.

But young Emmett chose work over further schooling. As a story in the *Macon News* would tell it eleven years later: "He finished the grammar grades and then pestered his mother and father so much that they were almost forced to let him go to work."

"Papa, I'm going to be a comedian." According to another, similar newspaper account from that time, published in the *Macon Telegraph,* "That's what Emmett Miller always told his father when he started to work at any job in Macon."

This account quotes his mother: "We knew that he was talented for the stage." And she goes on: "When he quit school and went to work he always said that he wanted to be a comedian. He worked with the Central of Georgia for about a year and a half."

Lena says that her son was "just a natural comedian, I guess. One of his teachers told me that in school he was just the monkey for the whole class." She recalled that Emmett's first stage appearance was at the Grand Theatre on Mulberry Street, when he performed "in a little skit put on advertising a soft drink."

The *News* says that Emmett "set his heart to become a black-face comedian" on his tenth birthday, when his father took him to see the Al G. Field Minstrels. The tale may be apocryphal, but, as we have seen, it was in the following school year that he flunked for the first time, and the distraction of a new and growing fascination may have contributed to that failing. To be sure, the masking and surrendering of one's personality in blackface minstrelsy seems often to have had a deep psychological appeal. The veteran minstrel Homer Meachum would speak of this appeal in almost pathological, almost addictive, terms: "A Nigger singer will always be a Nigger singer. You can put any kind of makeup on them, but they'll always come back for the cork."

The *News* also alludes to Emmett's participation as a teenager "in several amateur performances staged in Macon," and describes him as being "remembered by his many friends in Macon as 'Nigger' Miller, when he worked at the machinist trade in the Central of Georgia railway shops and later as an automobile mechanic."

"He was always an industrious boy," John Pink tells the *News*; and he "refused to lose the interest he always seemed to take in black-face comedy. Everytime a minstrel came to Macon, Emmett had to go, and while we didn't worry about the boy, mother and I often wondered if he really wanted to be a comedian. Then we would promptly forget it — until another show came to town, and it started all over again."

The fascination that black folk culture, real and imagined, held for whites ran deep in the homeland of Emmett Miller's youth. Joel Chandler Harris (1848–1908), from small-town Georgia, worked at a number of Southern newspapers, including the *Macon Telegraph,* before joining the staff of the *Atlanta Constitution* in 1876. His Uncle Remus stories, which began to appear in the summer of 1879, depicted a rich and relatively authentic world of black dialect, folklore, and humor that in many ways represented a marked contrast, and in some ways was a literary parallel, to the ersatz black folksiness, quaint dialect, and burlesque of the minstrel shows. That is to say that the character of Uncle Remus was essentially, like the idyllic vision of minstrelsy, a figment of white fantasy — Harris saw Remus as having "nothing but pleasant memories of the discipline of slavery" — but the tales and fables of Brer Rabbit that Harris told through Remus were the genuine stuff of black storytellers long before Harris. In 1883 Harris wrote to *The Critic* to say that, contrary to the stereotypes of minstrelsy, he had never seen a slave play a banjo. "I have heard them make sweet music with the quills — panpipes; I have heard them play passibly on the fiddle; . . . I have heard them blow a trumpet with surprising skill; but I have never seen a banjo." Harris left the *Constitution* in 1900 and started his own *Uncle Remus's Magazine*. He was the author of two novels and several volumes of short stories, but it was the Uncle Remus tales that brought him fame. For Ezra Pound, the phonetic wordplay of Harris's dialect was both an early source of inspiration and a lifelong source of fascination. It was from the Uncle Remus stories that Pound in the 1920s drew the nickname Possum for T. S. Eliot, the nicknames Tar Baby and Brer Rabbit for himself. Pound was born in 1885, the same year that Gus Cannon was born, the same year that Papa Charlie Jackson was born. It was the year that Alexander Graham Bell, Chichester Bell, and Charles Sumner Tainter developed the first practical and replayable record: a six-inch cylinder of ozokerite-coated cardboard that played at a hundred revolutions per minute and was capable of holding over eight minutes of sound in its engraved grooves. It was not until the spring of 1888 that Edison came forth with his own wax cylinders, which brought sound of a greatly improved quality and fuller volume.

If Macon can be said to have had a place in publishing, the journalist and author Harry Stillwell Edwards (1855–1938) and his publisher, the J.W. Burke Company, must be said to stand at the center of that place. Among Edwards's many books was *Eneas Africanus* (1919), the slim epistolary tale of "an old family Negro" who becomes separated from his owner in 1864 and finally finds his way back to his Georgia home after an eight-year journey through seven states, sheltered by kindly white folks along his winding way. He returns with a group of blacks in tow, presenting them to his master: "I done brought you a whole bunch o' new Yallerhama, Burningham Niggers, Marse George! Some folks tell me dey is free, but I know dey b'long ter Marse George." The tale of this "vanishing type" is "dear to the hearts of the Southerners, young and old," says Edwards in his little preface. "Is the story true? Everybody says it is." So popular was *Eneas Africanus* that in 1920 the Macon publishing company of J. W. Burke offered it simultaneously in five editions, ranging in price from fifty cents for the paperback to two and a half dollars for the illustrated ooze-leather edition.

In Edwards's tale, the owner of Eneas is a man named Tommey. Is it mere coincidence that the errant slave in William Faulkner's *Go Down, Moses* bears the name of Tomey's Turl?

Macon was the proud birthplace of the poet Sidney Lanier (1842–81). But the tales of Harris and Edwards held a place in the local cultural heart that the metaphysical conceits of Lanier did not reach. If Emmett Miller's cultural background is to be placed in a literary perspective it is this: he was born in the year that *Uncle Remus's Magazine* came to be, and he began his journey from Macon in the year that the journey of *Eneas Africanus* took the town by gentle storm.

On December 28, 1913, little more than a month before Emmett turned fourteen, his mother, on the eve of her fortieth birthday, gave birth to another son. The child, Lawrence Edward Miller, lived to the age of four and a half years, and on June 15, 1918, succumbed to diarrhea and enteritis.

The Macon directories of 1917 and 1918 (compiled when Emmett was, respectively, sixteen and seventeen) list Emmett as a chauffeur boarding at the home of his parents, at 1109 Oglethorpe. Though he came of conscription age nine months prior to the end of World War I, it appears that he was not called to serve. The 1920 directory lists him again as a chauffeur residing at the address of his parents. It would be his last listing for many years; by the time the 1920 directory was published, not long before his twentieth birthday, he likely was gone.

It is believed that he began his professional career in 1919. The

News story summarizes the first seven years of that career by saying that Miller played with the Neil O'Brien Minstrels, the Dan Fitch Minstrels, and, "for several months," on the Keith circuit. This all-powerful vaudeville empire stretched from the Palace Theatre in New York to the Grand Theatre in Macon, which had been a Keith Vaudeville showcase since its early days as the Macon Theatre. Both the Al G. Field Minstrels and the Dan Fitch Minstrels played Keith theaters. Fitch was handled by the Pat Casey Agency, an adjunct of the Keith operation.

Fitch's real name was Daniel R. Futch. He was born in Augusta, Georgia, on March 21, 1889. He had entered minstrelsy in 1907 as a member of Coburn's Minstrels, and had performed with the Neil O'Brien Minstrels and others. His own company, which first toured in 1921, operated more as a vaudeville attraction than as a traditionally structured, full-ensemble minstrel show.

It is *Billboard* magazine in its "Minstrelsy" column of August 30, 1924, that gives us our earliest glimpse of Miller and the Fitch company in action: "Dan Fitch's Minstrels received fine notices recently when they played a three-day engagement at the Rialto Theater in Poughkeepsie, N.Y. One paper declared that it was 'one of the best attractions in many moons,' having all the flourish and finish of an old-time minstrel show with the addition of new stuff. The performance consisted of the traditional first part and olio. The opening curtain revealed to the audience nineteen men in a circle, with four blackfaced end men. The singers, individual and chorus, were excellent and the comedians very funny. One of the hits of the show was Johnny Mack, female impersonator. Not until he pulled off his wig and remarked in a strong masculine voice that he was tired of the part did some in the audience feel sure that he was not a woman. The performance was brought to a close with a skit, 'Mandy's Syncopated Reception', [*interpunctio sic*] a rollicking number and a pleasing finale to a good performance. In the cast were Dan Fitch, Johnny Mack, Billy Everett, Charles Chiles, Ray Hart, Trevor Lewis, Nick Glenn, Fred Barnes, Art Hayes and Emmett Miller. A ten-piece jazz band furnished the music." Out of black-face, Miller also sang as a member of the troupe's vocal quartet, the Kings of Harmony.

A word about "Mandy's Syncopated Reception," about the catch-words "syncopated" and "syncopation," which will be seen to occur frequently in the popular press of the era. Strictly speaking, musical syncopation was the continuous superimposition of an irregular rhythm over a regular one. It was one of the defining elements of ragtime. To rag a song was to play it in syncopated style. In piano rag, the left hand kept the regular rhythm, alternating a low bass note with a midrange chord, producing a heavy accent on the first and third beats of the measure; and against this meter the right hand played a series of rhythmic displacements. In orchestral rag, groups of instruments took the parts of the left and right hands. But the connotations of syncopation went beyond ragtime, and were more than formal. From the 1890s to the 1920s, syncopation had come to signify the new spirit of rhythm itself, of jazz and blues and pop and all the colors of the Tin Pan Alley uroboros.

In addition to his work with Fitch, Miller is believed to have worked on the New York vaudeville stage with Cliff Edwards, and with the comedy team of Smith and Dale. Edwards (1895–1971), a comedian and singer from Missouri who was also known as Ukulele Ike, had been making records since 1922. His December 1923 recording of "Old Fashioned Love" contains the earliest recorded example of scat singing, an element of many of Edwards's record-ings thereafter. Will Friedwald points out in his book *Jazz Singing* (1990) that the vaudeville singer Gene Greene had used a half-chorus of mock-Chinese proto-scat in his 1917 Victor recording of

Irving Berlin's "From Here to Shanghai." (Cab Calloway, who recorded "The Scat Song" in 1932, also recorded a mock-Chinese bit in his "Chinese Rhythm" of 1934.) Greene, a baritone known as the Ragtime King, is also believed to have sung scat in his 1913 New York stage performances with ragtime pianist Charlie Straight of "King of the Bungaloos," written by Greene and Straight, and recorded by Greene for Columbia in 1911. While Jelly Roll Morton has attributed the invention of scat singing to an obscure black vaudeville singer named Joe Simms, it seems that Simms may have come along later than Greene. Whatever its ultimate source — and it seems to me only natural that scat singing, though unknown as such, had been in the air since the dawn of human song — one thing is certain: Louis Armstrong's lifelong claim to have inadvertently originated scat in his 1926 recording of "Heebie Jeebies" is patently absurd in light of the fact that Cliff Edwards had been singing scat for more than two years prior to that recording. Furthermore, a mere four months after Edwards scatted on "Old Fashioned Love," Don Redman scatted on Fletcher Henderson's recording of "My Papa Doesn't Two-Time No Time."

It may have been through Edwards's connections in the industry that on Saturday, October 25, 1924, at the Okeh studio in New York City, Miller made his first recording.

Produced by Okeh musical director Justin Ring (1876–1962), Miller's debut was a version, with piano accompaniment by Walter Rothrock, of Happy Lawson's 1921 "Any Time," which was Miller's signature song onstage. At least four takes were recorded, of which the fourth was subsequently chosen for release.

On November 7 he returned to the studio with Rothrock to record "The Pickaninny's Paradise," a 1918 song that had been introduced by the Courtney Sisters, and had been recorded by the Sterling Trio for Victor in early 1919. Miller recorded at least two takes of the song, and the second was chosen for release.

Now, what's the matter, honey, there's a tear in yo' eye — do
white folks say they don't know where you go when you
die?
Come to your mammy, dear, and listen here; I'll tell you
where those cullid chillun go when they leave here.

The song beckons the child to "Come lay your black kinky head in a bed on a pillow of white," as the singer unveils his vision of heaven, where will be found "sweet molasses all around."

"The Pickaninny's Paradise" was written by the Tin Pan Alley team of Sam Ehrich (1872–1927) and Nat Osborne (1878–1954). Ehrich, from New Orleans, was the song's lyricist; Osborne, a native of New York, wrote the music. Even in the year of its composition, six years earlier, "The Pickaninny's Paradise" was already something of an atavism, a throwback to an era of sentimental coon songs and sensibilities that the Jazz Age had rendered antiquated and passé. The coon song had grown more brash, as had the style of its singers, who had come to be known as coon-song shouters: a phrase echoed years later when black singers who developed a brasher style of big-band urban blues came to be known as blues shouters. And yet the figure of the pickaninny was clung to not only by the fading world of minstrelsy. Eleven months after Miller's recording, Ethel Waters would record a "Pickaninny Blues" for Columbia. Like the "Pickaninny's Slumber Song" of 1919, "Pickaninny Blues" of 1920 was a lullaby in the vein of "The Pickaninny's Paradise."

The word "pickaninny," from the Portuguese *pequeno,* meaning "little one," was more a theatrical term than a popular one. Like "darky," it was not often encountered in the realm of reality. In the early years of the twentieth century, it spawned the vaudeville slang "pick," referring to a black child who sang and danced onstage with a white headliner. "Picks" were most often used by female singers.

"After singing a few songs, they would bring out the picks," recounts Joe Laurie, Jr., in his book *Vaudeville* (1953); "I never saw any picks flop." In a song such as "The Pickaninny's Paradise," we enter into the eschatology of the picks.

These earliest Miller recordings, released as "Anytime" and "The Pickaninnies' Paradise" on Okeh 40239, were believed for a very long time to have been lost, and indeed often believed to have been never commercially released at all. However, in 1996 a copy of this first Miller record was brought forth by Richard J. Johnson, a collector in Aylesbury, England.

Johnson had acquired the record about twenty years earlier from the British jazz trombonist and bandleader Chris Barber. On a tour of the United States, Barber had found and purchased a vast storehouse of 78-rpm records, mostly jukebox stock but also many mint-state and still sealed in their various pressing-plant boxes and warehouse crates. The records spanned some forty years, from about 1910 to the mid-fifties, and every musical variety. Barber had the hoard shipped home to England and stashed in a three-story building in Harpenden, Bedfordshire, where they were sorted roughly into three categories and thus divided among the three floors: ground floor, jazz; next floor, blues and rhythm-and-blues; top floor, unknown and unsorted. Johnson visited the building three times. On his first visit, he bought nothing, as he had no money. On his second visit, he bought nothing, "as there was so much shellac I couldn't take it all in." On his third visit, he spent seven hours going through the boxes on the top floor. He left with two large bags crammed so full with heavy 78s that he could barely lift them. He hauled them nearly a mile to the bus stop, and after a two-hour ride, there was another half a mile to walk before he arrived home. But the fragile old records survived the journey intact. Among them was Okeh 40239. To the best of Johnson's recollection, the purchase price was thirty or forty pence, the equivalent today of about fifty cents, less in those days.

Checking the information on the label of Okeh 40239 against the discographical data in the standard reference work, Brian Rust's *Jazz Records 1897–1942,* it was apparent that no one, neither Rust nor his hundreds of correspondents, had ever actually seen this record, for it indicated Miller's musical accompaniment and the take number of each recording, and these disclosures were missing in Rust's work. Johnson passed this label information along to Rust, and it was incorporated in a later edition.

Twenty years later, perusing the notes of the 1996 Emmett Miller compact-disc collection, Johnson came upon the statement that Miller's first record "is so rare that no copies are known to exist." Johnson sent a cassette of the recordings to Lawrence Cohn, the album's executive producer. The tape was broadcast in Los Angeles by Ian Whitcomb on his KPCC-FM radio show on the evening of April 10, 1996, when Cohn appeared as a guest to promote the Sony CD.

Miller's first record makes it abundantly clear that he was already in 1924 one of the strangest and most stunning of stylists ever to record. In an age when scat singing was coming to represent a stylistic avant-garde of sorts, Miller's debut represented an avant-garde of its own, an altogether otherworldly voice, a bizarre malarkey of the soul that seemed a death-cry and a birth-cry, too: the last mutant mongrel emanation of old and dead and dying styles, the first mutant mongrel emanation of a style far more reckless and free than the cool of scat. The slurred arabesques, the yodel-like falsetto melismas: the attributes of Miller's brilliance as we know them are here, florescent and full.

These attributes are the driving force of "Anytime." Their presence is more spare in "The Pickaninnies' Paradise," their effect stranger and more subtle. The song's description of heaven grows ever more ghastly as it unfolds. There is a sweetness in Miller's voice as he sings of this place where — so hideous an image — "every bird in the sky has diamond eyes"; a sweetness that is cheap, theatrical, exuberant, disarming at once — and then, as if to signal and savor the sudden ominous descent of those birds, those fugitives, in this trite and tawdry heaven, from the hell of Hieronymus Bosch, the hell of Pierre Remiet, he completes the rhyme with a dire careening howl that contorts the simple innocence of the word "nice" into a cry whose effect, saccharine and strychnine at once, is altogether unsettling: "Now, ain't that *niii-yiii-yiii-yiii-yice?*" A pick-frightening melisma if ever there was one.

The suggestion is not that Miller designed it so, not that he knew from Hieronymus Bosch or from Remiet, or that he felt toward this mawkish song other than warmly and well. To the contrary, this distasteful song likely reflects to some degree his taste; its grotesque bathos, his poetic sense. He was, after all, a man whose literary grasp very likely fell short of that Macon bestseller *Eneas Africanus.* No, the suggestion is that impulse and a galvanic sensitivity to certain words, certain lyrical and musical colors, conspired in him to articulate, as startling sound, ambiguities and conflations of feeling that were otherwise inexpressible; the suggestion is that beneath his conscious artfulness, beneath his showmanship, something hidden, unknown if not unfelt, was subconsciously at work.

I think in this context of George Jones as a modern example: a cipher, a blank, void of self-awareness or verbal expression, and yet a singer from whose invisible depths torrents of perception and emotion emerge with impossible eloquence. Like Jones, Miller often recorded songs that were mediocre or worse. It is as if the songs, the words, do not matter; as if the feeling in the voice addresses what the songs merely suggest, or as if the songs merely provide a subterfuge. None of which means that Miller was not, first and foremost, an entertainer. His concern was showmanship, not expression, not art or creativity or any of the pretenses that are the sucker's-racket of today. Singing was not for him a way of dealing with his feelings; booze took care of that. But when he sang, something of brilliance sometimes emerged, something rare and true and immanent and wild, from beneath the counterfeit spontaneity and garish mannerisms of style.

In the summer of 1925, Emmett Miller emerged in Asheville, North Carolina. High amid the Blue Ridge and Great Smokies, Asheville was a town of some thirty-eight thousand, and a popular resort of the well-to-do, who were drawn to its atmosphere of culture and bucolic quiet, its mountain air and deep-blue skies, its shady winding streets and mansions. It was to a secluded rest home in Asheville that Al Jolson, the star of the day, would retreat in December of 1927, when he quit the show *Big Boy*. There were many theaters and a thriving local music scene; and the town long had been one of the principal and most profitable of stops on the minstrel-show circuit. It was in Asheville on September 11, 1915, that the Al G. Field troupe had its best day of business since its founding in 1886: four thousand paid admission for two shows at the City Auditorium, gross receipts over $2,500.

"I have always maintained," said Field, "that Asheville is the best show town in the South, if you give it a good show at the right prices. Our company always looks forward to its visits in this city with the utmost confidence. No matter what business has been elsewhere, we know that Asheville will top the list."

Asheville, for anyone (except perhaps Thomas Wolfe), was a desirable place to be. For a blackface singer, it was especially desirable. Miller, in the summer of 1925, was known as a "popular favorite with Asheville theatergoers."

A performer named Turk McBee is encountered repeatedly as a source of information on Miller in the writings of Charles Wolfe. In his essay in *Nothing But the Blues* (1993) McBee is Miller's "singing partner," who recalls that Miller met Jimmie Rodgers in Asheville. In a one-page article by Wolfe in 1994, "Miller and his partner, Turk McBee, relocated in Asheville; here they worked in clubs," and "McBee attests that Miller met Jimmie Rodgers (McBee called him 'that damn hillbilly Jimmie Rodgers') in Asheville, and claims Rodgers also learned a lot from Miller's singing." By the time of Wolfe's 1996 liner notes for *Emmett Miller: The Minstrel Man from Georgia,* McBee is Miller's "old friend and accompanist," and Jimmie Rodgers is described as "from Emmett's Asheville days."

There is no doubt that McBee did indeed claim to have been with Miller in Asheville. In 1979, Jeff Tarrer, a record collector and retired correctional-institution counselor, conducted a series of interviews with McBee, in which McBee certainly seems to recall some of the circumstances surrounding the Asheville sessions: the name of Miller's piano-accompanist, and Miller's alleged nickname for that accompanist. But McBee's claims should be considered with suspicion, as there is no evidence of his presence in Asheville, or of his having worked with Miller during this period. Above all, there is no evidence that Miller himself relocated in Asheville; no evidence of his being there in 1925 prior to late summer, and then only for a week or so. The evidence is that Miller had performed in Asheville in the past, as a theatrical performer on a professional vaudeville circuit, and that his 1925 visit to Asheville was again as such. He was not unknown; there was no playing around cafés and clubs.

Born on November 15, 1912, to one of the founding families of Greenville, South Carolina, Vardry McBee III was the son of a performer also known as Turk (1884–1945). The elder Turk had been a minstrel man himself, in the Field and Coburn companies; and the younger Turk had entered show business as a child. He was said to have played xylophone and tap-danced simultaneously at the age of ten. While it has been said that he performed with the Coburn Minstrels in 1925, there is no trace of the Coburn Minstrels appearing in Asheville that summer; and, in fact, there is no trace of McBee performing with the Coburn show until the summer of 1926. It is not until more than three years later, when Turk McBee and Emmett Miller both toured in the Dan Fitch troupe of 1928–29, that there is any hard evidence of McBee and Miller working together; and there is no further evidence of them working together until 1949. In the summer of 1931, when Miller took part in a disastrous attempt to revive the Field show, which had gone under in 1929, McBee was working as the youngest member of the John R. Van Arnham Minstrels, the last remaining major minstrel troupe still touring. At the time, *Billboard* praised eighteen-year-old McBee as "a natural born 'nigger singer.'"

McBee died on April 4, 1986, and the tales he told of working with Emmett Miller in Asheville date to the years of his drunken dotage. There is no denying that he and Miller knew one another. But in the summer of 1925, when Emmett Miller was in Asheville, Turk McBee, wherever he was, was twelve years old and very likely unknown to "his partner."

During his stay in Asheville, Miller is believed to have influenced local country singers such as the Callahan Brothers, who later based their 1934 recording of "St. Louis Blues" on Miller's arrangement. Homer "Bill" Callahan has been quoted as recalling of Miller: "He did some radio, but mostly he'd play around cafés, things like that. He had a band, but I don't remember much about that. We especially liked the way he did that 'St. Louis Blues.' We got a handle on our version from him."

Callahan's remembrance of Miller should be regarded with care. There was no radio station in Asheville when Miller was there in 1925; there would be none until WWNC ("Wonderful Western North Carolina") began broadcasting in February 1927. As for

Miller's playing "around cafes, things like that," Miller's only known engagements in Asheville were professional and theatrical: the Majestic, which had opened in 1912, was throughout the twenties Asheville's premier showplace.

It should be noted that Bill Callahan was only thirteen years old in 1925; his brother, Walter "Joe" Callahan, was only fifteen. I think it not unlikely that their 1934 version of "St. Louis Blues" may have been based as much on Miller's 1928 recording of the song as on any performance of it by him that they might have heard as adolescents.

Bill Callahan, whose boyhood memories of the period seem somewhat confused, is also alleged to have said that Rodgers visited Asheville often in those days, and has been quoted as saying of Miller that "There's no doubt that he influenced Jimmie."

But it is known that Rodgers did not move to Asheville until two years later, in January 1927, by which time Miller was gone. Nonetheless, when he did move to Asheville, Rodgers, who had not yet recorded, encountered and performed with local musicians such as Ernest Helton, a handyman by trade and music-maker by avocation, on whom Miller's influence and impression may still have been fresh and vibrant.

Regarding Miller, Rodgers, and the Asheville nexus, Nolan Porterfield, the author of the biography *Jimmie Rodgers* (1979), wrote in a 1995 letter to the *Journal of Country Music* that, "although I could never find any definite proof, I have long believed that Rodgers visited Asheville, N.C., before he moved there in early 1927, perhaps on several occasions, and he may well have been there when Miller was. But, of course, if Miller and Rodgers did meet at some point, in Asheville or elsewhere, shouldn't we consider the possibility, perhaps, that the influence ran the other way — or was at least reciprocal?"

The George Vanderbilt Hotel had opened in Asheville, at 75 Haywood Street, in July of 1924, the newest addition to the Foor-and-Robinson Hotels group, which already operated ten luxury hotels in six states, half of them in the Carolinas. A year later, when Ralph S. Peer, the director of production for Okeh, chose Asheville as the site for his next field-recording venture, he decided on the Vanderbilt as his center of activities. He arrived in town from New York and checked into the hotel in August 1925. With him in Asheville were: Charles L. Hibbard, recording engineer; G. S. Jeffers, general sales representative; and Polk C. Brockman, an Atlanta record distributor who had been instrumental in arranging earlier Okeh field recordings.

Peer (1892–1960), who would later produce Jimmie Rodgers's first recordings, for Victor, was in the early twenties the recording manager for Okeh Records. It was he who had produced Mamie Smith's bestselling "Crazy Blues" in 1920; he who had coined the term "race music"; and it was he who had traveled in 1923 to Atlanta, where, as assistant to Okeh's director of production, Fred Hagar (1874–1958), he recorded Fiddlin' John Carson, brought to his attention by Polk Brockman, who sold records out of his Atlanta furniture store. Carson (1868–1949) became the first star of what would come to be called hillbilly music, later country music. These sessions in Asheville were among the last that Peer produced for Okeh; he left the company later in 1925. Okeh, owned at this time by the General Phonograph Corporation, would be acquired by Columbia in the fall of 1926. After the takeover, the electrical recording process, adopted by Columbia in the spring of 1925, would be used for Okeh recordings as well.

According to Turk McBee, Jimmie Rodgers auditioned for Peer in Asheville at this time but was turned down. Again, everything McBee is alleged to have said may be true, but one is always wise to bear in mind Shakespeare's line about "old men of less truth than tongue." And one is wise, too, to bear in mind that drunkards and the truth are rare bedfellows at best.

The Vanderbilt had a roof garden, and a room on this top floor was set up by Peer as a studio. Equipment was installed, a supply of brown-wax master discs was laid in. Recording began on August 25, with Kelly Harrell singing to the guitar and harmonica accompaniment of Henry Whitter. Both men were from Virginia towns close to the Carolina border: Harrell from Fieldale, Whitter from Fries. Whitter was an established Okeh artist, here performing in a supporting role to Harrell, whose only previous recording session had been in January, for Victor, in New York. Thirty-five-year-old Harrell was that rarest of rural performers, a true folk artist, whose repertoire was built to some degree upon the remnants of antique balladry that had been carried across the Atlantic to the Southern colonies. His haunting recording of the murder song "Wild Bill Jones," made this August day in Asheville, would find new and more powerful life forty-six years later in James Dickinson's 1971 Atlantic album, *Dixie Fried,* a dark, gale-force reworking of old Southern music, a baptism of loud and dangerous rhythms, that stands as one of the great testaments not only of rock 'n' roll but also of its ancient and unfathomable roots.

First recorded in New York in the spring of 1924, for Columbia, by the North Carolina singer Eva Williams, "Wild Bill Jones," so deeply embedded in the American loam that it today bears a "Laws number," assigned to those ballads enumerated by the eminent folklorist G. Malcolm Laws, Jr., in his *Native American Balladry* (1964), has been recorded many times. Though the scholarly indices and accounts of Laws E10 date the song's earliest appearance to 1927, it is to the elusive earlier recordings by Eva Williams, Kelly Harrell, and their unknown antecedents, that Dickinson's version seems to be wed in its dark-winged power. While Dickinson was aware of the 1925 Harrell recording, he "never heard it. I feel sure Bob Frank did," he said, referring to the man from whom he got "Wild Bill Jones," a man whom he describes as a Memphis folk-singer "from the early sixties who made one record for Vanguard [*Bob Frank, 1972*] and disappeared into obscurity in San Francisco."

I know of nothing quite like Dickinson's transformation of "Wild Bill Jones" — that is to say his absolute understanding of it, and his surrender as a vessel to that understanding — except perhaps for the Rolling Stones' transformation, recorded in Muscle Shoals, Alabama, in 1969, of Mississippi Fred McDowell's "You Got to Move," itself a transformation, an understanding and a surrender, of an olden fatal spiritual raising. Dickinson was a part of those Rolling Stones sessions, too, which took place not quite four years after Dickinson, as the singer and piano-player in a group called the Jesters, provided Sam Phillips's legendary Sun label with one of its last gasps, a 1966 single called "Cadillac Man." (Dickinson, who was born at Baptist Hospital in Little Rock, Arkansas, on November 15, 1941, lived for most of his life in Memphis before moving to Mississippi in 1985.) He well remembers the three nights — December 2–4, 1969 — of those Rolling Stones sessions. "They cut 'You Got to Move' the first night. They were doing it two-piece on stage," he recalled. "This was the first time they had played it as a band." Dickinson had no role, he says, in the Rolling Stones' "You Got to Move," which Mississippi Fred McDowell (1904–72) had himself first recorded only in 1966. "I wish I could take credit," Dickinson says, "but I didn't really interact with them until the second night." His only "claim to fame along those lines," he says, "is 'hear him whip the women . . .' in 'Brown Sugar,' which Jagger had sung while tracking and was leaving out in the overdub. I remembered the line and Charlie Watts made me tell Mick."

There's a lot of respiration and perspiration connected with the making of phonograph records," reported the *Asheville Citizen* the next morning. "This was demonstrated in the recording laboratory of the George Vanderbilt Hotel yesterday when the Okeh Record Company began making a series of 'hill country records.' The laboratory is on the roof, a tightly enclosed room, which has been announced by officials of the recording company, to be as nearly perfect as any used by them in New York or elsewhere.

"In order to get perfect reproduction everything has to be 'just so.' At a signal from the producing engineer the disk begins whirling and the players begin playing and everyone begins perspiring. But the perspiration doesn't show up in the finished product. The recording device is like an ordinary phonograph mechanism in appearance. A thick wax disk rests on a circular bed that revolves when the motor is turned on. A needle or stylus bears down on the wax disk when the motor is turning. Five minutes and a new record is made. The wax disk is shipped, most carefully packed, to the factory where commercial records are made."

The story said "the company has found the atmosphere of Asheville to be the best in the country for the reproduction of the human voice and instrument music as well in the summer season."

Throughout the next seven days, at least a dozen more acts were recorded. After Harrell and Whitter came Ernest V. Stoneman, then Bascom Lamar Lunsford, the singing Asheville attorney and folklorist, and his fiddling brother, Professor Blackwell Lunsford.

Bascom Lamar Lunsford (1882–1973), from Turkey Creek, near Leicester, North Carolina, just a few miles from Asheville, had made some cylinder records as early as 1922 and had worked previously with Polk Brockman in Atlanta. Among the countless old songs that Lunsford collected and sang was a strange and eldritch piece that he had learned from a neighbor, Fred Moody, in the Carolina pines in 1901. It was called "I Wish I Was a Mole in the Ground," and Lunsford recorded it, for Brunswick, in Ashland, Kentucky, in the spring of 1928. In this song, from that place in a bygone century where dead voices gathered, came the warning that "a railroad man will kill you when he can and drink up your blood like wine." Here was a warning so plain and so inscrutable at once that, by some who heard and heeded, it would never, could never be forgotten. "All the railroad men just drink up your blood like wine," Bob Dylan conveyed that warning, in "Stuck inside of Mobile with the Memphis Blues Again." *Again* — "The Memphis Blues," that "first of all the many published 'blues,'" as W. C. Handy claimed — and again. From the forgotten shadowy pines of the nineteenth century to Fred Moody in 1901 to Bob Dylan in 1966: again, and again.

The banjo-playing singer Fisher Hendley had his debut here, at the Asheville sessions, with a song from the primordium of minstrelsy gone feral: "Nigger, Will You Work?," described in a subsequent Okeh catalogue as "quaint and amusing." Also recorded was Ernest Helton, the handyman-musician who later performed locally with Jimmie Rodgers. The sessions resulted as well in only-known recordings by a harmonica player named Jim Couch, and by the Foor-Robinson Carolina Club Orchestra, which was then performing nightly in the Vanderbilt ballroom under the direction of William Truesdale.

The orchestra recordings were made as the sessions wound down, on September 2. A story in the *Citizen* that morning spoke again of the presence in town of the Okeh men, of their recording of "folk lore songs of the mountain land and instrumental music of the hill country variety. They report large sales of similar records during the last few years. This company was the first to introduce negro folk songs by negro singers and also the first to discover the commercial value of the music of the mountain peoples as recorded on wax disc.

"The recording of the Foor and Robinson hotel orchestra will conclude the summer program of the Okeh people in Asheville.

"R.S. Peer, director of record production, before leaving for his home in New York City, expressed himself as greatly pleased with the results obtained here and with the co-operation given by local people. The Okeh company expects to make Asheville headquarters for summer recording on account of the superior quality of the air here, which is cool and dry and ideal for their purposes."

And the weather was indeed fair that day, with a cool low of sixty-two degrees and a balmy high of eighty-four. Though the morning *Citizen* made no mention of it, the *Asheville Times* ran a small item that evening revealing that the hotel orchestra was not the only act to record that day. "Test records were made today for the Okey [*sic*] Record company by Emmet [*sic*] Miller, blues singer appearing this week with the Musical Comedy revue at the Majestic theater. Accompaniments were played by Walter Rothrock, who made a special trip to the city for the purpose. Songs used by Mr. Miller included: 'You're Just the Girl for Me,' 'Bad Bill Is Sweet William Now,' and 'Love Sick Blues.' The same songs will be used in Mr. Miller's appearance at the Majestic."

Plans for Miller to record, as well as his opening at the Majestic Theatre, had been announced in the *Times* the previous Sunday:

"A popular favorite with Asheville theatergoers will appear at the Majestic this week when Emmet [*sic*] Miller and Harry Fitzgerald present their Musical Comedy Revue.

"Emmet [*sic*] Miller has amused local playgoers on previous engagements by reason of his histrionic ability, his clever mannerisms and the original matter utilized. Mr. Miller has been asked by the Okey [*sic*] Record company, who are recording in Asheville at present, to make several test records while in the city this week. Mr.

Miller's 'Blues songs' have been recorded before, and it is expected that good results will be obtained from these tests.

"Besides Miller, the featured players include Nan Fitzgerald, juvenile comedienne, in songs and dances; Eddie Hill, magician de luxe; Harmony Trio of singers. There is an unusually attractive and clever beauty chorus, special scenery and settings.

"The usual changes of bill will be made on Monday, Wednesday, and Friday, with screen programs on each bill."

In a Majestic advertisement on the next page, there was a full-figure photograph of Miller in blackface and a cap, one hand to his hip, the other to his head. His name was spelled right, and he was billed as "Asheville's Favorite Blues Singer" and "Okeh Record Star." Sharing the bill in addition to Nan Fitzgerald, Eddie Hill, the Harmony Trio, and the beauty chorus, were Birch and Birch ("Novel Musical Act") and Pat Third ("Dancing Fiend"). At matinee prices of ten cents and two bits, and an evening price of thirty-five cents, the show was advertised as "Asheville's Greatest Amusement Value."

Being "Asheville's Favorite," however, was apparently no great distinction. Ned Haverley, Benny Reed, Boots Walton, Slim Williams, and Happy Lawson, the author of Miller's signature song, "Any Time," were among the other minstrel and vaudeville acts that had played the Majestic earlier in 1925; and the stock Majestic advertising phrase "Asheville's Favorite" was applied to most of them.

Miller's show opened on Monday, August 31. There was a review in the next morning's *Citizen*:

"The Miller and Fitzgerald Musical Comedy Company opened a week's engagement at the Majestic Theatre yesterday to capacity houses. This show is one of the best to play Asheville in some time.

"Emmett Miller, the Okeh record star, assisted by Walter Rothrock at the piano, scored the outstanding hit of the show. 'Anytime' and 'Picaninny [sic] Paradise' were the two numbers used. These numbers are the first to be recorded for the Okeh record company, and are on sale now in several music stores in the city. Little Nan Fitzgerald, the juvenile singer and dancer, was a close second to Miller. She has a wonderful voice and has no peer as a dancer. Birch and Birch in musical novelties, Eddie Hill and the magic wonder, Pat Third and his spoon act all came in for hearty applause. The 3:30 o'clock and two night shows age in their several dance numbers. There will be a matinee today at 330 [*sic*] o'clock and two night shows at the Old Field cemetery at Beta, and Friday there will be another change of program."

That closing sentence gives pause. Presented to local historians, it gives profounder pause. Old Field was, and is, quite literally, a graveyard, out at the tiny town of Beta, in Jackson County.

Miller recorded four songs in Asheville that breezy Tuesday afternoon, September 2, 1925, the day after his triumphant (let us assume) engagement at the cemetery. The first of these songs was "You're Just the Girl for Me," written by Miller and Rothrock, although the title was that of a 1908 song by Junie McCree and Albert Von Tilzer. Next came "Big Bad Bill (Is Sweet William Now)," written in 1924 by Jack Yellen and Milton Ager, and recorded that year by Margaret Young (Brunswick), Ernest Hare (Okeh), Clementine Smith (Banner), Billy Murray (Victor), Joseph Samuels' Jazz Band (Perfect), and perhaps others. The third was "Lovesick Blues." The last was "I Never Had the Blues (Until I Left Old Dixie Land)," a song credited to Williams-Straight.

The lyrics of "Lovesick Blues" had been written by Irving Mills (1894–1985), a twenty-eight-year-old Russian émigré who would go on to sing with Duke Ellington and as the leader of his own group, Irving Mills & His Hotsy-Totsy Gang (which would at times include the Dorseys and other jazz musicians with whom Emmett Miller concurrently recorded). The music was by Cliff Friend (1893–1974) of Cincinnati. Together they had copyrighted the song on April 3, 1922, the second of three songs copyrighted that year bearing the same title. Later Friend held that, during the Depression, he sold his interest in the song for five hundred dollars.

Published by Jack Mills, Inc., as "I've Got the Love-sick Blues," the song was introduced by vaudeville singer Anna Chandler (1887–1957), a mezzo-soprano described both as a purveyor of "popular and semi–high class songs" (a 1917 Columbia Graphophone Company catalogue) and as "an early-day blues singer" (her *Variety* obituary). Her photograph appeared on the cover of the original, five-page edition of the sheet music, along with the exhortation, "Get this Number for Your Phonograph and Player Piano." But it was another vaudeville singer, the contralto Elsie Clark (1899–1966), who first recorded the song, for Okeh, on March 21, 1922, prior to its copyright. A Mills advertisement for the song in the May 27 *Billboard* proclaimed, "Tons of Testimonials. Hundreds of Hoorays for this Marvelous Double for Any Combination. Great Comedy Patter and Sensational Harmony Number. Each Rendition Spells W-O-W! Good - Better - Big!" Three weeks later, an item in the June 17 *Billboard* reported that "Lovesick Blues" was being performed in the new show at the Boardwalk, New York's latest cabaret novelty. That summer, Jack Shea also recorded the song, for Vocalion. An often-repeated story held that the song had originally been pitched by Mills to Al Jolson, and in the end went to Shea as a Jolson sound-alike.

But it was Emmett Miller's version, recorded these three summers later in Asheville, that served as the foundation for the song's immortality. As reported in the *Times,* Miller's lone accompaniment on "Lovesick Blues" and his other Asheville recordings was Walter Rothrock, the pianist who had recorded with him in New York the year before.

It is Turk McBee's memory of Rothrock's name — and of Miller's alleged nickname for Rothrock: Mister Hot Rock — that lends credence to McBee's claims of having been with Miller in

Asheville at the age of twelve. Then again, these are details that may have been shared by Miller at a later time. Rothrock's name, in any case, appeared on the labels of the records he made with Miller.

From Miller's Asheville recordings, two Okeh records were issued. The first was "Lovesick Blues" coupled with "Big Bad Bill," released in November 1925; the second was "I Never Had the Blues (Until I Left Old Dixie Land)" coupled with "You're Just the Girl for Me," released in December.

Most of the records made in Asheville were released in Okeh's 45000 hillbilly series. The records by Kelly Harrell, by Jim Couch and by the Foor-Robinsin orchestra, both never to be heard from again, and by Miller were issued in the straight 40000 series. Of these, only the hotel orchestra and Miller were not included in the Okeh Old Time Tunes catalogue.

For a long time, it was believed that these records, like the New York recordings of 1924, were forever lost. Discussing the Asheville recordings, the liner notes to the 1996 Columbia/Legacy compact-disc collection *Emmett Miller: The Minstrel Man from Georgia* state that "no copies are even known to exist." But in these same notes, the track information for Miller's 1929 recording of "Big Bad Bill (Is Sweet William Now)" is illustrated by a label photograph not of this later recording but of Miller's "lost" 1925 record of the same song. This Okeh label, reduced and murkily screened and barely legible, nonetheless is clearly of the old style predating both the electrical-recording era and Okeh's takeover by Columbia from the General Phonograph Corporation, whose imprint is visible on the label. Furthermore, under magnification, it reveals the legend "Recorded in Asheville, N.C." (This same puzzling label, rendered even murkier, is used to illustrate the track listing for "Sweet Mama.") In the summer of 1996, I brought this to the attention of Lawrence Cohn, the executive producer of the CD. Larry told me that the source of the label illustrations was the California collector

Gene Earle. I called Gene, who told me that he had lent all his Miller records to Sony for photographic purposes, including both versions of "Big Bad Bill." Sony used the earlier label by mistake, not noticing that what was being photographed was a record whose very existence was questioned by the text at hand. Thus Okeh 40465 — "Big Bad Bill" coupled with "Lovesick Blues" — is now known to survive in at least two private collections, the other, besides Earle's, being that of Al Haug of Minneapolis, who about 1990 picked it up in a store for under ten dollars. I was made aware of Haug's record by a letter I received from Minneapolis in early 1996: "Dear Mr. Tosches," it began. "Hello my name is Paul Dandy and I am a 16 year old musicologist and historian with my studies focused on the great Emmett Miller. I have been researching Miller for about 6 years . . ."

Ironically, also among the records that Gene Earle lent to Sony was a copy of the first Miller record, Okeh 40239, assumed to be lost until the copy owned by Richard Johnson of England was brought forth some time later. Earle told me that both records, Okeh 40239 and 40465, had been in his collection for a long time, though he could not really recall when or where he got them.

At least two copies of the other Asheville record, "I Never Had the Blues (Until I Left Old Dixie Land)" coupled with "You're Just the Girl for Me," are now also known to exist. They came to light in 1997: one was in the possession of an Australian collector, the other in the stock of a record dealer in New York.

Listening to Emmett Miller's 1925 "Lovesick Blues," we can perceive the vocal trademarks that influenced Jimmie Rodgers (1897–1933), Bob Wills (1905–75), and others. His wry, bizarre phrasing, his eccentric timing, his startling falsetto flights in the middle of vowels, his uncanny swoons of timbre and pitch — these were only the most accessible elements of the singular essence that set him apart, in his own day and forever. These elements are present in all of his Asheville recordings, as they are in his New York recordings of the previous year. Even the most lackluster of them — "I Never Had the Blues (Until I Left Old Dixie Land)," where Walt Rothrock's startling piano-work renders Miller's singing mundane by comparison, and "You're Just the Girl for Me" — are distinguished by wild and stunning break-voice effects. In "You're Just the Girl for Me," Miller begins in a natural voice, which is as straight and as colorless as the lyrics he sings — the only lyrics he is known to have written — but increasingly that strange break-voice force can be heard straining to overtake singer and song: time and tempo shift and are shaken, uneasily at first, then somewhat maniacally; and, in the end, all attempt at sweetness and sentiment is forsaken as Miller's voice flees with a hurried yowl from his own stillborn song.

Though his baritone voice was noticeably deeper in 1924–25 (perhaps to accommodate the acoustic recording process), his style did not appreciably change from these earliest records to his last commercial recordings of 1936. Whether this style was his own or (more likely, it now seems to me) derived from an even more obscure and forgotten progenitor is something that remains unknown, the only true Miller mystery, the enigma of the Ur-Miller, yet to be fully explored. What we do now know is that, from 1924 to the end of his career, that style evinced neither evolution nor innovation.

To be sure, Miller was not the first blackface minstrel to yodel, if that is what we are to call his break-voice falsetto bleat. Matt Keefe had been yodeling through the 1885 "Sleep, Baby, Sleep" since at least 1904, when he sang it with the Lew Dockstader troupe; and by 1908, in a Cohan & Harris Minstrels program, Keefe was identified as a singer of "Yodle Songs." By 1925, when Miller was still relatively unknown, the singing of Ola Elwood, Willard H. Weber of the J. R. Van Arnham Minstrels, Morris Nelson of the Coburn Minstrels, and especially Wichita-born Al Tint, known widely as "The Yodeling Minstrel," had established yodeling as a routine aspect of blackface performance.

In my book *Country,* in a chapter titled "Yodeling Cowboys and Such," I devoted some pages to the course of old-fashioned, Tyrolean-style yodeling from early-nineteenth-century British stage performances to its place in American music. Since then, the research of Bart Platenga of the Netherlands has greatly expanded upon this history, and while he generously acknowledges as a source those pages in *Country,* I can confidently state that their breadth and detail have been superseded by those of Platenga's study, which has been published in Volume 8/9 (1998–99) of the *American Music Research Center Journal,* under the title "Will There Be Yodeling in Heaven?"

But it was Emmett Miller who employed the yodel as more than a novelty. It was Miller who cultivated it as something plaintive and disarming, something that would become — in Jimmie Rodgers's "Blue Yodel" (1927) and all his subsequent blue yodels, in Van and Pete's "Yodel Blues" (1928), in the yodeling of Jimmie Davis and Hank Williams and Jerry Lee Lewis, as well as in the wondrous black yodeling of Tommy Johnson's "Cool Drink of Water Blues" (1928), of Stovepipe Johnson's "Devilish Blues" (1928), of the Mississippi Sheiks' "Yodeling Fiddling Blues" (1930), of the Rhythm Wreckers' version of Rodgers's "Blue Yodel No. 2" (1937) — an expressiveness pure and free. We call it yodeling only because there is no other word for it. Its influence can perhaps be heard even in the lupine wail that became the vocal trademark of Howlin' Wolf in the early 1950s. Ray Charles recalled learning to yodel as a teenager, when he performed with a hillbilly band called the Florida Playboys. In his study, Bart Platenga evinces the yodeling in the vocal effects of Leon Thomas, notably in Thomas's work with Pharoah Sanders.

It was Ralph Peer who, assuming the same role for Victor as he

had for Okeh, first recorded Jimmie Rodgers, in 1927. Like Bob
Wills, who worked blackface in Fort Worth in 1929, Rodgers was
not without experience as a blackface performer.

The influence not only of Miller but of minstrelsy in general was
pervasive in Rodgers's work. "In the Jailhouse Now," recorded by
Rodgers in early 1928, had been previously recorded by four black
acts — by Whistler and His Jug Band, as "Jail House Blues," in the
fall of 1924; by Earl McDonald's Original Louisville Jug Band, as
"She's in the Graveyard Now," in 1927; twice again in 1927, under
the title that Rodgers used, by Jim Jackson and by Blind Blake —
but its ultimate source lay in minstrelsy, and the true popularizer of
the piece seems to have been Rody Jordan of the Al G. Field Minstrels, who performed it as "He's in the Jail House Now" during the
1924–25 season, the season when Rodgers worked blackface in a
traveling medicine show. (Ernest Rogers, a white singing guitarist,
journalist, and stage performer of Atlanta, claimed to have sung the
song on radio as early as 1922, five years before he began making
records, such as "I Got the Misery Blues" and "The Mythological
Blues," for Victor. And as we here wander through these parentheses, we might also pause to note that Jimmy Dorsey and Stan King
would play on a version of the song by Boyd Senter and His Senter-
pedes in 1929, while they were recording with Miller.) And in July
1930 at Victor Hollywood Studios, Rodgers recorded a minstrel
routine called "The Pullman Porters."

The summer of 1933 was a hard and pivotal time for Bob Wills,
who struggled that season between bad fortune and good, leaving
Fort Worth and the Light Crust Doughboys, under bad circumstances, and forming the Texas Playboys in Waco. Charles R.
Townsend, Wills's biographer, mentions no further blackface performances by Wills after 1929. However, two small and obscure
items in *Billboard,* not to be found in Townsend, present intriguing
possibilities. The first, from August, mentions a "Bob Willis" ap-

pearing at movie theaters in Houston with Jimmy "Slats" Allard and His Showboat Minstrels. The second, from October, amends the spelling and specifies the role: "Bob Wills, the middle man," has appeared with Allard at the Palace Theatre in San Antonio, and will be appearing next with him in Fort Worth (where, it is known, Wills had worked blackface four years before).

But neither Rodgers nor Wills would become known as a blackface performer. Emmett Miller, however, would never be known otherwise, and his name and his art, for years, would be buried with the memory of blackface itself.

His star shone briefly, for less than three years.

Nineteen twenty-six: the year the Black Bottom overtook the Charleston, the year that *Billboard* first alluded to the "jazzing-up" and modernization of minstrelsy.

A program book for the tenth-anniversary jubilee of the National Vaudeville Association Benefit Fund, held at various theaters in New York on May 2, 1926, includes a full-page Pat Casey Agency advertisement for the Dan Fitch Minstrels. Pictured beneath a portrait of Fitch is an ensemble photograph of the eighteen-member troupe. Seated at the far left are two men in blackface, another at the far right. Presumably these are the interlocutor and end-men. The one at the far right, seated somewhat apart from the rest of the group, bears a distinct resemblance to Miller, though positive identification is impossible.

On Sunday, July 25, 1926, Miller opened an engagement at the Capitol Theater in Miami. The standard contract, executed through the Gus Spiegelberg Sun Booking Agency, "Successors to Virginia Carolina Managers Circuit" of Atlanta, stipulated "the exclusive services of the said Artist in his specialty or act, entitled" — and here, typewritten, followed the phrase "Yogeling [*sic*] Blues singer."

The Capitol, located at North Miami Avenue and Third Street, self-proclaimed "Miami's Own Theater — Direction Wolfson-Meyer Theater Corporation," gave advance notice of Miller's appearance in a *Miami Herald* advertisement of Friday, July 23:

COMING SOON
EMMETT MILLER — FAMOUS YODELING BLUES SINGER
And Maker of Okeh Phonograph Records

In the *Herald* of the following day, the Capitol announced the next day's new program:

STARTING TOMORROW
BILLIE DOVE AND FRANCIS
X. BUSHMAN IN
"THE
MARRIAGE
CLAUSE"
On the Stage
EMMETT MILLER
The Famous
YODELING BLUES SINGER
And Maker of Okeh Phonograph Records.

(Francis X. Bushman, born in 1883, was celebrated in 1926 for his role as the centurion Messala in *Ben-Hur* of that year. He would appear four decades later, in 1966, the year of his death, in Samuel

Z. Arkoff's American International Picture *The Ghost in the Invisible Bikini*. Such is show business, such are showmen. As for Billie Dove, born Lillian Bohny in 1903, she was in her day as popular as Clara Bow, and her box-office power outdrew that of Mary Pickford, Gloria Swanson, and Greta Garbo. The singer Billie Holiday, forsaking her birth name of Eleanor, named herself after her.)

A *Herald* item on Monday, captioned *YODELING BLUES SINGER ON PROGRAM AT CAPITOL,* began: "Emmett Miller, the Yodeling Blues Singer and maker of phonograph records, was well received last night at the Capitol Theater. His numbers were all of popular variety and made a big hit with the audience."

Wednesday's *Herald,* under the caption SINGER OF BLUES AT CAPITOL THEATER, presented a photograph of Miller, in blackface, black tuxedo and tie, white shirt, white gloves, white hat with black hatband. He is seated, legs crossed, gazing casually but earnestly: the image of suave, urbane sophistication, as if the blackened face and rhomb-ovate of the exaggerated, whitened mouth were but aspects of that sophistication, serving merely to define, rather than to render bizarre or ludicrous or to add even the slightest hint of whimsy to, the nature of that sophistication. It was as if the black of his face and the black of his tuxedo were worn with equal dignity, as if the dignity of the former elucidated the dignity of the latter, distinguishing his air not only as elegant showman, but, further, as blackface showman.

The *Miami Daily News* that day, in an item headed YODELER PUT ON CAPITOL BILL, stated that "In addition to the usual picture program, Emmett Miller, the yodeling blues singer, will appear at each performance. Miller is well known in the south, where he has been appearing recently in his special singing entertainment act."

The *Herald,* Friday, July 30: "Emmett Miller, yodeling blues singer, is appearing at the Capitol Theater today and tomorrow for the last times. He was booked for four days but his engagement was extended to a full week." In actuality, the original contract, dated July 16, six days before Miller's opening at the Capitol, had clearly specified an engagement of "one week."

There are two extraordinary aspects to these Miami shows. One is how ungodly hot it must have been in the dead of the south Florida summer inside the Capitol. (Air-conditioning had only recently come to theaters, in 1925, in New York City.)

The far more provocative aspect to these shows is the billing of Miller as the Famous Yodeling Blues Singer, and, in accord with this new stage sobriquet, the recurrent press references to him as [italics mine] "*the* yodeling blues singer."

The phrase "Yodeling Blues" was the title of a song in the spring of 1923. The composition was credited to the ever appropriative Clarence Williams, who accompanied on piano the first recording of the song, by the vocal duet of Sara Martin and Eva Taylor, in May of 1923. The song was also recorded, the following month, by Williams's protégée Bessie Smith. The phrase, title, and song had nothing to do with yodeling or otherwise inflecting the blues, but rather with the notion of blues caused by the sound of yodeling: a piece of Tin Pan Alley foraging at its most meager.

But it is with the Miami engagement of July 1926, that the phrase "yodeling blues" does indeed appear to be for the first time applied to a style, an inflection, of singing: the style and inflection of singing that Emmett Miller had given voice to since at least the earliest recorded evidence of it, in 1924, and, as fully developed as that earliest evidence is, almost certainly for some years predating that evidence. That style, that inflection — that wild rushing flight of swarming inflections — eludes and defies any other more accurate single word. And yet it cried for a name. For while powers need no names, nothing can be sold without a name.

Thus, sometime between the spring and summer of 1926, either from wile and wit within or bestowed, or raised from the common, spreading descriptive of the fleeting masses of his fleeting fame, Emmett Miller became the Famous Yodeling Blues Singer.

Miller was in Asheville again in the late summer of 1926, as he had been in the late summer of 1925. Labor Day week found him performing at the Majestic, four shows daily as an "extra added attraction" to the feature pictures *Bigger than Barnum's* (September 6–7) and *The Regeneration of Brian Kent* (September 8–9). Advertisements billed him as "Emmett Miller — Blues Singer" and "The Okeh Record Star."

Perhaps Miller was still in Asheville when the Al G. Field Minstrels came to town later that month. The show this season starred Blackface Eddie Ross, the veteran interlocutor Leslie Berry, singers Billy Church and Phil Pavey, and eccentric dancer Bob Conn, who was a newcomer to the troupe. The company's arrival was anticipated by the *Asheville Times* in its "Stage and Screen" column of Sunday, September 19:

"The coming week end will find the Auditorium again tenanted. This time an old favorite among the traveling troupes which come to Asheville will be with us for two days. The Al G. Field's Minstrel show has been one of the events of the city's dramatic season since long before the old auditorium burned and in the days when Field himself was alive and one of the chief performers. The show today is a monument to a great entertainer and its success is no doubt largely due to the principals [*sic*] of good showmanship, which the founder practiced.

"The success of the production here is annually a thing to be taken for granted. Residents of Asheville who rarely go to any sort of theatrical entertainment are inevitably to be seen among the audiences when Field's minstrels come to town.

"This year the watchword of the troupe is 'bring on the jazz.' It is the fortieth anniversary of the organization and the show has been dedicated to snappy syncopation. Three shows will be given, the first Friday evening at the usual theater hour."

There was a photograph of portly, smiling Billy Church, "silver toned tenor" of the troupe.

Opening night sold out, with tickets priced at fifty cents to two dollars. "Eddie Ross is by all odds the star of the show," reported the *Times* reviewer on Saturday morning. "His monologue is a classic and his banjo playing about as near perfect as such things can be." The review went on to praise Billy Church, Phil Pavey, Leslie Berry, and "the blackface boys of the dancing chorus who step off in unison the meanest Charleston ever trod upon the boards of the old Auditorium."

The Field troupe was the last of the grand old minstrel shows, the show with which Dan Emmett had performed his final engagement, at the turn of the twentieth century.

Field, whose real name was Alfred Griffith Hatfield, was born near Morgantown, Virginia (later West Virginia), on November 7, 1850. He entered minstrelsy at twenty; at the age of thirty-five, in October 1886, he formed his own outfit. Headquartered in Columbus, Ohio, Field advertised his show, at the time when young Emmett allegedly first saw it, as "America's Representative Organization" and "the largest and most complete organization of its kind in the world." In the early twentieth century, Field was the grand old man of minstrelsy. Known affectionately as Al G., he drove a white horse in his troupe's parade through every town and city, bowing to the crowd from the regal high-seated phaeton to which his horse was hitched. Though Field himself was gone — he had been laid to rest in a Knights Templars ceremony in the spring of 1921 — the outfit that bore his name lingered on, under the management of his nephew Edward Conard.

The *New York Herald* had written of Field's death as the death of minstrelsy itself. In a piece headlined "Black Face Minstrelsy

Passes," the newspaper said: "Whether Field's minstrels, now that its originator and proprietor is dead, will continue is definitely not stated." It concluded: "Black face minstrelsy did its full share to make the world forget its cares and troubles. By its passing vaudeville was the greatest gainer, but there are still old timers who with a questionable allegiance to movies and modern plays doubt if the theatregoer benefitted greatly by the change."

The Field Minstrels came to the Grand in Macon almost every fall, and sometimes in the spring as well — as in March of 1925, when the Field show arrived in Macon barely a month after Neil O'Brien's minstrels came through.

O'Brien, born in Port Dickinson, New York, in 1868, was himself a Field alumnus (1896–98). His own troupe of 1925 — the fourteenth annual edition of the O'Brien show — featured, as it did the year before, Sugar Foot Gaffney of LaGrange, Georgia, and Billy Beard of Columbia, South Carolina. Known as the Party from the South, Beard was another Field alumnus. John Pink Miller later said that Beard, during a stay in Macon, predicted that Emmett "would some day be a famous comedian."

Lee Roy "Lasses" White, the Southern Sunflower, had also been a Field headliner. In 1924, with the backing of W. T. Spaeth, he had formed his own Lasses White All-Star Minstrels, which also played Macon.

Bert Swor was one of the celebrated blackface performers of the day. Born in Paris, Tennessee, in 1871, he spent twenty years, on and off, with the Field show. In most of those years, as in 1925, he was its star.

It was likely sometime soon after this season's Macon performance, late in 1926, that Miller became a member of the Al G. Field Minstrels.

"Do you remember," reminisced Miller's fellow Field minstrel Bob Conn a dozen years later, "back in 1926, when Emmett Miller almost had his hand severed by a pelican for trying to take the bird's meat away from him in Florida? Also, when Emmett almost caused a riot over a dice game at the old Fairfax, now the Paramount, in Miami? I was fired on account of the incident, and Blackface Eddie Ross and Emmett Miller quit the show because I was canned. However, we all ended up at the end of the season, still with the Field show."

It is this reminiscence by Bob Conn that dates Miller's earliest association with the Al G. Field Minstrels. Conn himself was new to the troupe in 1926. A review of the Field show late that summer in the *Telegram* of Youngstown, Ohio, described Conn as "a 'find' among the newcomers." Miller was not yet with the show; and, though he performed in Asheville on September 6–9, he was not with the show when it played the Asheville Auditorium on September 24–25; and he was not with the show when it played Macon. The itinerary of the troupe wound southward every summer, following warm weather, ending in Florida. There is no reason to doubt Conn about the year: it must for him have been a memorable year, his first year with the show; and his reminiscence was not all that far removed from it in time. He also mentions Blackface Eddie Ross in conjunction with Miller. Ross was with the troupe in 1926, but not in 1927. Miller was not with Field in 1928; and in 1929 the Al G. Field Minstrels disbanded in midseason. Nineteen twenty-six is the only year that Ross and Miller could have been together in Florida as members of the Field troupe. Thus, unless Conn imagined the whole thing — pelican, dice game, and all — late in the season of 1926 is when Miller joined the troupe.

Sally Hinson's research has further revealed that Miller was in Asheville yet again in the late spring of 1927, when he performed at the Majestic during the week of June 6. An advertisement billed him as "Late of Al G. Field Minstrel," further evidence that he had hooked up with the troupe at the close of its previous season.

This presents the possibility that Emmett Miller and Jimmie Rodgers actually may have met after all — not in 1925, as has been conjectured, but almost two years later, in June of 1927.

Rodgers was indeed living in Asheville at this time. In fact, on the Monday night of May 30, a week before Miller opened at the Majestic, the Jimmie Rodgers Entertainers made their debut on WWNC. Rodgers's show was very short-lived. Only two weeks separated the first program from the last, on June 13; and there is no listing for Rodgers on the Monday night of June 6, when his hour slot seems to have been given over to "Old Time Music by Hayes-Lunsford." But it was long-lived enough to place him in Asheville at the time of Miller's engagement at the Majestic.

Miller by this time was a celebrity of sorts in town — "Asheville's Favorite Blues Singer" and "Okeh Record Star" — and Rodgers surely should have wanted him on his struggling little Monday-night radio show. Miller's opening at the Majestic on the Monday of June 6 may have offered a mutually advantageous opportunity; though, as the evidence is that there was no Rodgers broadcast of June 6, it is conceivable that Miller was a guest on the previous, first show. It is conceivable as well that there was no Rodgers broadcast of June 6 because Rodgers joined the Miller bill at the Majestic. The WWNC studio was located in the Flat Iron Building, at the corner of Wall Street and Battery Park Avenue, just a few blocks from the Majestic, which was located at the corner of College and Market Streets.

Perhaps Bill Callahan's childhood remembrance of Miller doing "some radio" was a recollection of this later time; perhaps Rodgers's phantom visits of 1925, recalled by Callahan in his old age, were but an understandably confused memory of Rodgers's actual residency in 1927, when Callahan was fifteen. In fact, his recollection of Miller — "He did some radio, but mostly he'd play around cafés, things like that. He had a band" — is more accurate of Rodgers in

Asheville in 1927 than of Emmett Miller at any time. It also echoes Rodgers's own remembrance of his early days in Asheville, as recounted in an interview with the *Asheville Times* in late 1929, when he returned to play the City Auditorium as one of the country's most celebrated performers: "I managed to make a living by entertaining, playing for dances, and giving programs," he said, "but it was hard sledding."

Thus if Rodgers and Miller met in Asheville, it was likely in early June of 1927. By the end of that month, they both were gone.

By no means the least persuasive argument for the possibility of a Miller-Rodgers radio encounter is that, as far as is known, Turk McBee made no claim to have been there. His father, however, made news of sorts that summer, when an item captioned "Turk McBee Improving" appeared in *Billboard:* "Greenville, S.C., July 16 — Vardry T. (Turk) McBee, widely known theater man, is slowly improving in the Emma Booth Memorial Hospital from the effects of blood poison, arising from an infection on his lower lip."

On the Saturday of July 9, 1927, a month after Miller's shows in Asheville, the *Citizen* of Columbus, Ohio, published a pre-season report on the Al G. Field Minstrels, then preparing for rehearsals in nearby Newark. The troupe this season included several performers from the previous season: the singers Carl Graves, Harley Newland, and Phil Pavey, as well as the veteran interlocutor Leslie Berry. But the majority of the minstrels were newcomers. The show's singers included Stan Chapin, Russell Neff, Charles Page, and an Alpine yodeler named Harry Clark. The dancers, under the direction of Eddie Uhrig, included Jack Ault, Maurice Bair, Leo Doran, Warren Dugan, Frank Miller, Garner Newton, and Jack Warner. The featured comedians included Billy Redd, Paul Taylor, and Drane Walters. Some members had more than one role: Garner Newton was a comedian as well as a dancer; Paul Taylor a singer as well as a comedian; Berry, Neff, Page, and Pavey sang together as the Harmony Four. There was also a tightwire act, Roy and Hughie Mellnotte. The troupe's musical director and bandleader was O. A. Meredith. Both he and Eddie Uhrig, the dance director, were new this season.

The *Columbus Citizen* report noted the presence of "Emmett Miller, a black-face comedian whose frolics enhanced the show for a brief period last year and who has been regularly signed for this season." Rehearsals began in Newark on July 11, and the show opened at the Newark city auditorium on Saturday, July 30, coinciding, "as is the time-honored custom," with the week of the Hartman State Fair.

By August Miller was also performing again as a vaudeville solo act: a long engagement at the Park Theatre in Erie, Pennsylvania, August 1–13, and shows in New York.

Jimmie Rodgers had left Asheville in late June in search of work. In Bristol, Tennessee, on August 4, while Miller was performing in Erie, Rodgers made his first recordings, for Ralph Peer of Victor.

From Bristol in August, Rodgers went to Washington, D.C., where he remained until November.

In its issue of August 27, *Billboard* reported on a Field show in upstate New York: "Emmett Miller, vocalist with the Al G. Field Minstrels, singing *Anytime,* at the Colonial Theater, Utica, N.Y., put it over with a bang, according to *The Observer-Dispatch* of that city, which states that patrons of the theater would not let Miller rest until he had given four encores of the song. Further comments, in part, on the show the newspaper says: 'Humor was at its highest pitch during the skit, *The Abode of the Spirits.* In a bootleggers' camp in the Everglades, Drane Walters and Miller demonstrate negro laziness to the nth degree. Charles Page, whose desire to quote Shakespeare brings the line "Sit Down, Ham", sends the audience into gales of laughter. The piano moments in *Silver Threads Among the*

Gold, sung by Harley Newland, accompanied by the chorus, satisfied lovers of old-time ballads: Newland's sweet tenor reached the higher register at the close of the song, while the chorus hummed softly and produced a demand for two encores. Opening, the orchestra is at the rear of the stage, elevated above the singers against the background of a city sky line. The musician [*sic*] style of playing, with the singers predominating, offered a new type of accompaniment to the songs. O. A. Meredith, leader, has developed a peculiar rhythm with his band of players that gets away from the blare and noise of jazz, but keeps all the sensation of syncopation. *Radio Troubles* is far from what the title implies. The Mellnotes, Roy and Hughie, on the tightwire, introduce their bit clothed in series of surprise antics.' "

In early September a *Billboard* correspondent attended a Field show in Akron. "Mr. Conard has assembled a very capable company," he wrote; "has developed some new stars, contracted some he has sought for many years, and advanced others from the ranks. Taken all in all, it is a most creditable production, lacking none of the careful costuming and staging as in former years and from all indications the show should experience a winning season.

"The opening number of the show this season is very simple, yet impressive, and seldom has a first part been so replete with features. *Up High* is the way the first part has been programmed, the entire company taking part.

"Heading the fun contingent this year are Emmett Miller, Paul Taylor, Drane Walters, Billy Redd and Garner Newton. Miller has long been sought by Mr. Conard, but not until this season could he be suitably cast. Miller carries the bulk of the comedy of the olio and is one of the best principals the Field show has ever featured. *Any Time* is Miller's big song hit and he never fails to get several encores. His work in the afterpiece 'The Abode of Spirits' is typical of Mr. Conard's olio features and Miller does his lines in a manner that keeps the audience in a fit of laughter for the 20 minutes the skit runs.

"Billy Doran, who for several years has been responsible for the dance numbers on the Field show, has given up the minstrel game for dance instruction work in New York. Eddie Uhrig, a Field veteran, has charge of the 'hoofers' and has worked out some very pleasing numbers. His dancing squad includes Warren Dugan, Jack Ault, Garner Newton, Frank Miller, Maurice Bair, John Warner and Leo Doran.

"Emmett Miller and Phil Pavey open the olio with a talking skit. The dancers follow with a short number and then Paul Taylor and Drane Walters fill a spot. Hughie and Roy Melnotte [sic] offered a novelty wire act which is just fair. 'The Abode of the Spirits', a satire on prohibition, is very amusing and is probably as entertaining as any presented by the Field show in recent years. 'Moonlight' is the title of the dancing specialty which follows and this goes into the finale in which the entire company takes part, Harley Newland assuming the lead singing role. Leslie Berry, a veteran with the show, fills the role of interlocutor in his own inimitable style.

"*Silver Threads Among the Gold* is well done by Harley Newland. Phil Pavey sings *At Dawning, Forgive Me* is Carl Graves' feature song, and *When You're Lonesome* is being creditably rendered by Russell Neff. *I'm Looking Over a Four Leaf Clover* is the first ballad of the first piece sung by Stan Chapin. The Harmony Four, Phil Pavey, Russell Neff, Leslie Berry and Charles Page, get a nice lot of applause and are one of the best numbers in the afterpiece."

The show played Asheville on September 16–17. Its anticipated arrival headlined an article on current and forthcoming attractions in the *Times* of Sunday, September 11:

"With the approach of fall comes an increased interest in all forms of theatrical entertainment, even the movies — which, like the poor, we have with us always. The nights become too chilly for auto-riding and sparking (as the mid-victorians [*sic*] called it); the old folks stay at home, and so the proper thing to do is to "Take Your Girlie to the Movie" (sung to any of the popular airs — They're all alike anyway.) [*interpunctio sic*]

"The first sign of the opening of the theatrical season is Al G. Field's Minstrels, which will begin a two-day run this week at the Auditorium. Hedged about with almost a half century of tradition, this institution played for our fathers and filled a place in the average American's credo similar to that held by the Democratic party, castor oil, and the Methodist church. While not holding such an important place in the esteem of the youth of today, particularly that group which is vaguely termed 'modern youth,' Field's Minstrels still is able to pack houses wherever it goes.

"This season the minstrels turn to aviation with shrewd insight into the American taste for up-to-the-minute stuff, even in entertainment. One of the principal scenes is set atop a skyscraper, with the tops of other buildings in silhouette, the performers supposedly arriving by airplane. Thence follows the burlesque of aviation."

It was indeed a year for aviation. Captain Charles Lindbergh, a United States air-mail pilot, had won a twenty-five-thousand-dollar prize offered for the first nonstop flight from New York to Paris. Flying alone in his monoplane, the *Spirit of Saint Louis,* Lindbergh left New York on the morning of May 20, arrived in Paris on the evening of the following day. Receiving him in Washington on June 11, President Coolidge had raised him to the rank of colonel; on June 13, an estimated two thousand tons of ticker tape and shredded paper rained down upon him as he rode up Broadway in Manhattan in his parade of triumph; and on June 18 the United States Post Office issued a special ten-cent air-mail stamp commemorating his flight.

The *Times* article went on to discuss the Keith vaudeville bill at the Plaza, Norma Shearer in *After Midnight* at the Imperial, and an extra added attraction at the Majestic: "Alleh Rageh, foreteller of world events and discerner of your middle name." The great Rageh was "scheduled to drive blindfolded through the streets of Asheville" on Monday.

An accompanying piece appeared on the next page, headlined "Field Minstrels Atop Skyscraper":

"'Up High' is the title given the latest edition of the Al G. Field Minstrels, which is scenically set with roof garden entertainment atop a skyscraper.

"In silhouette appear the top-flight stories of other tall buildings, inspiring monuments to the skill of our craftsmen, their outlines softened by the silvery radiance of the full moon.

"The entertainers have arranged a varied and pleasing program for the occasion and a hilarious evening for all is under way, each endeavoring to out-do the other in his own inimitable style of entertainment.

"The guests, absorbing the spirit of the assemblage, presently participate in the festivities to the delectation of all. The varied innovations introduced in this novel depiction of a minstrel first part stamp it as a black and white revue of the most appealing type. In this hour of rapid entertainment, a melange of mirth and melody par excellent [sic] is presented by a group of stylists unexcelled.

"The vocal number presented by Emmett Miller, stellar comedian in his own inimitable style, is one of the high spots of the evening."

An advertisement in the *Asheville Citizen* on the eve of the show billed Emmett Miller as "Well Known in Asheville"; an ad in the next day's *Citizen* billed him as "The Well Known Asheville Favorite." The review in that morning's *Citizen* was headlined "MILLER STAR OF MINSTREL SHOW":

"Emmett Miller, with a captivating personality, was the stellar attraction of the forty-first annual presentation of the Al G. Field's Minstrels at the Auditorium last night. The performance met with general approval of the capacity crowd, although it must be confessed it was the excellent performance of this young artist that kept the production from mediocrity.

"Miller, who recently played at the Majestic theater in tabloid, proved himself a capable comedian and worthy of the important role given him by the management. He was ably assisted by Drane Walters, Billy Redd, Garner Newton, and Paul Taylor.

"The singing was not up to the usual standard and the production was without a capable soloist. Such favorites as Jack Richards and Billy Church were sadly missed by the crowd. Another favorite, John Healy, was unable to come with this year's show on account of advanced age. His place as 'Old Black Joe' was taken by Paul Taylor.

"The usual half-circle was the first part, while the second part was a series of short sketches, including a vaudeville number and an excellent dancing act. Leslie Berry, one of the best interlocutors in the history of minstrelsy, handled the first part in a capable manner. It was the direction of this veteran that kept the show going at a fast clip.

"The selection of songs were excellent, and the singers were well received, especially Phil Pavey, Carl Graves and Russell Neff. However, it was Emmett Miller's 'Any Time' that provoked the most applause.

"The comedians had a fine line of new jokes and the audience was kept in a general uproar. Billy Redd's 'Poetry of Songs' was generously applauded, while Drane Walters proved himself to be an able second to Miller."

The review praised the dancers and the Mellnottes, whose wire-walking act was doubling as part of the Keith show at the Plaza; the dialogues of Drane Walters and Paul Taylor, Emmett Miller and

Phil Pavey; the Harmony Four, consisting of Pavey, Russell Neff, Leslie Berry, and Charles Page.

"Much comedy was furnished in the Abode of the Spirits, a short sketch dealing with the manufacture and sale of whiskey, and featuring Miller, Walters, Redd, Newton, Taylor, Bair and Page."

Two days later, on September 19, the Field troupe appeared at the Auditorium Theatre in Winston-Salem, North Carolina. On the eve of the shows, the *Winston-Salem Journal* ran a Field publicity photograph of Miller wearing the same undersized hat and contorted droll expression that Bert Swor had worn in his Field publicity photo years before. It was captioned "Musical Comedian," and a legend beneath it read: "Emmett Miller, well known in Winston-Salem, coming to the Auditorium with Al G. Field's, matinee and night, September 19." A brief item accompanying the photo further described Miller as "a comedian unexcelled in the impersonation of the Southern negro." Drane Walters was also lauded, as "equally skilled in darkey delineation." Described as "the fastest and funniest afterpiece ever presented with a minstrel show," the negro absurdity, "The Spooks' Rendezvous," was said to be "based on the superstitions of the Southern negro." The setting sounds similar to that of the show's regular afterpiece, "The Abode of the Spirits," but the emphasis seems to have been shifted from distilled spirits to otherworldly spirits. Instead of "a bootleggers' camp in the Everglades" — the backdrop of "The Abode of the Spirits" — here "the scene is a swamp in Florida, where two scary [*sic*] boys find themselves surrounded by 'hants,' as they call them, the mysterious noises emanating from the surrounding darkness causing them moments of despair and helplessness."

The review in the *Winston-Salem Journal* of September 20 made no mention of "The Spooks' Rendezvous"; the afterpiece was "The Abode of the Spirits."

The subheading of the review was an effusion of acclaim: "Emmett Miller Proves Big Star, Carrying Burden of Work of Show."

The review conveys a sense, if somewhat befuddled, of the vaudeville mélange that minstrelsy in its decadence had become: "The program opened with an 'Aerial First art' filled with Ethiopian Envoys who went through dances and jests of doubtful vintage; with boys from gay 'Paree' who sang by turn and flourished themselves before the audience in rustling velvet and gorgeous trappings; with Dixie Dukes who gave their hearers a sort of musical, conversational, comical dramatic salad, intended to give the correct seasoning to the courses that followed."

I take it that "Aerial First art" is typographical sputum for "aerial first act," referring to the theme of this season's show. As to the flaunting of the boys in their gorgeous trappings, precise and confident decipherment eludes me.

"Interspersed at frequent intervals with songs done to a turn by Emmett Miller and Paul Taylor," the show nevertheless left much to be desired. "Emmett Miller and Phil Pavey rescued the performance from dullness a number of times, together and singly, and especially grateful was the audience when they appeared for a 'few moments' in the last half. In the latter half Miller added to his popularity gained in the first division of the program with his inimitable singing. He never let himself out far enough to show his range but he displayed his vocal abilities in a multitude of calisthenic exercises, syncopated close harmony, and interpretive exhibitions which netted himself and his accompanist encore calls a-plenty."

"But those who had seen Al. G. Field's Minstrels through the past several years sighed for days of 'Auld Lang Syne,' when 'Silver Threads Among the Gold,' 'Any Time,' 'Everybody's Smiling Down in Dixie' and ever 'Crazy Words' were fairly recent and were being sung by artists who did not appear on the program last night."

"Silver Threads among the Gold" predated the Field Minstrels; it was from 1873 and had not been "fairly recent" in half a century. But what here intrigues is the reference to "Any Time" as a favorite number sung by a Field performer, or performers, before Miller's time. We know that it was Miller's "big song hit" during this season, and the fact that he had recorded it almost three years ago as his first recording suggests that it had been his signature song for quite some time. But from whom in the context of the Field show had he inherited it in 1926 or 1927? The song was only five years old in 1926. Bert Swor, who headlined the Field show in 1920, headlined as well in 1922 and 1925; Eddie Ross headlined in 1926. During this time, there were many featured singers, such as the yodeler Ola Ellwood. In the fall of 1926 alone, Phil Pavey, Dolph Kestor, Harley Newland, Carl Graves, Jack Richards, and Billy Church worked as singers in the troupe. Had Miller's performance of the song in 1924 or earlier been inspired by a rendition witnessed at a Field show?

The troupe performed in Durham on the evening of September 20. "The New Field Show Is Good" declared the *Durham Morning Herald* in the headline of its review the following day.

"Al G. Field's minstrel show paid its annual visit to Durham last night and gave delight to an audience of minstrel fans at the city auditorium. It marked the opening of the 1927–28 theatrical season locally. In fact, it is almost the custom for Field's to open the Durham season. But, it is a different Field's show this year. It has been almost completely overhauled and revamped as to personnel. Gone are the old stars such as Swor, Healy, Church, Richards and others familiar for a generation of minstrel fame. A few years ago it was said what would Field's minstrels be without Swor, or Healy, or Church, or Richards? Many would have answered that it wouldn't be much of a show. Last night's presentation was a full and satisfactory answer."

The anonymous reviewer horsewhipped into service an analogy of new blood from the minor leagues rejuvenating baseball or football teams whose star players have faded. The present show represented a similar example of rejuvenation: "better team work than has been witnessed in many a year. Aging Billy Church wasn't missed. Conceited Richards has been replaced. Swor and Healy are most missed, but not as you would imagine after seeing the new show. The most noticeable absence was the 'Old Black Joe' act. It is true that the act is still on, but it is not the same as of old."

There was no question as to the star of the new season: "Few black-face comedians ever received such an ovation here as Emmett Miller got last night. It reminded one of the palmy days of Al Fields [sic], Lew Dockstader, Primrose, 'Honey Boy' Evans, 'Lasses' White and Bert Swor. Mille [sic] is a successful successor to those famous minstrel men of old."

The reviewer did not find the production so lavish. "There was more of the minstrelsy than usual, and less attempt at gorgeous scenic effect. At one time the Field show was threatening to become a musical comedy composed of males. The minstrel features of old were sliding out of the picture. But there are signs of a drift back toward pure minstrelsy in the new Field show."

From Durham, the troupe traveled north to play Richmond, Virginia; then south again, for two nights and a matinee, September 22–24, at the Strand Theatre in Salisbury, North Carolina; then on to Raleigh, North Carolina, for two nights, September 26 and 27, at the State Theatre. An advance publicity item appeared in the *Raleigh News and Observer* of September 21:

"Minstrelsy of the newest and best type is the aim of the producers of the forty-first annual edition of the Al G. Field Minstrels, which will appear at the State Theatre, Monday and Tuesday nights, September 26 and 27.

"Since the founding of the famous amusement institution, the traditions of this splendid form of entertainment have been retained. The plaintive melodies of the Southland, mingled with the peppy tunes of today, the levee dances of slavery days and the daring dances of today, go to make a modernized minstrel melange entertaining to all.

"Particular attention has been paid to the selection of comedians comprising the staff of laugh-getters. Emmett Miller, 'The man with the clarinet voice,' heads the list of fun-makers, and the brand of comedy served by this young delineator of the southern negro is in a class of its own.

"'Up High!' is the title of the first part, scenically set with roof garden environment atop a modern skyscraper.

"The vocal portion of the entertainment is capably presented by a corps of well-trained singers, handsome young men with personality aplenty, gorgeously costumed and delivering solo and ensemble numbers in a manner that sets a new high mark in minstrel melody." Published with the item was a photograph of Drane Walters in blackface and splayed high collar.

Two days later a small Field advertisement gave second billing to Miller, "Clarinet Voiced Comedian," beneath Hughie and Roy Mellnotte. On the eve of the troupe's opening, a larger ad described Miller similarly as "The Funny Clarinet Voiced Comedian," and more publicity appeared in an item on the opposite page: potted praise for this "famous organization, now well nigh the last of its kind and claimed to be the best," an institution that always offered "something up to the minute and full of innovations, while at the same time adhering to those time-honored forms and traditions of the art, without which it would cease to be what it professes." Here again Miller — "a face new to minstrelsy, but one of the cleverest blackface comedians of the present day" — was the Man with the Clarinet Voice, the star of the show. But here he was not alone: "Another delineator of the Southern Negro who captivates the audience with his droll mannerisms is Drane Walters. Then there is Billy Redd, from Virginia, and Garland Newton, from Kentucky, who are thoroughly versed in the art of Negro interpretation.

"A dozen singers of note go to make up the vocal contingent, chief of which are Phil Pavey, a silvery lyric tenor; Harvey Newland, who sings the old songs of minstrelsy in a manner all his own; Stan Chapin, a robust tenor of great power and range; Harry Clark, the Alpine yodler; Russell Neff, high baritone of splendid quality; and a well-trained chorus of powerful and harmonious voices."

It is interesting that nowhere among these "singers of note" is mention made of Miller. This time, instead of a grinning Drane Walters, there appeared the Field publicity photograph of a grinning Miller in his undersized hat: "Ernest [*sic*] Miller, Clarinet Voice Comedian with Al G. Fields [*sic*] Minstrel [*sic*]."

While the headline of the *News and Observer*'s review of September 27 also shunned the plural — "Field Minstrel Has New Star" — the subhead got the name right: "Several of Stars Missing But Emmett Miller's Work Features." The amicable reviewer described "a crowd which all but filled the theater," then, like his colleague in Durham, turned to baseball metaphor: "The new star about whom revolves the chief fun-making in the attraction is Emmett Miller, a Southerner who only a couple of years back was touring this section on a tabloid circuit. Miller, known as the 'boy with the concert [*sic*] voice,' easily was the Babe Ruth of the Field company last night and time after time he circled the bases of applause as his stuff went over big with the audience. He has brought his shuffling walk and his 'thousand frogs on a log' story to minstrelsy, and they, with his 'coronet' [*sic*] voice, are the main guns in his artillery of fun-making."

Ungainly praise issued forth as well for the opening ensemble production, "Up High," and for its "harmony makers, clad in colonial costume." (Might these have been the "boys from gay 'Paree' who sang by turn and flourished themselves before the audience in rustling velvet and gorgeous trappings," described in Winston-Salem?) Harley Newland's performance of "Silver Threads among the Gold" was "the best rendered and best received of the solo numbers. Phil Pavey, Carl Graves, Russell Neff and Stan Chapin are the other sweet singers whose numbers were well received.

"Nine black-face dancers of ability, whose work was in keeping with their name of 'Synchronous Steppers,' gave the company a feature which drew much praise. In one of the oleo acts these steppers appear on a darkened stage with black costumes trimmed with phosphorent [*sic*] cloth, in a weird dance."

"The Abode of Spirits" carried "quite a few laughs. The funmakers went into the mothballs for some of their cracks, but even these seemed to go over well." Hughie and Roy Mellnotte, the tight-wire act, "added quite a bit of novelty." The Harmony Four "were another oleo attraction."

The show was in Charlotte for a matinee and evening performance on Thursday, September 29. Its coming was advertised as early as September 18, with special mention made of Emmett Miller, "Clarinet Voice Comedian," and Drane Walters, "The Virginia Reel Kid." Further publicity appeared in the *Charlotte Observer* of September 25, in an item headed "Newest Type of Minstrelsy in Field's Show," drawn from the same press release that had been used by the *Raleigh News and Observer* four days earlier. An ad on the opposite page described "The Funny Comedian Emmett Miller" as "Well Known Locally." The *Charlotte News* of that day ran the photograph of Miller that had appeared in the Winston-Salem paper a week before.

The review of the show in the *Observer* described the Field blackface comedians as "led by Emmet [*sic*] Miller, the minstrel of minstrels," and went on to describe the reaction of the crowd to Miller and "Thousand Frogs on a Log," which apparently served as a running joke throughout the show: "An audience filling the balconies and half filling the auditorium seemed to never tire of giving encores to the stuttering Emmet [*sic*] and his ebony supporters in their boot-legg [*sic*] breeches or gold braided coats.

"Other minstrels and singers came in for their share of applause, but Emmet [*sic*] overshawoded [*sic*] them.

"All night Emmet [*sic*] grumbled and growled about a 'thousand frogs on a log.' Early in the evening the interlocutor attempted to recite something about a 'thousand frogs on a log.' Instantly Emmet [*sic*] was growling in disgust, 'Can't get no thousand frogs on no log. If you had said seventeen or eighteen hundred that might 'er sounded reasonable.'

"Finally, the mention of a 'thousand frogs on a log' was sufficient almost to throw the audience into paroxysms of laughter."

The review in the *Charlotte News* compared the show to "the shoddy performance of has-beens that were here last season" under the banner of the Field troupe:

"They can't come back, says an axiom of the prize ring, but that's not true generally, and Al G. Field's Minstrels have proced [*sic*] this year that it isn't applicable here.

"Last season the company that performed under the name of Al Field must have made the spirit of the illustrious blackface roll and toss in its grave. It was a travesty on the ancient and honorable troupe that had for so many years packed 'em in throughout the Country. But a general house-cleaning has been made, and Al Field Minstrels have come back."

The reviewer lamented the loss of "the immortal duet team" of Billy Church and Jack Richards, the absence of a Bert Swor or a Lasses White. "But with Emmett Miller leading the end men, the five negro comedians produced laughs aplenty. Miller caught the audience's fancy from the first with a clever voice control and a rare string of pokes [sic], and Drane Walters and Paul Taylor were not far behind him."

Again Miller is nowhere mentioned as a singer. His performance of "Any Time," noted earlier this season in Utica, Akron, and Asheville, and implied in Winston-Salem, is absent from accounts of the Field shows in Durham, Raleigh, and Charlotte; and, as Miller comes to the fore in the troupe's releases and advertisements, it is always as a blackface comic — as the clarinet-voiced comedian, not as the clarinet-voiced singer.

A week later, the Field Minstrels arrived in Atlanta for three days, October 6–8.

Atlanta had always been one of the Field show's biggest and most important engagements, but the state of minstrelsy had fallen on such hard times in recent years that the troupe had not even played Atlanta in 1926.

This year, the city was in a festive mood. It was the week of the Southeastern Fair and the week of the World Series. The weather was summery, the temperature in the eighties. Mayor Ragsdale had proclaimed Thursday, October 6, a half-holiday, Atlanta Day. The Fair's dairy-cattle and swine shows would take place that morning, the greyhound and grand-circuit races that afternoon. The Field Minstrels would open at the Erlanger Theatre that night.

It was the troupe's anniversary: on this date forty-one years ago, the Field Minstrels had given their first performance, at Marion, Ohio. And on this same night, October 6, 1927, *The Jazz Singer* opened — an ominous event for minstrelsy, and for vaudeville, too.

Echoing the sentiment of the Winston-Salem paper, the *Atlanta Constitution* the next morning was lukewarm in its review of the Field show:

"Many glorious stage traditions are wrapped around the name of Al G. Field, and for more than a third of a century that master showman brought every year an organization of singers, dancers and comedians whipped together under intelligent direction to the point where they always provided an evening of rare diversion and nearly always succeeded in packing the house to capacity. As much can hardly be said for the version appearing under the Field banner this season." The reviewer went on to say that "as far as being a show that will compare in any way with the grand old shows of former days it is rather weak. At a $2.20 top it does not compare with the old 'best show in the world for a dollar' offered by Al G. Field himself."

But "Emmett Miller, a blackface comedian with a trick voice, was the one bright and shining star of the evening. His work in the first part, his gags and song saved the first part. His specialty with Phil Pavey in some real close harmony singing, was another real number. And his comedy in the last burlesque was as funny as anything seen here in years."

A trick voice! What a wonderful and perfect phrase, unimproved in all the metaphorical groping that in recent years has sought to capture and describe the essence of that voice.

The *Atlanta Journal*'s reviewer that day was equally profuse in his praise of Miller. "Generally speaking," he wrote, "the show moves on two separate planes. There are plenty of good, standard minstrel men, who sing and dance and answer interlocutory questions in credible fashion, and then there is Emmett Miller." The reviewer reported that "Mr. Miller's first three words drew a big laugh, though no one really heard them, or cared much what they were. Thereafter his presence on the stage was marked by a constant titter, punctuated by frequent booms, which is all that needs saying about Mr. Miller. He 'caught on' and he stayed on, making a distinct success of a moderately good minstrel show." The review concluded that "Maybe it isn't as good as it used to be, but those who buy their entertainment by the night, without expecting a historical background along with it, will be well satisfied by Emmett Miller and company."

Present in Atlanta were field-recording men from Okeh Records, there to record the black preacher Rev. J. M. Gates. They were in town recording Gates for four days; they finished on October 6. It is possible that they attended Miller's triumphant opening that night, and maybe they carried word of it back to the Okeh office in New York. It had been more than two years since he had recorded for Okeh. Back then, the label had been owned by General Phonograph, now it was part of Columbia. He most likely had been forgotten at Okeh, if he ever had been much noticed at all. But in little more than three months hence, he would record again for Okeh.

An item in the theater listings of the October 8 *Constitution* noted that "Emmett Miller, a newcomer this year, has made a deep impression with minstrel fans, and has firmly established himself as a prime favorite."

The next stop was Macon, where the troupe would serve to open the city's 1927–28 theatrical season. In many ways, this victorious homecoming would be the brief shining moment of Miller's career.

As early as October 2, there had been stories in the local papers: "Former Macon Boy Has Comedy Role in Fields [*sic*] Show" (the *Telegraph*), "Macon Boy Now Headliner of Field Minstrel Show, Realizing Young Ambition" (the *News*). The latter informed that Emmett was a "blackface comedian, known as the boy with the 'clarinet voice,' who sings with a semi-yodle," and that there "are many cracks that Emmett makes which create an uproar, and the biggest hand comes, perhaps, when he sings that popular hit, 'I Want My Rib,' which is said to bring down the house."

Trick voice. Clarinet voice. Semi-yodle. All the technical schizo-canto terminology one ever needed to approach Miller's singing had lain awaiting discovery amid the faded, crumbling newsprint, the ads for blackfaced white men and the ads for guaranteed skinwhiteners, of almost seventy years ago. (One account, in the *Macon News* of October 2, 1927, said that it was "the New York newspapers" that first described Emmett as "the man with the clarinet voice"; but any such evidence from New York newspapers is yet unknown.)

The Field advertisements that followed on October 4 and 5 highlighted only one performer by name: "Emmett (Nigger) Miller with half hundred singers, dancers, acts, comedians and specialty people." The *Telegraph* ran a photo of Emmett, clean-cut and wholesomely forth-smiling, in a suit, white shirt, and tie. The *News* ran the Field publicity photo of him in blackface, the same one that had appeared in the Winston-Salem paper. This picture, bearing the caption " 'Nigger' Miller," also appeared in the *Telegraph* on the Sunday morning of October 9. A Field advertisement on the same page proclaimed that "The Macon Boy — Clarinet Voice Comedian, EMMETT MILLER is a Member." The *News* that day, like the *Telegraph* before it, noted that Laurence Stallings, another native son of Macon, was the author of the story on which King Vidor had based the picture *The Big Parade,* about to open at the Capitol. But it was Emmett that received the greater glory. For those who were still unaware, the *News* explained that "Emmett Miller, known to his hundreds of friends here as 'Nigger,' is the son of Fireman J. (Pink) Miller, driver for Chief W. S. Blanton, and who has been in the service for more than 20 years. Emmett is billed as the headliner in Field's minstrels because of his 'clarinet voice.' He has not failed to get the biggest hand at any place he has appeared."

That Sunday, the troupe arrived in Macon from Atlanta in their private Pullman cars. In the evening Emmett visited his parents at their home at 570 First Street. "He drove there," reported the *Telegraph,* "in a Packard car which had been placed at his disposal during his stay here by A. S. Reese, local agent of the Packard company." At half past eleven the next morning, October 10, there was a parade by the troupe, and in it Emmett and his father rode together in the Packard: down Mulberry Street, from the Grand Theatre to Broadway, on to the corner of Cherry and Third, where a free noon concert was given by the Al G. Field Gold Band, conducted by the troupe's musical director, O. A. Meredith; then on to the new municipal auditorium on Cherry, then Poplar, Second, and back to the Grand. The first show, a special matinee, was at three that afternoon, with the regular show at half past eight that night. In the afternoon, between shows, Emmett bought his parents a Studebaker.

The *Telegraph* declared next morning that Miller "'ran away,' in the fullest sense of the phrase, with last night's show." The overflowing crowd's response to Miller could not be attributed solely to "his being a 'home boy,'" said the reviewer. "Miller plays the part of a negro as few have done. He is almost in a class by himself. His slow, easy-going antics portray the negro as Georgians can best appreciate him. His speech is typically that of the negro. His vocal abilities are enhanced by what one might term an 'impediment,' which factor strikes a happy chord with his audience, and it does not have to be a home-town audience at that." Last night's audience "could not get enough of Miller. He stopped the show several times. His particular hit of the evening was Any Time, in which he found occasion to use his 'impediment' to the best advantage. On this number he was encored repeatedly. Miller scored a second time with Phil Pavey in a clever bit of patter and a tuneful number, the pair singing a duet to the accompaniment of Pavey, who strummed a ukulele." In conclusion, the reviewer wrote, "One comes away from the performance with the feeling that the good old Field's of long ago has departed and that Miller is the show in its entirety. Could he but dance, Miller would be a sensation." All the same, the reviewer found Pavey, not Miller, to be "the most pleasing songster of the troupe."

That phrase: *what one might term an impediment.* Trick voice, clarinet voice, semi-yodle. The technical vocabulary grew.

The *News,* no less ardent in its praise of Miller, made note of a certain misting in the eyes of his mother, who sat with John Pink in the lower right box. His parents had seen him perform professionally only once before, when he played Atlanta "a year or two ago" with the Dan Fitch Minstrels.

That Georgia autumn was the beginning, and in many ways the apex as well, of Emmett Miller's short-lived glory.

Unknown and unknowable as the truth regarding possible contact between Jimmie Rodgers and Emmett Miller may be, the fact remains that neither of the recordings that Rodgers made at his first session, in August 1927, evince the faintest influence of Miller. While he yodeled on one of these — "Sleep, Baby, Sleep," a nineteenth-century stage song that he had sung on his radio show — it was a yodel of the old-fashioned sort, far from the blue yodeling that would distinguish his work beginning with his next session, in Camden, New Jersey, on November 30.

Writing after her husband's death, Carrie Rodgers would say that Jimmie had consciously decided against recording one of his blue yodels at his first session, feeling that it might distract attention from the qualities of voice and guitar that he wanted to impress upon Victor.

The truth of Carrie Rodgers's account is doubtful, and it is more likely that Rodgers had not yet developed his blue yodel at the time of the first session — perhaps because it had been inspired only so recently, by his exposure to Miller's singing in Asheville less than eight weeks before. Then again, perhaps Rodgers's blue yodel had been long gestating, inspired by an earlier exposure to Miller in the course of his medicine-show or railroad travels, or through Miller's recordings. Of course, there may have been no exposure to Miller whatever, or there may have been exposure without influence, and Rodgers's blue yodel may have been developed by him independently and apart from Miller; or he may have stolen it, or derived it, from a source that is wholly unknown. It is interesting that at this same session, second session, on November 30, 1927, Rodgers followed his "Blue Yodel" with a recording of "Away out on the Mountain," a song by Kelly Harrell, who, like Miller, had recorded for Okeh at the Asheville sessions of 1925.

It is irrefutable that, as Jerry Lee Lewis said, again and again, Jimmie Rodgers was, essentially and above all, a *stylist*. There were, as Jerry Lee saw it, only four stylists that ever mattered a damn: Jimmie Rodgers, Al Jolson, Hank Williams, and himself. Of these four, only Williams was a songwriter of significance; and, even in his case, his biggest success, far from being an original composition, was a version of Emmett Miller's rendition of "Lovesick Blues."

Were it not for the black sources from which Rodgers drew, there would have been no substance through which to wreak the rare brilliance of his style. That spider of which Rodgers sang in his 1931 "Let Me Be Your Sidetrack," that spider crawling up the wall to get his ashes hauled, had been a familiar blues image, and could be heard as recently as 1929, in the Triangle Quartette's "She Done Quit Me Blues" and the Monarch Jazz Quartet's "What's the Matter Now?" But it is often impossible to tell if the farther, more distant sources, the wellsprings of those black sources, were of ultimately black, white, or shared origin. A song such as "Frankie and Johnny," which Rodgers recorded in the summer of 1929, dated, it is believed, to an actual murder that went down in St. Louis in October 1899 (though, as the scholar Paul Oliver has pointed out in his history of the song, there were old-timers who "claimed to have heard the song as early as 1850" — another time, another murder, or merely a shadowing, or a foreshadowing, in a ballad with a theme as ancient as the strophes of tragedy. The 1899 murder of seventeen-year-old Allen Britt, described in a *St. Louis Post-Dispatch* notice as "an ebony-hued cake-walker," by his girlfriend Frankie Baker, "also colored," would likely account for the title, "Frankie and Albert," under which early versions of the song were recorded, such as Coley Jones's of 1927, Charley Patton's of 1929. Mississippi John Hurt's version of 1928 was simply called "Albert." A two-part recording of the song in its earliest known black incarnation as "Frankie and Johnny" was made in Dallas by Nick Nichols in December 1929. If the song's origin lay in St. Louis, the song came circuitously to these Mississippi and Texas singers; and if the title "Frankie and Albert" reflected that origin, it must be noted that the title "Frankie and Johnny," by which it became widely known, was the title under which it was first published, in 1912, by the vaudeville performers Ren Fields and the Leighton Brothers. A 1921 Columbia recording of "Frankie and Johnny" by the Paul Biese Trio credits the Leighton Brothers as the song's composers. The popular white entertainers Ted Lewis and Frank Crumit, who was the vocalist on the Paul Biese Trio version, both recorded successful renditions of the song in 1927 — recordings whose success predated the first black recording of the song under any title. Whatever its true origin, in a real or fabled murder or fancy of the 1840s or 1850s, or in the documented St. Louis killing of 1899, in antebellum blackface minstrelsy or a *fin-de-siècle* St. Louis brothel, the allure of the song and its characters proved long-lived. In 1930, they entered literature: *The Saga of Frankie & Johnny,* with fine engravings by John Held, Jr., was published by the New York house of Walter V. McKee in both a general edition of 2,500 copies and a signed and numbered edition of fifty copies. Brook Benton had a modest hit with "Frankie and Johnny" in 1961; Sam Cooke had a big hit with it in 1963. Bob Dylan brought it back round, as "Frankie and Albert," in 1992.

Jerry Lee Lewis himself recorded "Frankie and Johnny," in 1958, when he also made his own first recorded version of "Lovesick Blues." As the self-proclaimed last of the four great stylists, he rocked the spirits of the dead with whom he suffered to share his stature. And, yes, of course, Jerry Lee was right: Jimmie Rodgers was a great stylist, a term that Jerry Lee used with reverence and moment. And he was the greatest of thieves as well. From black, from white, from those whose color was lost to the shadows of the past: he took and he wrought.

Emmett Miller and the Field show were in Atlanta when Rodgers's first record was released, in early October. The following month, Rodgers left Washington for New York, and on November 30, in Camden, he recorded his first "Blue Yodel."

Rodgers's possible movements outside of Washington during that autumn of Miller's glory remain unknown, and I cannot help but wonder if — between the Bristol session of August and the Camden session of November — he was exposed to any of Miller's many acclaimed performances, either in the Northeast or the South.

Facts may be meaningless, and facts may say much. But here are some facts to ponder:

In the spring and hot days of 1926, Jimmie Rodgers, struggling to get by, had not yet made a record. During that time, Emmett Miller was the Famous Yodeling Blues Singer. Within two years, Miller was descending, and his title of glory, the Famous Yodeling

Blues Singer, was all but forgotten. Jimmie Rodgers, ascending, was now wealthy and famous as America's Blue Yodeler.

In "Echoes from the Okeh Recording Studio," an article published in the December 1927 issue of *The Phonograph Monthly Review,* Tommy G. Rockwell, the Louisiana-born recording manager of Okeh Records, is pictured with chief recording engineer Charles L. Hibbard, music supervisor Justin Ring, and other members of the Okeh recording staff:

"Our department," states assistant recording engineer Peter Decker, "under Mr. T.G. Rockwell, searches to find such numbers as we may define as hits. Of course, it is almost impossible for anyone to determine what a hit is, but by receiving all numbers first off they can at any rate pick such numbers that look best to them and take a chance."

In December of that month, Rockwell sent the following Western Union telegram from New York to Emmett Miller in care of the Field Minstrels in Columbus, Ohio:

WIRE ME CARE OKEH RECORD COMPANY ELEVEN UNION SQUARE NEW YORK WHERE I CAN REACH YOU BY TELEPHONE AND TIME WANT TO TALK TO YOU ABOUT COMING TO NEW YORK FOR RECORDING.

A month later, on January 15, 1928, Miller returned to the Okeh studio, not to sing, but to record three comic blackface dialogues with Roy Cowan.

"Wat's dish 'ere w'at dey calls de fonygraf — dish yer inst'ument w'at kin holler 'roun' like little chillun in de back yard?" Uncle Remus was asked in "The Phonograph," one of the sketches in *Uncle Remus: His Songs and Sayings,* published in November 1880. "It's a mighty big watchyoumaycollum," Remus answered. Before long, from up North, there were other answers spoken similarly.

Minstrelsy, coon songs, and blackface humor were a staple of the recording industry since its birth. The first recording star was George Washington Johnson, a black man known as the Whistling Coon. His 1891 Columbia recordings of "The Laughing Song" and "The Whistling Coon" were probably the bestselling cylinders of the early 1890s. Some of Edison's most popular cylinders were minstrelsy: banjoist Vess Ossman's "Darkey Tickle" (1896), "Nigger in a Fit" (1896), and "Little Pickaninnies" (1899); Arthur Collins's "Nigger, Nigger Neber Die" (1899), "Every Race Has a Flag but the Coons" (1900), and "Coonville Cullid Band" (1904); Ada Jones's "Songs My Mammy Sang for Me" (1905), "Bull-Frog and the Coon" (1906), and "If the Man in the Moon Were a Coon" (1906). W. C. Handy had recorded an Edison cylinder of "Cotton Blossoms" with Mahara's Minstrel Band in Helena, Montana, in 1897. In early 1903, Columbia issued a twelve-disc, half-hour minstrel-show extravaganza, "An Evening with the Minstrels," produced by Len Spencer (1867–1914), one of the most prolific and renowned of the day's recording artists.

The earliest known recordings made in the South by a performer of color were those of the Creole entertainer Louis "Bebe" Vasnier, who had worked in minstrelsy in the 1880s in an act called Johnson and Vasnier's Colored Minstrels. It was in New Orleans in 1891 and 1892 that Vasnier recorded a series of "Brudder Rasmus" sermons, such as "The End ob de World," and minstrel songs, such as "Coon with a Razor," as cylinders for the Louisiana Phonograph Company. Vasnier, who was born in Louisiana in May of 1858, vanished from history within a decade of his recordings. What little has been discovered of this enigmatic character has for the most part been through the impressive and painstaking research of Tim Brooks, whose collection contains the only Vasnier recording yet to be unearthed, a Brudder Rasmus bit called "Adam and Eve and de Winter Apple." By the time this unique and fragile cylinder came into his possession, in 1993, more than a century after it came to be, the recording had deteriorated to little more than rough hiss and surface noise.

Vasnier is known to have moved by 1898 to St. Louis, which, like New Orleans, was a fertile Mississippi River breeding-ground of the blues. The last trace of his career was a small advertisement for himself in the July 14, 1900, issue of *The Freeman,* a black newspaper of Indianapolis. Beneath his name and the phrase *"Singing and Dialect Comedian Sketch and Song Writer,"* the notice read in part:

> *Natural facial expressions, in five different dialects, no make up — Negro, Dutch, Dago, Irish and French. I sing in all. The only colored musician who can do it. "De proof of de eating was in de puddings." "Sure it's the like of me dat can do it." "I tella fo you no lie." "Je ne mant pas." Address: LOUIS VASNIER, 110 S.14th Street., St. Louis, Mo.*

Negro Dialect Recitations, a thirty-cent paperbound collection of 1887, included a selection titled "Brudder Johnson on 'Lectricity'":

"Speakin' ob 'lectricity," it began, "Mr. Edison tole me it can't go froo glass; but den, don' yer see, a man can't cork hisself up in a glass bottle all de time." De sermons ob Brudder Rasmus were de uncorking ob dat bottle ob what Brudder Johnson spoke. Why, de man could eben do a Dago, widout no make up.

A 1901 Columbia catalogue lists minstrelsy records such as "De Sweetest 'Backer Is Nigger Twist," "Jolly Darkeys," and "No Coon Can Come Too Black for Me" (a song popularized by the minstrel team of Walter Smart and George Williams in *The Octoroons,* a black variety show of 1895). In its 1917 catalogue, Columbia still advertised coon songs, but a bit more demurely. Under the heading Coon Songs, as under the heading Minstrel Records, the reader is advised to "See: Negro Songs and Plantation Airs," where will be found airs such as "Nigger Love a Watermelon, Ha! Ha! Ha!" and "I'se Gwine Back to Dixie," but not records such as "Nigger Blues" by the "exclusive Columbia artist" George O'Connor, a tenor known for his "humorous dialect songs." The composer of "Nigger Blues," described elsewhere as a fox trot, was Miller's friend Lasses White. The black minstrel Bert Williams was also claimed by Columbia as an exclusive artist.

In its 1920 catalogue, under Coon Songs and Specialties, Victor printed the following:

> NOTE — By "coon songs" are meant up-to-date comic songs in negro dialect. The humor of many of these songs cannot be called refined, and for that reason we have distinguished them from old-fashioned darky humor, these songs being listed under "Fisk Jubilee Quartet," "Negro Songs," and "Tuskegee."

Victor had its own Victor Minstrel Company, and under Minstrel Records in the same catalogue, is found the following:

> NOTE — Lively and entertaining "tabloids" of minstrelsy, full of snappy repartee and tuneful singing. Don't get these minstrel records expecting to hear sweet and soothing music — it isn't that kind! But the records are good entertainment for a jolly party who likes vigorous singing and perfectly obvious jokes, the point of which can be grasped by the average person without the aid of a map! Rousing bits of comedy and melody by a talented bunch of singers and comedians.

The Metropolitan Orchestra, the first of the studio orchestras, recorded "Coon Town Capers (A New Negro Oddity)" for Berliner in early 1897; "Who Dat Say Chicken in Dis Crowd?," a show-stopper from the 1898 black musical *Clorindy, or the Origin of the Cakewalk,* was recorded by this Berliner orchestra in January 1900.

"Who Dat Say Chicken in Dis Crowd?" was the work of two black men, the composer Will Marion Cook and the lyricist Paul Laurence Dunbar, who certainly must be counted among the peerage of coon-songsters. Cook (1869–1944) had studied violin at the Oberlin Conservatory, the University of Berlin, and the National Conservatory of Music under Antonín Dvořák. Dunbar (1872–1906), a forefather of the Harlem Renaissance, was the author of four novels and several respected collections of poetry, which ranged from light dialect verse to stuff of the thou-art variety. In the teens, two of his poems were recorded by others as black-dialect recitations for Victor, and the Irish tenor John McCormack recorded his song "Who Knows."

Bert Williams and George Walker, who billed themselves as the Two Real Coons, began their recording career for the Victor Talking Machine Company on October 11, 1901. Two-man blackface routines by whites became an important part of the industry seven years later, in the fall of 1908, when the team of Billy Golden and Joe Hughes began recording together.

Golden, born William B. Shire in 1858, began his recording career as a singing comic in 1891, when he had a hit with "Turkey in de Straw." A Victor Records catalogue of 1920 said of Golden: "No one could ever approach him in this kind of work — in fact, the hearer forgets all about Golden and hears only a jolly old darky with an infectious laugh." Indeed, while Victor had coupled its Golden recording of "Turkey in de Straw" with a recording of "Nigger Loves His Possum" by the duet of Arthur Collins (1864–1933) and Byron Harlan, Columbia had coupled one of *its* Golden recordings of "Turkey in de Straw" with a recording by Bert Williams, a real coon. This integration via two-sided disc brings to mind the vaudeville act known as the Blue Grass Boys, contemporaries of Golden and Hughes: "Will and Jim, black and white, tall and slim," they advertised in 1911.

With Joe Hughes, who joined him in 1904, and with two later partners, Jim Marlowe and William Hughes, Golden dominated the blackface-dialogue field until 1921, when actual black performers entered it: the Chicago-based song-and-dance team of Flournoy Miller (1887–1971) and Aubrey Lyles (1883–1932), both of whom were from the South and were active on the B. F. Keith vaudeville circuit by 1910; Moss and Frye; and others, including the lyricist Andy Razaf and the pianist and composer James P. Johnson. Together in December of 1926, a lean time for both of them, they recorded blackface routines for Cameo under the name of the Two Watermelon Seeds.

Golden died in 1926, the year that the blackface team of Charles Correll (1890–1972) and Freeman Gosden (1899–1982) began their recording career. They had developed their act, known as Sam 'n' Henry, the year before, working in the Chicago revue *Red Hot,* deriving it perhaps from Miller and Lyles, who had developed similar characters, Steve and Sam, in an earlier blackface routine, "The Mayor of Dixie," that they had performed in Chicago with the Pekin Stock Company.

The use of the name Sam in blackface comedy had been popular since the early days of minstrelsy. It occurs throughout *Christy and Fox's Complete Melodist and Joke-Book* of 1858, as, for example, in the dialogue called "The Blues," which begins:

"Julius, what's the matter with you this evening — you seem so down-hearted."

"Sam, I got a touch ob de blues."

"The blues — what do you call the blues?"

"I will 'deavor to 'splanify it to you. You see, de blues am dis, Sam . . ."

Correll and Gosden began recording for Victor in Chicago in December 1925; WGN of Chicago began broadcasting them as Sam 'n' Henry in January 1926. Their early recordings are a curious blend of whiteface comedy, blackface comedy, and whiteface singing. On "All I Want to Do," recorded in March 1926, there is not a trace of blackface: they sing in straight whiteface harmony and perform a routine in which Gosden refers to himself as Gos, to his partner as Charlie. On the flip side, "Let's Talk about My Sweetie," recorded the same day, they sing whiteface, break into spoken blackface dialect as Sam 'n' Henry, return to whiteface song. Their next session, in April, was devoted exclusively to Sam-'n'-Henry dialogues. Here the dialect voice of Sam has settled, intensified since the previous session; Henry's voice, deep and full, remains the same. At the following session, in May, they divided their work into two clear-cut categories: whiteface Correll-and-Gosden duets and blackface Sam-'n'-Henry dialogues.

In March 1928 Correll and Gosden would move to a competing Chicago station, WMAQ, changing the name of their act and show from Sam 'n' Henry to Amos 'n' Andy. Some years later, when Correll and Gosden were reportedly paid a million dollars each by CBS for the television rights to *Amos 'n' Andy,* Flournoy Miller was put on the payroll as a consultant in the search by Correll and Gosden for black actors to portray their characters. This perhaps suggests that characters developed by Miller and his partner had indeed been the inspiration for the Correll-and-Gosden act that eventually became *Amos 'n' Andy.* In the end Alvin Childress was cast as Amos. Spencer Williams, Jr. (1893–1969), a writer-producer-director of low-budget all-black films (*Blood of Jesus,* 1941, and *Jivin' in Be-Bop,* 1947, are representative titles), was cast as Andy. Williams and Flournoy Miller had worked together as actors in all-black Westerns in the late thirties; one of these, *Harlem Rides the Range,* was written by them. Tim Moore, a former minstrel, was cast as King-fish Stevens.

In the teens, Bert Swor, the Field star, had worked with another blackface performer, Charles Emmett Sellers (1887–1934), who went by the name of Mack. A 1914 program for B. F. Keith's Palace Theatre lists Swor and Mack fifth on the bill, their act described as "Realistic Impressions of Southern Negroes." The partnership of Swor and Mack ended. Swor spent the 1915 season with the Field troupe, and subsequently served in France during World War I. Sellers teamed in 1917 with George Searey (1881–1949). Known as the Two Black Crows, Moran and Mack began recording for Columbia in the spring of 1927. Correll and Gosden performed to piano accompaniment only when they sang. On Moran and Mack's records, a pianist provided opening and closing music, and played abstractedly in the background as they performed their routines.

The first Two-Black-Crows release, "The Early Bird Catches the Worm," was a tremendous hit. In this routine, Moran goes by the name of Amos — a year before Correll and Gosden rechristened Sam 'n' Henry as Amos 'n' Andy — and brags of being "head man" in the Neil O'Brien Minstrels. The blackface of the Crows was subdued: the dialect was subtle, and the Amos character maintained an essentially whiteface voice. In later Mack-and-Moran records, after Correll and Gosden changed the name of their act, the Crows' Amos became Willie.

The success of Correll and Gosden, of Moran and Mack, made blackface dialogue one of the sensations of the recording industry in 1927, and it directly led, in the first days of 1928, to Okeh's interest in similar material by Miller and Cowan. Even the inspiration for Miller's choice of the name Sam may have been derived more directly from the growing popularity at the time of Correll and Gosden's Sam 'n' Henry than from minstrel tradition. In fact, in the first of Miller's dialect recordings, "Thousand Frogs on a Log," Roy Cowan is addressed as Harry. One could not get much closer to Sam 'n' Henry than Sam 'n' Harry.

Accompanying Miller and Cowan was an unknown pianist, who provided music very similar to that of the Moran-and-Mack recordings. Here, as in all future blackface recordings by Miller, Sam is played with a languid, stammering drawl: obviously the persona he had cultivated through the years in minstrelsy. An occasional stammer, an even deeper torpor are distinguishing qualities of Charlie Mack's blackface persona; but Miller's stammer more closely resembles a mannerism affected by a fellow Georgian named Herschel Brown. It can be heard prominently on Brown's first Okeh record, "Talking Nigger Blues," recorded in Atlanta on July 30, 1928.

The origins of the "talking-blues" idiom, a virtually unchanging sing-song style of wry comic rhyme — familiar to modern ears through Bob Dylan's 1963 "Talking World War III Blues" — are lost in the prerecorded mists of musical miscegenation. The earliest recorded example is by Chris Bouchillon, a singing, mandolin-playing foundry-worker from Greenville, South Carolina, who recorded his "Talking Blues" for Columbia in 1926.

"Ain't no use in me workin' so hard," cadenced Bouchillon, "I got a woman in the white folks' yard."

Released in early 1927, Chris Bouchillon's "Talking Blues" became one of the hit records of that year, and as such did much to bring to wider public awareness, and to render seemingly novel, a captivating form that likely had been around, in songster tradition and on the minstrel circuit, longer than could ever be known — a form so playfully simple that its age might be measured in centuries rather than in years.

The influence of Chris Bouchillon's "Talking Blues" can be heard within months of its release, in the identical metrical sing-song of the Spooney Five's "Chinese Rag," recorded in Atlanta in early No-vember of 1927. And it was also in Atlanta in the wake of Bou-chillon's successful "Talking Blues" that Herschel Brown recorded "New Talking Blues," followed by "Talking Nigger Blues," on a hot day in the summer of 1928. As in Bouchillon's performance:

"There ain't no use in me workin' so hard, I got a gal in the white folks' yard."

Along with a variation:

"There ain't no use in me workin' so much; I got a gal that brings me the mush; she works for the white folks down in Caroline; she brings me everything from molasses to wine."

The gal in the white folks' yard, a figure of the songster tradition that dated at least to the late nineteenth century, was encountered on record as early as 1902, in "Poor Mourner" by the Dinwiddie Colored Quartet. By the time of Herschel's Brown's "Talking Nig-ger Blues," Luke Jordan had reclaimed the line for black singers. "I got a girl, she works in the white folks' yard," sang Jordan, follow-ing it with other familiar elements, in his "Cocaine Blues," recorded for Victor in Charlotte, North Carolina, in the summer of 1927, and done in 1929 by the white country singer Dick Justice in his "Cocaine." The song was an echo, musically, of the raggish "Don't Let Your Deal Go Down," which was more associated with old-timey white country singers, though black singers, such as Jordan, made use, widely and loosely, of the breakdown-rag on which it was built, as can be heard not only in Jordan's "Cocaine Blues" but also in his "Pick Poor Robin Clean," recorded at the same session. Lyri-cally, the song was an echo of the minstrelsy tributary, a comic turn in which the furniture-repossession agent is descried as the Arch-fiend: "If it ever was a devil born without any horns, it must've been the furniture man," sang Jordan in his 1927 "Cocaine Blues," and the line was repeated almost verbatim in Justice's "Cocaine" of 1929: "If there ever was a devil born without horns, it must've been a furniture man." The latter is the exact variation to be heard in the 1930 "Furniture Man," by the male black songster Lil McClintock. It is revealing that the two black recordings — Jordan's circumstantially, McClintock's explicitly — exhibit a more evident closeness to a minstrel source than Justice's recording. In Charlotte on that summer day in 1927, Jordan followed his recording of "Cocaine Blues" immediately with a recording of "Traveling Coon"; and McClintock's recording makes use of the word "coon" and, more liberally, the plural "coons." Meanwhile, in a variation called "Riley the Furniture Man," recorded in Atlanta in 1927 by the white hillbilly string band known as the Georgia Crackers, the word "nigger" was present, but there was no reference to the "devil born without horns."

Recordings such as Papa Charlie Jackson's "All I Want Is a Spoonful" (1925) harkened back to songster celebrations of cocaine in the last years of the nineteenth century and first years of the twentieth century, when cocaine, like heroin, was still commonly and legally consumed in the form of various potable tonics. As the spoonful of liquid became a spoonful of white powder, the old songster evocation proved endlessly enduring.

New York Herald, September 29, 1913, front page: 10 KILLED, 35 HURT IN RACE RIOT BORN OF A COCAINE 'JAG' — DRUG CRAZED NEGROES FIRE AT EVERYONE IN SIGHT IN MISSISSIPPI TOWN. — THREE WHITE MEN AMONG THE DEAD — "As a result of two negro boys, brothers, going on a cocaine 'jag' here today a race riot was started in which three white men were killed and five seriously injured; seven negroes were killed, one of them being lynched, and about thirty wounded.

"A serious clash between the races was prevented by the arrival on a special train of a company of national guardsmen from Natchez.

"The trouble started at about two o'clock this morning and continued intermittently until ten o'clock, when Will Jones, the younger of the two boys who started the firing, was lynched just after the soldiers arrived. His brother, Walter Jones, had been shot and killed by citizens earlier in the day."

One recalls the eponymous lost-to-the-mist figure of the song "Wild Bill Jones," staggering toward bottomland beneath the moon, gun in hand and murder in heart.

Harriston, where the Jones brothers' cocaine spree took place on this Sunday morning of September 28, 1913, was a small rural town in Jefferson County, in the southwestern part of state, bordering the Mississippi River and adjacent to Copiah County, where two-year-old Robert Johnson, the future Delta blues legend, lay in his mama's arms.

Cocaine, an alkaloid obtained from the leaves and young twigs of the coca plant, was nothing new. It had been around, and its properties, both as a local anæsthesiant and as a stimulant, had been known since the 1870s. By the 1890s, it was passing from pharmacopoeian elite to hoi polloi fringe. In the second of his published Sherlock Holmes tales, "The Sign of Four," which was published in the February 1890 issue of *Lippincott's Monthly Magazine,* Arthur Conan Doyle showed the fictional master detective of his fiction in a more revealing light.

"Sherlock Holmes took his bottle from the corner of the mantelpiece, and his hypodermic syringe from its neat morocco case. With his long, white, nervous fingers he adjusted the delicate needle and rolled back his left shirtcuff. For some little time his eyes rested thoughtfully upon the sinewy forearm and wrist, all dotted and scarred with innumerable puncture-marks. Finally, he thrust the sharp point home, pressed down the tiny piston, and sank back into the velvet-lined armchair with a long sigh of satisfaction."

"Which is it to-day," inquires his assistant and house-mate, the good Doctor Watson, "morphine or cocaine?"

"It is cocaine," Holmes tells him, "a seven-per-cent solution. Would you care to try it?"

Doyle was knighted in 1902, thus becoming Sir Arthur Conan Doyle. The following year, when he resumed publishing Holmes stories, which he had quit in weariment a decade ago, Holmes no longer used cocaine. Its use in the real world was widespread by then, among the chic and the dregs alike of London, Paris, New York, and every other cosmopolitan city. The days of the seven-percent solution were passing. "They buy the 'coke' in the form of powder and snuff it up the nose," wrote the muckraking liberal progressive Ray Stannard Baker in his 1908 book *Following the Colour Line: An Account of Negro Citizenship in the American Democracy.*

As the event of 1913 in rural Mississippi illuminates, it did not take long for the white powder to reach not only the Southern cities but the Delta towns, plantation fields, and backwoods as well.

In that year, the writer Arthur B. Reeve, in his detective story "The Dope Fiends," pioneered a much more down-and-dirty type of cocaine fiction than that which had been opened with the opening, twenty-three years earlier, of Holmes's neat morocco case.

From the songster tradition of light-hearted stuff such as Luke Jordan's "Cocaine Blues," Dick Justice's "Cocaine," and the Memphis Jug Band's rollicking "Cocaine Habit Blues" of 1930: it was a tradition that lingered through cocaine references in the buoyantly suicidal "Knockin' Myself Out," recorded in 1941 by the jazz-blues singers Lil Green, Yack Taylor, and Jean Brady. (This song's lovely lyric "I'm gonna kill myself, I'm gonna knock myself out gradually by degree" can be traced in essence to John Estes's 1930 "Milk Cow Blues," recorded in Memphis in the spring of 1930. While Estes's "Milk Cow Blues" contains no bovine allusion whatsoever, it does refer to being "sloppy drunk" and "slow consumption killin' you by degree.") It was a tradition in which the Holy Modal Rounders rejoiced in their berserk 1967 version of Jordan's "Cocaine Blues"; a tradition whose most elegantly playful sprout, Cole Porter's 1934 "I Get a Kick out of You," with its line "I get no kick from cocaine," would endure through countless versions. The white powder also inspired an ever-darkening musical course, evolved from another traditional "Cocaine Blues," which came to be associated with Reverend Gary Davis (1896–1972).

Though Davis's first recording of "Cocaine Blues," in 1957, was a wordless guitar instrumental, in which could be heard echoes of Luke Jordan's "Cocaine Blues" of thirty years past, Davis also developed lyrics for his "Cocaine Blues." Before Davis recorded the song with these lyrics, Bob Dylan had encountered a stage performance of it by Davis, likely at the Indian Neck Folk Festival, held under the aegis of Yale University, at the Montowesi Hotel in Branford, Connecticut, on May 6, 1961: an emanation of that grossest and most degrading of all minstrelsies, which was the celebration of the primitive, the romance of *rusticitas,* by young, "liberal," white Americans seeking escape from vacuousness through the delusive pseudonegritude of the "raw, hard truth" of the blues. Dylan took to Davis and to the song immediately. He can be heard singing it on a crude recording made in a Minneapolis apartment three days before Christmas of that year, before Davis himself was recorded singing it; and ever since, through the ensuing years to the present day, Dylan has been performing and transmuting the song, from a naïve dactylic overreaching of his own immature minstrelsy to a stormfront of endlessly permutating implications and intensities.

In Johnny Cash's own manic version of "Cocaine Blues," from the album *Johnny Cash at Folsom Prison* of 1968 — the year before Cash collaborated with Dylan on the latter's *Nashville Skyline* album — his line "I took a shot of cocaine and shot my woman down," delivered with the rhythm of a semi-automatic, is met with a wild exuberance from his inmate audience, the likes of which response even the wiliest songsters of old could have brought forth only rarely. (As for *Nashville Skyline,* it was at the final session for that album, on February 18, 1969, that Dylan recorded Jimmie Rodgers's "Blue Yodel" and "Blue Yodel No. 4.")

But let us turn from the white powder and return to the white folks' yard from which we have somewhat strayed. Or have we strayed? For is not the breeze that carried them both — that low breath of unexplored true history — one and same?

All told, Herschel Brown works "the white folks' yard" into "New Talking Blues" no less than four times.

The white folks' yard does not figure into "Talking Nigger Blues," which is distinguished by a background of blues lines by guitarist L. K. Sentell and by Brown's stammering delivery — an effect that is as evocative of Emmett Miller as the piece's drawn-out, tired monologue is of dying blackface comedy itself. If "New Talking Blues" derived from Chris Bouchillon's success of 1927, it seems no less likely that "Talking Nigger Blues" derived from Emmett Miller's success of that same year.

At a subsequent Okeh session in 1929, Brown recorded "New Talking Blues No. 2" — "There ain't no use in me workin' so hard, because I got a gal in the white folks' yard," he here declares again, twice, in a performance that is distinguished from his first "New Talking Blues" only by slicker and more suggestive turns of phrase: Brown brags of blindsiding his woman, of "spendin' her jack"; tells of taking her to church, where she "began to shake that thing" in front of the preacher, and of seeing her "in her nighties; she stood between me and the light and good gosh almighty."

("You wear those dresses, the sun come shinin' through," as Jesse Stone wrote and Big Joe Turner sang twenty-five years later in "Shake, Rattle and Roll." As for shaking that thing, it had been going on in recordings since Papa Charlie Jackson's "Shake That Thing." Jackson's record, made in the spring of 1925, proved so catching that four other black singers, all of them female, covered it within less than a year — Eva Taylor; Ethel Waters, who claimed to have been performing the piece since 1921; Viola McCoy; and Viola Bartlette — and the power of its essence so enduring that the legacy of "Shake That Thing" lived well into the R&B era. Tampa Red, who sang of a girl who shook that thing for the judge and put the cops in jail, in his 1932 "No Matter How She Done It," was still invoking the image in 1950, in "Love Her with a Feeling.")

At that same session, Brown recorded "Nigger Talking Blues No. 2." Here, even more, he sounds like Emmett Miller: not just in his affected blackface stammer and the tired, drawn-out dying black-face nature of the monologue, but in other, subtler effects that could be heard in the speech-to-song pieces of Miller's recent Okeh recordings. Here, too, as in "New Talking Blues No. 2," the language is more raw, not so much slicker and more suggestive, but rather crudely harsh: the phrase "nigger woman" occurs three times, as if in a sort of base and desperate attempt to revive a dead racket by stripping it of all subtlety and pretense — of removing the last frayed and faded gaudy sequins of quaint modesty from, of stripping bare beneath the glare, the exotic dancer whose theater has emptied with the râle of a bygone day. It should be noted, however, that, less than a year earlier, in his "Can't Put the Bridle on That Mule This Morning," the black blues singer Julius Daniels was even more liberal in his use of the word "nigger," as was Peg Leg Howell in his "Skin Game Blues" of 1927.

Daniels, born in 1902, was an interesting character, a delta of influences and rich alluvium unto himself: like Furry Lewis in his 1928 "Kassie Jones" and Jimmie Rodgers in his 1930 "Blue Yodel No. 9," Daniels, in his 1927 "Richmond Blues," had his name written on his shirt — the flaunted sartorial mark of the Chink-laundered streetcorner sheik who hustled rather than worked. Though "Richmond Blues" is in many ways a direct forebear of Rodgers's song, the name-on-the-shirt couplet had been encountered many years earlier by the folklorist Howard W. Odum, who published it in *The Negro and His Songs,* the 1925 book he wrote with Guy B. Johnson. (The couplet, as illustrated in my book *Country,* had a long subsequent history, through rockabilly into modern country music.) In his "Crow Jane Blues," also from 1927, Daniels asked the same question that Henry Thomas asked in "Red River Blues," which Thomas had recorded less than three weeks earlier and many states away: "Which-a-way do the Red River run?"

It is from the talking blues of Chris Bouchillon and Herschel Brown that the later various "talking blues" of Woody Guthrie derive. In the first of these, a version of Bouchillon's "Talking Blues," Guthrie transforms "the white folks' yard" into "the rich folks' yard." Bob Dylan, in turn, derived his "Talking New York" (1961), "Talking Bear Mountain Picnic Massacre Blues" (1962), "Talkin' John Birch Paranoid Blues" (1962), and "Talking World War III Blues" (1963) directly from Guthrie's "talking blues." From 1926 to 1963, from Bouchillon to Brown to Guthrie to Dylan, the routine remains the same.

While the classic, benign, and insouciant talking blues, with its central figure of the gal in the white folks' yard, was common to both black songsters and blackfaced white minstrels, the "talking nigger blues," as exemplified by the recordings of Herschel Brown, were — like most twentieth-century songs prior to the 1980s that flaunted the word "nigger" — purely the stuff of white minds and makers. That the classic talking blues came from either the black songster tradition or an emulation of it is attested by the "gal in the white folks' yard": a figure that could not have originated as a self-referential expression among white singers. Whether that figure was invented by whites to further blacken in burlesque a style — the talking blues — that spread from the black tradition to captivate whites, and then was appropriated in turn by black songsters themselves, such as Jim Jackson, can never be known. The boast of the "gal in the white folks' yard," which Jim Jackson recorded as part of his "What a Time," exactly a month after Brown recorded "Talking Nigger Blues" — and which Luke Jordan had used a year earlier in his 1927 "Cocaine Blues," in which "a girl who works in the white folks' yard" brings him "everything that she can steal" — dated at least to the 1890s and was likely popularized through minstrelsy, which was an influence on Jackson, the black songster-bluesman, as well as on Chris Bouchillon, Herschel Brown, and others. The figure was taken up almost exclusively by male singers; but in her 1929 "I Hate a Man Like You," Lizzie Miles sings, neither benignly nor lightheartedly, but beautifully and powerfully, from the viewpoint of the sacrificing woman in "the white folks' yard." Mention of "the white folks' yard" occurs on record as early as "Poor Mourner," recorded by the Dinwiddie Colored Quartet at their first session, for Victor, in the fall of 1902; and it occurs as well in the first recording of another early black vocal group, the Excelsior Quartette's "Kitchen Mechanic Blues," recorded for Okeh in early 1922.

The importance of the early Southern black vocal groups, such as the Dinwiddie Colored Quartet, which recorded only twice, at sessions a day apart at the end of October 1902, and the Excelsior Quartette, whose few recordings were all made in the spring of 1922, cannot be overestimated, either as evidence of the multifarious musical miscegenation and cultural pollinations from which their repertoires and styles were derived, or as seminal influences on what was to come.

The progenitor of these black vocal groups was the Fisk University Jubilee Singers, which was formed at Fisk University in Nashville in 1867, the year after the founding of the university itself. It was the success of the Fisk Jubilee Singers' first concert tour, in 1871, that inspired the emergence of similar groups from other black educational institutions, such as the Tuskegee Institute Singers, from the university founded by Booker T. Washington, in Tuskegee, Alabama. The connection between black schools and black vocal groups continued into the next century: the Dinwiddie Colored Quartet, for example, performed to raise funds for the John A. Dix Industrial School in Dinwiddie, Virginia.

The Fisk group originally consisted of a number of men and women — as many as eight — and its repertoire originally was one of spirituals, as was that of the Tuskegee Institute Singers. Both of these groups remained dedicated almost exclusively to spirituals, but in time the groups themselves came to reflect the dominant configuration of the less exclusively spiritual groups whose formation they had inspired: the male quartet. It was as the Fisk University Jubilee Quartet that the Fisk singers first recorded, in 1909, and as the Fisk University Male Quartet that they recorded from 1915 to 1920. The Tuskegee Institute Singers recorded first, in 1914, as a "double male quartet," but by 1926, when they recorded after a hiatus of more than a decade, the group had become the Tuskegee Quartet.

"We take pleasure in presenting these examples of Negro Folk Songs by the Tuskegee Institute Singers," declared the *1920 Catalogue of Victor Records.* The group sang "these old inherited 'Spirituals' as did their grandfathers, in deep reverential spirit." The catalogue spoke of "weird harmonies" and observed: "Another curious fact is that while the early music of the Egyptians, Orientals, Greeks, Indians and practically all primitive peoples is almost invariably in one part, yet set any three or four negroes singing at any time or place and you will instantly hear an accompanying harmony in one or more of the voices." We should not here pause to wonder upon what the Victor copywriter's knowledge of the unknowable harmonics of ancient Greek music was based, or upon the sweeping description of ancient cultures as "primitive"; but the notion of the music of the Tuskegee Institute Singers being a direct emanation of a primitive culture is absurd.

As they had taken the names of their masters, so blacks in America had taken their religion as well. The forgotten gods and spirits of Africa were a vague and underlying ancestral presence in the palimpsest Christianity that slaves had rendered from the church-stuff religion of their Baptist and Methodist masters, most of whom never knew that the word "religion" was not to be found in any bible, or that the pagan Latin word, *religio,* whence it came, denoted the supernatural powers of magic and of sacred place: concepts much closer to the purer spiritualities of Africa than to the debased and pious spirituality connoted by "religion" among America's settlers.

As you sow, so shall you reap. Though the phrase as such, like the word "religion," never occurs in either the Old or New Testament — it is the pagan Cicero who first articulates it thus ("*Ut sementum feceris ita metes*"), in his *De Oratore* of 55 B.C. — the notion itself, and the metaphor of sowing and reaping, pervade the Bible. "The good book tell you: reap just what you sow," sings the bluesman Tommy Johnson in his 1928 "Bye Bye Blues." Our first encounter in English with anything the likes of this dictum is in a piece of poetry from about the year 1421: "Eche dedly synne is a dedly knyf," we are told. "For he shal repe Þat he sewe." The phrase became a dominant one, with the power as if from Scripture, through American gospel music. "You're Going to Reap Just What You Sow," sang the Fisk University Jubilee Singers in an unissued Columbia recording of 1919. "You Shall Reap Just What You Sow" sang the blues queen Alberta Hunter in 1923. "As you sow, so shall you reap," sang Bing Crosby in "Someday Sweetheart" in 1934; "and what you reap is gonna make you weep." James Luther Dickinson, "The Judgement," *Dixie Fried,* 1972: "As you sow, shall you reap; what you reap is gonna make you weep."

Though great Shango was forgotten, the power of his thunder lingered. It reverberated in the blood when the Mississippi sky broke open with a blast and a serpent of lightning; and it reverberated in the Word. The risen Christ was mighty *vodu,* and in His cross there was more of meaning, more of *religio,* than any bible-toting bossman ever knew. *This* — not the permutations of European harmonies or songs such as "Swing Low, Sweet Chariot," which both the Fisk and Tuskegee groups sang — was the true legacy of that ancestral spirit, and primitive only in the sense that all true magic is primitive. And yet it is the absurdity inherent in the likes of that old Victor catalogue that still imbues our misknowing today.

Songs of Stephen Foster — "My Old Kentucky Home," "Old Black Joe" — were as far as the Fisk singers ventured from spirituals. To judge by their few recordings, the Tuskegee singers ventured not even that far. But those little-known, immensely but deceptively important quartets whose emergence the Fisk and Tuskegee groups inspired were a true amalgam of the sacred and the profane.

Described in an early Columbia catalogue as "men of color," the Standard Quartette, who recorded from 1891 to 1897, sang not only the likes of "Swing Low, Sweet Chariot" and "My Old Kentucky Home," but as well the likes of "So, Bo, Give Me Them Two Bits" and "Little Alabama Coon." In early 1894, more than eight years before the Dinwiddie Colored Quartet, they recorded a Columbia cylinder of "Poor Mourner," which is lost to us, as are all but a few of the Standard Quartette's recordings.

In the recordings of the Excelsior Quartet, it all comes together in a maelstrom, not only of the sacred and the profane, but of minstrelsy, vaudeville, jazz-blues, and songster hokum: from "Walk in

Jerusalem Just Like John" to "Kitchen Mechanic Blues" to "Roll Them Bones" to "Jelly Roll Blues" (which had been recorded a year before by the Norfolk Jazz Quartet, one of the most prolific of the many early black vocal groups associated with that Virginia city). Regarding "jelly roll" as a slang term connoting, as *The Oxford English Dictionary* has it, "the female genitalia or vagina," its first use in song dates to W. C. Handy's "St. Louis Blues" of 1914. "I Ain't Gonna Give Nobody None o' This Jelly Roll," copyrighted by Clarence and Spencer Williams in 1919, was recorded by Mamie Smith in 1922; and several months later, in 1923, the same writers provided Bessie Smith with "Nobody in Town Can Bake a Sweet Jelly Roll Like Mine." Furry Lewis's "Jelly Roll" came in 1927. By then, recorded twelve days previously, Peg Leg Howell had come forth with "New Jelly Roll Blues." In 1936, the song entered white country music through a "New Jelly Roll Blues" recorded by the Texas singer Al Dexter.

(Dexter, who was born in 1902 and died in 1984, told me that he wrote "New Jelly Roll Blues" on the way to his first recording session — a claim of provenance no doubt similar to that of Peg Leg Howell's. "Did you get that song from a black guy?" I pressed him gently. He responded, "No. Well, yeah, I guess so." Then, at the age of seventy-three, he began to sing it.

(And, speaking of early black vocal groups, slang terms for the female genitalia or vagina, and errant pullulations in country music, mention might here be made of the Old South Quartette's "Pussy Cat Rag" of 1928. While "pussy" as slang for — again, *The Oxford English Dictionary* — "the female pudendum" dates at least to the 1870s, the Old South Quartette's recordings set a precedence for its use as a double-entendre song device. From there, it was not far to Bo Chatman's 1931 "Pussy Cat Blues." The leap to country music came with a Western-swing recording called "Pussy, Pussy, Pussy," recorded in 1939 by the Light Crust Doughboys, and in

1940 by Bill Boyd and His Cowboy Ramblers. When the bluesman Tampa Red, evading notice by the *OED,* made the trans-species metaphor move with "Let Me Play with Your Poodle," in 1942, the country singer Hank Penny followed with a hillbilly-swing version in 1947, the year that Lightnin' Hopkins took up the doomed cause of the *Pudelhund-qua-Pfläumchen* metaphor with his down-home "Play with Your Poodle."

(But enough of this. Jelly roll, pussy, poodle be damned. They are all the stuff of drab and ill-writ songs, worth nought more than mere snicker or sneer to the dimmest-witted of pastors. Thus these parentheses close and we return to where we long ago once were.)

The affinity to minstrelsy of the early black vocal groups was close. The Unique Quartet, who recorded for Edison between 1890 and 1896, performed with the Georgia Minstrels, Primrose & West, and other minstrel troupes. Their only surviving recording, "Mamma's Black Baby Boy," an Edison cylinder of 1893, is also the earliest surviving recording of any black vocal group; and it is minstrelsy through and through. At the time of their recordings, in 1902, the Dinwiddie Colored Quartet were appearing in the *Smart Set* stage company of Ernest Hogan, the author of the minstrel classic "All Coons Look Alike to Me."

The Old South Quartette, a group from Richmond, Virginia, recorded "The Watermelon Song" and "The Bonnie Blue Flag," an exhortation to rally round the old flag that flew over Richmond in its days as the capitol of the Confederacy. These Edison cylinders from late 1909 were released as by Polk Miller and His Old South Quartette. Miller, who died in 1913, was a white pharmacist who played banjo and had a stage show of "Stories, Sketches, and Songs" that presented a minstrelsy vision of black life before the Civil War. Polk Miller's was an odd form of minstrelsy, and perhaps should not strictly be termed as such, for he did not perform in blackface (and thus perhaps may be considered a progenitor of the corkless minstrelsy of the 1960s as practiced in all sincerity and goodwill — those same virtues claimed by blackface minstrels of yore — by John Hammond, Jr., by Koerner, Ray, and Glover, at times even by the early Rolling Stones, and by so many others.

Mark Twain was reportedly among Polk Miller's admirers. According to the Cincinnati *Commercial Gazette* of October 15, 1894, Twain had introduced Polk at Madison Square Garden. "Mr. Miller is thoroughly competent to entertain you with his sketches of the old-time Negro," Twain was reported to have said. "I not only commend him to your intelligent notice but personally endorse him." Polk's recordings with the Old South Quartette may be the earliest union of black and white voices on record.

The Kings of Harmony, the Dan Fitch quartet in which Emmett Miller sang in 1924; the Harmony Four, of the Al G. Field Minstrels — it is interesting that these and other white minstrel counterparts to the black vocal groups never performed in blackface: as if to imply that the business of singing unto the Lord must never be degraded by the least hint of mockery, or, perhaps, by the least hint of blackness — a foreshadowing of the irreligious but reverent minstrelsy without blackface to come in the sixties. And yet it can be said with certainty that the gospel music of these white minstrel quartets was more a tepid-souled adulteration of the black-quartet sound than a tepid-souled adulteration of the true white spiritual-singing tradition as exemplified by twenties recording groups such as Allison's Sacred Harp Singers and the Alabama Sacred Harp Singers, with whom they likely had as little in common as did popular white gospel quartets of the teens such as the Chautauqua Preachers' Quartette and the Columbia Stellar Quartette. As the fearsome fires of hell and the harrowing dark night of the soul, as well as the more austere nineteenth-century sacred-harp style shared by blacks and whites, would define the many forms of Spirit-driven black music that in the late 1920s — from the Rev. J. M.

Gates's "Death's Black Train Is Coming" of 1926 to Blind Willie Johnson's "Dark Was the Night, Cold Was the Ground" of 1927 — subsumed the restrained sacred singing of the early black vocal groups, so it was the grim and dire hymnal of a religiosity, exemplified by groups such as Allison's Sacred Harp Singers, which few dared, or could, set aflame, that came to define the sound and sensibilities of country music's theology, from the Carter Family to Hank Williams. If white sanctified music was the music of the grave — and how wonderfully so, in the case of Hank Williams — black sanctified music was the music of the Judgment Day quaking that would shake and sunder the grave. Of the few country singers who have felt and foreseen and conveyed that shaking, Jerry Lee Lewis comes foremost to mind.

As for the groomed and tuxedoed minstrel-revue quartets in which Emmett Miller and others sang so straightforwardly, theirs might have been an offering to some envisioned Almighty, a caricature, if you will, in god-face: a forerunner of the *Head of Christ,* as painted by Warner Sallman in 1940 and reproduced more than five hundred million times since, that has become the omnipresent Jesus, resplendent in fair waves and rhinoplasty, of American brand-name Christianity.

Though the Excelsior Quartette came to be one of the first black vocal groups marketed specifically to the so-called race audience, and seemed to be associated with Mamie Smith, whose "Crazy Blues" of 1920 was the explosion that marked the dawn of that race market, the Quartette's true background, like Miller's, was in coon-song vaudeville. It is not improbable that their paths crossed.

As these rare and obscure recordings by the early black vocal groups shed light on the evolution of American music in the dark days before recording history whence the sound of these groups evolved, so too they can be heard to have forehowled, at times astoundingly, what lay ahead.

"Rock 'n' roll me in your arms," sang the Male Quartette on a Little Wonder record, "The Camp Meeting Jubilee," that has been dated to about 1910, a record that incites "all you niggers down yonder in the mournin' pew for to wake up" to salvation, a record that can be described as nothing else, and nothing less, than gospel-jive. Of the Male Quartette, beyond this lone and wild sounding, nothing is known. The lead singer, whoever he was, shows the distinct influence of Al Jolson, or, perhaps the distinct influence of the unknown influence on Jolson, white or black, or white-as-black, black-as-white or, as here, black-as-white-as-black.

Found in the Excelsior Quartette's 1922 "I Am the King of the Sea," the warning that "your foot might slip and your soul will be lost" served as inspiration for Julius Daniels's 1927 "Slippin' and Slidin' Up the Golden Street." Slippin' and slidin', out of the primordium, endlessly rocking: "Slippin' and Slidin'," Little Richard, 1956.

In the Southern Negro Quartette's "Anticipation Blues" of 1921, the amalgam of the early black vocal groups is encountered at its most stunning. Amid its stylistic schizophrenia, the Quartette careens from straight vaudeville to wails that are bizarrely out of time, from a rhythm-and-blues era — Junior Parker, Bobby Bland — not yet envisioned.

Another, far more frenetic Southern Negro Quartette recording of 1921, "Sweet Mamma (Papa's Getting Mad)," is essentially a black-as-white performance — again, the Jolson style comes to mind — but it is black-as-white gone berserk, with the wildest harmony conflagrations to be heard on any of these forgotten recordings. And, amid its frenzy, something else: traces of a warbling yodel that seems to presage Emmett Miller's first recordings of little more than three years later, but which likely was already emerging from Miller's throat. It is interesting that Miller later recorded his own version of "Sweet Mamma."

The Monarch Jazz Quartet, in 1929 recordings such as "What's the Matter Now?" and "Pleading Blues," are possessed of a jive-and-wail spirit that black vocal groups would rarely recapture until more than two decades later, in the music of groups such as the Clovers, the Dominoes, and the Royals.

Slip and slide. Primordium and continuum. From the Fisk Jubilee Singers in 1867 to the Unique Quartet of 1890 to the Southern Negro Quartette of 1921 to the Mills Brothers quartet of 1931 to the Ravens quartet of 1946 to every rhythm-and-blues and doo-wop quartet that followed. There exists an underground recording, "Rotten Cocksuckers' Ball" by the Clovers, one the great early R&B vocal groups, who began recording in 1950. This furtive recording is shocking in more ways than one, for its sound is far closer to that of the black vocal quartets of the teens and twenties than to that of the age that the Clovers themselves helped to define with hits such as "Fool, Fool, Fool," "Lovey Dovey," and "Your Cash Ain't Nothin' but Trash" (the latter written by Jesse Stone, whose long and amazing career had its roots amid minstrelsy). There is even an archaic air to much of the song's vulgarity that suggests that "Rotten Cocksuckers' Ball" may possibly have been an errant part of the underground black-vocal-group legacy inherited from olden days, dating perhaps to "The Darktown Strutters' Ball" of 1917.

Yes, slip and slide. It all began back there: in gaslight, in the days before phonograph records, in that reverberation of Shango in the blood, in darkness, in thievery, in false face and true, and in that common universal soul, that hypostasis, that νοῦς of which Plato spoke, and of which, one way or another, every great singer, thief and holy vessel at once, has sung.

But I was talking about the talking blues, and was about to say:

Though traces of the talking blues can be found in a very few black recordings of the period — by "Talking" Billy Anderson, who recorded in Atlanta in 1927; by Coley Jones, who also first recorded in 1927, in Dallas, and who, like Chris Bouchillon, played a mandolin — the early talking blues, as we know them, are a white phenomenon, and really are not blues at all, except in name. The anomaly is Herschel Brown, whose "Talking Nigger Blues" and "Nigger Talking Blues No. 2," while the whitest of all the talking blues — that is to say, the most blackfaced of them — nonetheless are built upon a blues music that far transcends anything associated with the blackface tradition.

More precisely, I was talking about a stammer — an artificial stammer — and was about to say:

Whether Brown learned the stammer effect from Miller's shows or from the recordings Miller made in January 1928, or — possible but unlikely — Miller took it from Brown's shows, or each stole it independently from an earlier act, or, as suggested by its shared occurrence in Moran and Mack, it was a traditional blackface trait, is not something we are likely ever to know. Available facts concerning Brown are few. He made several washboard-band recordings under various names, for Columbia in 1927, for Victor and Okeh in 1928; performed with his washboard band in 1932 as a hillbilly act on WGST in Atlanta. As for that shared stammer, an interesting observation by Sally Hinson:

"I'll admit to you that over the years, I've watched more than a few Elvis movies," she wrote in 1996, after I had drawn her into my pursuit of the ghost of Emmett Miller, "and I always noticed how Elvis would affect a stammer, particularly when beginning a sentence with 'I.' He would repeat the 'I' a couple of times and when he did it, he was often in a situation where he was being disingenuous. This always made me think of black folks, of 'Amos 'n' Andy,' etc. Good old Southern boy that he was, I knew Elvis had soaked up a lot of black influence along the way. Now I can see a clear line stretching directly from the minstrels of yore to the Southern red-neck/hillbilly performers. To me, this stutter is the vocal equivalent of the old darky with head hung low, shuffling his feet and trying to score a point or just stay even."

Two of the January 1928 dialogues, "Thousand Frogs on a Log," which was one of Miller's most popular stage routines, and "Brother Bill," were coupled as Okeh 40976, advertised in the Okeh Race Records catalogue, and released on February 15, 1928, at a price of seventy-five cents. The third, "On the Rock Pile," was never released. Like all of Miller's masters, it is now lost.

At the opening of "Thousand Frogs on a Log," we can hear the unique, high-rising yodel by which we know him. The line, sudden and surreal, he delivers in this fashion — *"I don't want no more your greasy cabbage weed"* — has nothing to do with what follows: it is a calling card, intended only to announce his presence; the manner of its delivery was already well established as the virtuoso effect by which he was known and for which he was celebrated.

In the exchange that follows, Miller complains of a howling cat whose cries had kept him awake the previous night.

"Buh-but I stopped him," he says.

"How?" asks Cowan.

"I cut his tail off."

"Oh, man, you can't stop no cat from howlin' by cuttin' off his tail."

"Stopped this one, 'cause I cut it off up to his neck."

This bit about the cat would turn up the following summer on the first of Correll and Gosden's Amos-'n'-Andy records, "Is Everybody in Your Family as Dumb as You Is?"

In "Brother Bill," evoking a character who sported "a rattlesnake for a whip, barb wire for a necktie," Miller foreshadowed imagery that would turn up twenty-eight years later in Bo Diddley's "Who Do You Love?" This should be no less surprising than to discover that Bodiddily was the name of a character portrayed by Emmett Anthony in *Liza,* an all-black musical comedy of 1922 — a name that seems to have been appropriated within the year by a scat singer who performed under the name Bo Diddly at the Royal Gardens in Chicago in 1923.

A second blackface-dialogue session followed six days later. On this Saturday, January 21, Miller and Cowan were accompanied by the fuller background music of a saxophonist, clarinetist, pianist, and drummer, identified as E. Payson Re and His University Five.

Edward Payson Re (1906–78), known as Payson Re, was a pianist then at the outset of his career. He performed also in the late twenties with the California Ramblers, the prolific East Coast dance band with which the Dorsey brothers, Stan King, and others recorded; and, beginning shortly before World War II, went on to lead the house band at the Stork Club for twelve years. The most well known musicians he was associated with were the cornet-player Bobby Hackett, who played in Re's band at the Megansett Tea Room in North Falmouth on Cape Cod in the summer of 1933, when Hackett was eighteen, and Pee Wee Russell, who played clarinet with Re at the Megansett Tea Room the following year.

The two routines recorded with Re's group that winter day were "Sam and His Family" and "Hungry Sam."

In "Sam and His Family," Cowan, addressed here by his actual name of Roy, remarks that Sam is looking well, then inquires after his wife.

"Sh-sh-she ain't wit' us no mo'," Sam says.

Cowan, taken aback, asks: "What was the cause of her death?"

"You mean, what-what caused her to die?"

"Yeah."

"Sh-sh-she got so mean, we had to kill her."

After some confusion, the flustered straight man tries again to ascertain the cause of death: "What was the complaint?"

"Man, there wasn't no complaint. Ever'body was satisfied."

The routine shifts temporal planes. The wife is still living. Sam complains about her in the present tense.

"Son, you don't seem to like your wife."

"Wuh-well, I used to, Roy, buh-but sh-she done got too fat."

"Wha' you mean?"

"Well, right at the present time, the only thing she can buy ready-made to fit her is an *um*-brella."

But the wife sure could dance; "yuh-you oughta see her do the Shimmy."

"The Shimmy?"

"Yassuh. She walk right fast, stop right quick, and let nature take its course."

The Shimmy by this time was passé. It had been overtaken years before by the Charleston, and now the Black Bottom had overtaken the Charleston. The joke, which works only with the Shimmy, suggests for at least this part of the routine an origin of about 1922–23, when the Shimmy was in vogue.

In "Hungry Sam" one of the jokes involves the recollection of a drunk and disorderly Sam gleefully attacking a man at a dance the night before:

"Why you knocked that man down and stomped him right in the face. The very devil must have told you to do that."

"Th-the what?"

"The devil musta told you to do that."

"The devil mighta told me to knock him down, buh-but stompin' him was my own *i*-dea."

Some months later, an almost identical joke turns up in Moran and Mack's "Two Black Crows in Jail," recorded in October for Columbia:

"You knocked that man down with a brick."

"Well, what business is that of yours?"

"Yes, and you wasn't satisfied with knockin' him down; you deliberately jumped on him."

"Well, that's all right. Ain't I a-sorry?"

"Yes, but I don't blame you. That wasn't your fault. No, that was the devil made you knock that man down."

"Yeah, the devil mighta made me knock him down, but that jumpin' on him was my own idea, that's what it was."

In *Country* I traced an obscure rockabilly flip side back through its folk antecedents to an origin in the Orpheus myth. The same could be done with nonsense such as this. To remark on the occurrence of a blackface bit preceding an occurrence elsewhere by a matter of months, or even years, does not necessarily imply provenance, theft, or influence. In terms of material, I suspect that there is little of originality in any of these blackface recordings, and that the sources of much of this material are lost in the uncharted mists of an older time. That Miller is credited on his Okeh record labels with the authorship of his routines attests less to originality than to the common practice of putting one's name to material that lies in the public domain beyond exclusive copyright.

As we shall see, Miller's routines evince a marked penchant for dead wives. The face-stomping bit will be repeated as well; and running down an old man while drunk-driving an automobile will also be celebrated. Dialect comedy in general had never been overly genteel. Ralph Bingham began his 1915 Victor recording "Jests from Georgia" as follows: "This old world is full of funny things, if you only look for them. Here are two little jests from Georgia. Some time ago, they were hanging a colored fellow . . ."

Jimmie Rodgers's "Blue Yodel," rush-released in February 1928, was an immense hit.

On a late-spring Tuesday, June 12, Miller entered the studio again, this time for the first of the seven sessions that would result in his finest work, the recordings for which, today, he is remembered. Most of these recordings, made with the Dorsey Brothers, guitarist Eddie Lang, drummer Gene Krupa, and others, would be released as by Emmett Miller "Acc. By His Georgia Crackers."

Might Okeh's renewed interest this spring in Miller as a singer, not merely as a blackface comic, have derived in part from Victor's success with Rodgers?

Asheville. Jimmie Rodgers. Emmett Miller. The summer of 1927 and the fall of 1927. That strange blue yodel that both wove through the breeze.

In the end, Rodgers's fame and fortune flowered with unimagined abundance, as the wisp of Emmett Miller's brief moment in the sun faded to nothing. Rodgers died young, and Miller lived on nearly thirty years more, the one more a ghost in life than the other in death.

Jimmie Rodgers was one of the great luminaries of American music, a profoundly important link between the shadows of a relatively unknown cultural heritage and all that we have come to know as popular music. Between those shadows — of minstrelsy, vaudeville, urban pop, and deep Southern music, both black and white — from Hank Williams to Jerry Lee Lewis to Bob Dylan and beyond, Rodgers has been a central force, a tie that binds. Dylan, who was born eight years to the very day — May 21, 1941 — after Rodgers's final tuberculosis-racked recording session, has long considered Rodgers an inspiration, a progenitor. Dylan wrote in 1996 in the liner notes to *The Songs of Jimmie Rodgers: A Tribute*: "If we look back far enough, Jimmie may very well be 'the man who started it all' for we have no antecedent to compare him. His refined style, an amalgamation of sources unknown, is too cryptic to pin down." Though Rodgers's recordings remain as wondrous today as they were three-quarters of a century ago — as ever new as, say, Dylan's *Highway 61 Revisited* and *Blonde on Blonde* remain after half that span — they are for the most part unheard by those who well know and embrace his spiritual progeny. From his earliest disciples — Jimmie Davis, Gene Autry (back in the late twenties and early thirties, when they were both blue-yodeling singers of lowdown smut), and Ernest Tubb (to whom Dylan paid wry homage in his 1965 book, *Tarantula,* written during the time of *Highway 61 Revisited* and *Blonde on Blonde*) — to Lefty Frizzell and Jerry Lee Lewis and Dylan himself, the influence of Rodgers has been a powerful underground current that has nourished black music as well as white: from the Mississippi Sheiks in the thirties to Fats Domino in the fifties. The most startling modern evocation of that ageless power can be heard in one of the recordings on the tribute album that Dylan put together: John Mellencamp's performance of Rodgers's "Gambling Bar-Room Blues."

Rodgers was an urbane and sophisticated character whose image was that of a hillbilly singer. It was to Hank Williams, who was in fact a hillbilly singer, that much of Rodgers's spirit passed. As with Rodgers's, Williams's legacy, and his own ageless powers, would reach far beyond his time and knowing — through George Jones; again through Jerry Lee Lewis, again through Dylan, who found in him a fountainhead — to the obscure transcendent beauty of *Hanky Panky,* the 1994 album by the The, in which Matt Johnson so beautifully and chillingly brings forth the marrow of doom from the bones of Williams's songs, capturing the hidden soul of those songs as no one — not even Jerry Lee, not even George Jones — ever has.

Mellencamp, whom I had never before given a passing prick of the ear, gives in his end-of-the-century version of Rodgers's 1932 "Gambling Bar-Room Blues" a haunting illumination, deep magic and slow, hard grave-digging rhythm, of what Dylan calls Rodgers's "raw essence," an essence he perfectly describes as a "nectar that can drill through steel" — an illumination that strangely, tenuously brings to mind Dylan's "Isis," a song of reincarnation and unknowing, which in turn brings — strangely, tenuously, with its fiddling by Scarlet Rivera — Rodgers's "Gambling Bar-Room Blues," with its fiddling by Clayton McMichen, and — strangely, tenuously, with its final piano flourish by Dylan — the great reincarnator himself, Jerry Lee Lewis, who, inspired and inspirer, brings the spirits of Rodgers and Dylan together.

Rodgers shared the credit for the composition of "Gambling Bar-Room Blues" with Shelly Lee Alley (1894–1964), a Houston-based musician and friend of Rodgers whose professional relationship with Rodgers dated at least to Rodgers's recording, in January 1931, of Alley's "Travellin' Blues," to which the Alley brothers, Shelly Lee and Alvin, brought the distinguishing and influential sound of their twin jazz fiddling.

But "Gambling Bar-Room Blues" is really and purely the perfection of Rodgers's earlier, 1930 recording of "Those Gambler's Blues," which is really "St. James Infirmary" — also known as "St. James Hospital," "The John Sealy Hospital," and "The Dying Gambler" — which is really the old American ballad "The Dying Cowboy," which was really the old Irish ballad "The Unfortunate Rake."

As for the medical-institutional nomenclature of some of the song's American variants, it is apocryphal that the best-known title referred to the adjunct of a church that operated amid the whorehouses and saloons of the Storyville district of New Orleans during the dawn of jazz and blues. "St. James Methodist Church," writes Al Rose in his *Storyville, New Orleans,* was "a Negro religious center and one of the most prosperous Protestant places of worship in Louisiana. According to a common story, the church offered first-aid services and modest hospital facilities and thus became the inspiration for the widely performed *St. James Infirmary Blues.* Unfortunately, this colorful and imaginative association is not true; indeed, the song has no connection with New Orleans whatsoever."

Rose, however, makes no mention of St. James Hospital, which was active in New Orleans as far back as the Civil War. It was a white hospital, but it must be held in mind that the song, in its origin, was white as well.

The John Sealy Hospital was also a real place, founded in 1890 in Galveston, Texas, west along the coast from where the Mississippi flowed into the Gulf.

The cowboy singer Carl T. Sprague had recorded "The Dying Cowboy," for Victor, in June of 1926. Louis Armstrong had sung "St. James Infirmary" in 1928. The Hokum Boys had recorded "Gambler's Blues (St. James Infirmary Blues)," for Paramount, in the fall of 1929. The blues singer Mattie Hite had recorded "St. Joe's Infirmary (Those Gambler's Blues)," for Columbia, in January of 1930, less than six months before Rodgers recorded "Those Gambler's Blues." Drawing from the tributaries of "The Dying Cowboy" and "St. James Infirmary," Blind Willie McTell derived his "Dying Gambler" of 1935, his "Dying Crapshooter's Blues" of 1940. Bob Dylan's 1983 "Blind Willie McTell" reaches through those McTell songs to both echo and trace those same tributaries. "I'm staring out the window of the old St. James Hotel," sings Dylan in his song. The St. James Hotel, near both Highway 61 and the Mississippi River, is located on Main Street in the town of Red Wing, in Dylan's native Minnesota.

And, of course, that is what all of this is — *all* of this: the one song, ever changing, ever reincarnated, that speaks somehow from and to and for that which is ineffable within us and without us, that is both prayer and deliverance, folly and wisdom, that inspires us to dance or smile or simply to go on, senselessly, incomprehensibly, beatifically, in the face of mortality and the truth that our lives are more ill-writ, ill-rhymed, and fleeting than any song, except perhaps those songs — *that* song, endlessly reincarnated — born of that truth, be it the moon and June of that truth, or the wordless blue moan, or the rotgut or the elegant poetry of it. That nameless black-hulled ship of Ulysses, that long black train, that Terraplane, that mystery train, that Rocket "88," that Buick 6 — same journey, same miracle, same end and endlessness.

Lightnin' Hopkins's nasty, sidewise "I saw you ridin' around, you was ridin' around in your brand-new automobile," from his wry, lie-down-hip 1949 "Automobile," somehow becomes, in 1966, Bob Dylan's nasty, sidewise "well, I see you got your brand-new leopard-skin pill-box hat." Some people are so cool, *so* lie-down hip, that they can steal the right breezes simply by breathing: the pranayama of holy theft, the pranayama through which Virgil drew into himself the air that Homer had breathed, and through which Dante drew Virgil's.

For it is all the same air, passed to the living from the dead: an errant wisp of a sigh from Sappho in the drawn breath of a lover thousands of years down the line. Brand-new automobile, brand-new leopard-skin hat. *Das Ewig-Weibliche,* and her bitch daughter, remain eternal: in a Mesopotamian skirt of snakes, in a brand-new car, or a brand-new pill-box hat, they, like all the deities of our creation, remain eternal, in whatever guise. Sometimes the hat indeed, as Max Ernst said, makes the man. Sometimes the man makes the hat. Sometimes the man is the hat; sometimes the hat is the man. And sometimes the hat is simply a good place to aim the gun.

It is said that the blues cannot truly be defined. It seems right, then, that the full beauty and force of one of the first great phrases so quintessentially and timelessly of the blues — "*sunt lacrimae rerum,*" from the first book of Virgil's *Aeneid* — has through the ages been a mystery as well as a majesty of expressiveness. *Sunt lacrimae rerum.* [There] are tears [for] things. [There] are tears [of] things. [There] are tears [from] things. Bare bones that cannot be rendered. Every attempt at faithful translation, literal or through wildly grasping poetic liberty, has failed. *Rerum* has been posited as "trials," the oddly singular "misfortune," and all manner of other — what else to call them? — *things* that the word never remotely denoted in Latin. The poet John Dryden's famous translation of 1697 avoids the problem entirely: it is as if the phrase never existed. A modern scholar of language comes vaguely close in explicating *lacrimae rerum* as "the sense of tears in mortal things," but this cannot serve as translation, for the verb *sunt* is plural and "the sense of tears in mortal things" is a nominal phrase that is inescapably singular. *Lacrimae rerum.* The ambiguity of the unstated genitive preposition is immense. The ambiguity of the all-encompassing "things" is insurmountable; and real or imagined echoes of "*natura rerum,*" by which Cicero expressed the sum and magnitude of the human universe, and of Lucretius's "*rerum natura,*" taken to mean "the nature of things," cannot but be heard in Virgil's words, for through such echoes his words may have been cast not only to signify the tears caused by and shed for things, but to evoke as well a world in which all was sorrow, a world in which the nature of all things was sadness. This is the natural and numinous world that is glimpsed throughout the *Aeneid,* as when echoes of mourning, the amber-weeping pines, and their sea-like billowing ("*arbore fluctum,*" X, 207) are brought together by the poet's magic of black and gold. *Fluctum. Fluxus.* Flux. Flow. Everything flows, as Heraclitus said. Every thing.

Lacrimae rerum. A phrase of illimitable nuances of meaning, illimitable nuances of feeling; a phrase of illimitable possibilities, blue and vast as the sky itself. *Lacrimae rerum.* The sky is crying.

Inhale one vision, exhale another. To steal consciously is the way of art and of craft. To steal through breath is the way of wisdom and of art that transcends.

All of it, which we can hear if we seek it, and if we open ourselves to it; all of it, which can obliterate and redeem; all of it, which is ours to hear, as the true sound and music and rhythms of

Homer and Sappho are not; all of it, descended from that lost song — as lost to us as the sound and music and rhythms of that far more ancient source. The same wind that bellied the sail of that black-hulled ship in the rosy-fingered dawn is the wind that blew through the trees in Asheville, the wind that stirred and caressed, stirs and caresses us all: Jimmie Rodgers, Hank Williams, Jerry Lee Lewis, Bob Dylan — and forgotten, at the source and heart of that continuum, Emmett Miller. From Hector's plaint — "your lyre and your love-tricks" — to "Lovesick Blues" to "Love Sick."

As Mary Wack has observed, in her look back to classical antiquity at the outset of *Lovesickness in the Middle Ages,* "Ancient literature and medicine agreed in their descriptions, if not their evaluations, of eros experienced as illness." She reminds us that, as the legends went, "It was the madness of love that drove Sappho to leap to her death, and love that robbed Lucretius of reason."

The Old Testament book that has come to be known as the Song of Solomon and as the Song of Songs, unique in the Bible as a collection of love poetry, has confounded scholars who have sought to determine its origin in time. Though it is believed to have come forth sometime between the fifth and the third centuries B.C., there are many who believe its elements to be far more ancient, derived from sources as old as Sumerian love poetry of the nineteenth century B.C. and earlier, and Egyptian love poetry of the fourteenth century B.C. and earlier. Though only forty Egyptian love songs survive from the fourteenth century to the twelfth century B.C. — the span of the Nineteenth and Twentieth dynasties, when Egypt likely first encountered Israelite tribes — the theme of lovesickness is present among them. This theme blooms full in the refrain (2:5 and 5:8) of the Song of Solomon: "I am sick of love." It is a refrain that Bob Dylan echoed more than two thousand years later: "I'm sick of love." In the spoken interlude to her 2001 version of Prince's "When Doves Cry," Patti Smith returned to the Solomonic source of this refrain.

Sick of love, sick of life. From barroom to barroom, an endless howl and endless smiling dance beneath a Venus ever rising. Mask of tragedy, mask of comedy, mask of blackface. Prosopon — πρόσωπον — mask; in Latin, *persona*. Singer and song, mask and melos, ever changing, ever the same. To have seen Sappho lift her skirt in that breeze; to have heard her raise her voice in song in that breeze. To have heard Hesiod yodel madly at the bitter fates. A breeze through Lesbos, a breeze through the Carolinas, a breeze through the here and now.

The beautiful old Flat Iron Building still stands. The Majestic, which became the Paramount, shut in 1959; the Vanderbilt is now an old-folks' home. Perhaps in some dusty subterranean corner of Asheville something from those summers of seventy years ago and more still lies awaiting discovery.

Though surely unintentional, the name that Emmett Miller of Macon gave his backup group — the Georgia Crackers — seems a wry jazz-age echo of that band of Macon sons barely remembered as the original Georgia Minstrels — a name already echoed in the twenties, straightforwardly and without any wry twist, by black touring companies such as J. F. Murphy's Georgia Minstrels, Richard's and Pringle's Georgia Minstrels, and by white companies such as Rusco and Hockwald's Famous Georgia Minstrels, J. C. O'Brien's Georgia Minstrels. As for *cracker,* Miller was certainly not the first entertainer to use it as a moniker. A performer known as Cracker Quinn, of Durham, North Carolina, had worked with Dan Fitch as partner in a blackface act during Miller's years with the Fitch troupe; and a string band, whose music bore no resemblance to Miller's, had recorded under the name of the Georgia Crackers for Okeh in 1926. Blackface Eddie Ross, Miller's friend from the Field troupe, performed a banjo number known as "Ross' Florida Cracker," which he recorded for Victor late in 1923. A hillbilly string band calling themselves the Georgia Crackers had recorded six songs for Okeh in Atlanta in 1927, the year before Miller's first Georgia Crackers session in New York. In its own rough-hewn way, this hillbilly string band, from predominantly black Hancock County in central Georgia, echoed the same sources that informed their more sophisticated contemporary Jimmie Rodgers and his black counterparts: those motes of vaudeville, minstrelsy, and the black songster tradition aswirl in the effulgence of that beautiful thievery that in the hands of one became the blues, in the hands of another country music. It was the nineteenth-century fiddle-based string bands, black and white, through which the mongrel motes swirled. It was the symbiosis and synergy and estuary of those nineteenth-century fiddle-based string bands, black and white, that brought forth, simultaneously, before the ascendancy of the guitar, what came to be called the blues and country music. It was the music of those fiddle-based string bands, black and white, that was the true indigenous and autochthonous sound of the nineteenth-century South, mother and wild bride and fickle daughter, enticer and enticed of all that swirled, of that eventual bastard song, neither black nor white, both black and white, of the midnight bottomland crossroads and the great lighted dazzling of Broadway alike. It was the likes of Emmett Miller and others that haunted both commingled midnights.

"The Coon from Tennessee," as recorded by the Georgia Crackers string band, shared elements with Jim Jackson's "I'm Gonna Start Me a Graveyard of My Own," recorded almost a year later. It is interesting that Jackson recorded a "Love Sick Blues" in 1929 — a "Love Sick Blues" that bears no resemblance to the song that

Miller had recorded. Maybe he could only remember the title. Maybe it was an earlier, different "Love Sick Blues," culled from another tent-show or minstrel stage. Similarly Ernest Tubb's 1936 recording "Mean Old Bed Bug Blues" bears no resemblance beyond its singular title to the Irene Higginbotham song recorded some years earlier by Lonnie Johnson, Bessie Smith, Furry Lewis, and others.

And, so, "Georgia cracker." The term itself, of course, is a common one, dating at least to the late eighteenth century. According to an accepted, but dubious, etymology, it was applied to poor white inhabitants of the Georgia and Florida backwoods because of their dietary staple of cracked corn. "The Crackers of Georgia," a study by Delma E. Presley in *The Georgia Historical Quarterly* (1976), traced its usage to 1784, when it appeared in reference to outlaws, specifically in the back settlements of the Maryland colony: "hardy banditti well known by the name of Crackers." The 1972 Supplement to *The Oxford English Dictionary,* however, cited an earlier occurrence of *crackers* in a letter of June 1766, in which it was explained as "a name they have got from being great boasters; they are a lawless set of rascalls on the frontiers of Virginia, Maryland, the Carolinas and Georgia, who often change their places of abode." The Georgia jurist, educator, and author A. B. Longstreet (1790–1870) wrote endearingly of the poor rural whites known as crackers in *Georgia Scenes,* an 1835 collection of humorous sketches whose purpose, he said, "was to supply a chasm in history which has always been overlooked — the manners, customs, amusements, wit, dialect, as they appear in all grades of society to an eye and ear witness of them." The term came to be embraced colloquially by Georgians as a source of humor and self-effacing pride; and by the mid-nineteenth century and well into the twentieth, Georgia was known as the Cracker State. In the early 1930s, Erskine Caldwell, another Georgia author, would show a darker and more sordid side of cracker life in his popular novels *Tobacco Road* and *God's Little Acre;* but only later did *cracker* become the pejorative epithet that it is today, a class slur leveled by other whites or a racial slur cast by blacks.

The musicians at the first Georgia Crackers session were: Jimmy Dorsey, alto saxophone and clarinet; Tommy Dorsey, trombone; Stan King, drums; Eddie Lang, guitar; Leo McConville, trumpet; and Arthur Schutt, piano. Four recordings were made. Of the origin of the first of these, "God's River Blues," nothing is known other than that its authorship is credited to someone named Baskett. The song appears not to have been copyrighted; the credited author may in fact have been an obscure songwriter named Billy Baskette. "God's River" was probably deemed a weak performance, as it was shelved by Okeh for more than two years, not to be released in America until the fall of 1930. It would, however, be released earlier in England, as the flip side of the British Parlophone issue of "Lovesick Blues," recorded later this day.

The second Crackers recording, "I Ain't Got Nobody," dates to an April 1914 copyright as "I Ain't Got Nobody and Nobody Cares for Me." The copyright credits the music to Charles Warfield, the lyrics to David Young, and the arrangement to Marie Lucas. A 1915 manuscript copyright credits the same song, its title shortened, to Spencer Williams and Dave Peyton; and in a 1916 published copyright, the music is credited to Williams and Peyton, the lyrics to Roger Graham.

Several weeks previous to Miller's recording of "I Ain't Got Nobody," W. C. Handy had featured the song, along with "St. Louis Blues" (highlighted by a Fats Waller organ solo) as part of the "Jazz Finale" of his Carnegie Hall concert of April 27, at which Handy's orchestra was joined by the Jubilee Singers. In the program notes, the authorship of "I Ain't Got Nobody" was credited to Spencer Williams alone.

The song was recorded in New York as "I Ain't Got Nobody

Much" by the singer Marion Harris for Victor on August 9, 1916. Harris, born in Henderson, Kentucky, in 1896, was one of the great vaudeville singing stars. "I Ain't Got Nobody Much" was the song with which she began her recording career, and it was claimed that the record sold in the millions. She recorded the song again, as "I Ain't Got Nobody," for Columbia in April 1920, five months before she recorded a new song called "Sweet Mamma (Papa's Getting Mad)," which Miller would record at the final Crackers session. Harris died in her room at the Hotel Le Marquise in New York in April of 1944, in a fire believed to have been caused by her smoking in bed.

Blonde and lanky, Harris was known as the Queen of the Blues, a title later used by Columbia to promote big black Bessie Smith. When Paramount usurped the title to promote Ida Cox, Columbia raised Bessie to Empress of the Blues. Smith recorded "I Ain't Got Nobody" in the summer of 1925; Cox recorded it that fall, as did a band called the Tennessee Tooters, whose personnel included the future Georgia Crackers bassist Joe Tarto. Cliff Edwards recorded it in the spring of 1926.

In the spring of 1927, Sophie Tucker (1884–1966), who had started out in blackface, also recorded the song, for Okeh. The personnel of Miff Mole's Molers, who accompanied Tucker on "I Ain't Got Nobody," included both Jimmy Dorsey and Eddie Lang, who now, little more than a year later, were in the same studio recording the same song with Miller. In the summer of 1928, Arthur Schutt, Joe Tarto, and Stan King worked in the Okeh studio with both Mole and Miller. In a blur, the British release, by Parlophone, of one of Miller's records from this summer would be issued with a label that credited accompaniment to Miff Mole's Molers rather than the Georgia Crackers.

Harris, Smith, Cox, Tucker — the versions of "I Ain't Got Nobody" by these women are all wondrous in their ways, but it is

Miller's version that transcends. In the following year, the Monarch Jazz Quartet recorded a version of the song, also for Okeh, also in New York. This black group's 1929 treatment of the song offers a tantalizing suggestion of Miller's stylistic influence. But Miller's recording exceeded comparison with any other. Not until Louis Prima wed the song to "Just a Gigolo" in 1956 would there be a recording of "I Ain't Got Nobody" that approached the wild originality and sublime sociopathic air of Miller's.

Milton Brown (1903–36), the most imaginative of the Western-swing musicians, was at this time — June 1928 — a member of a tuxedo-clad Fort Worth trio who called themselves, with a snazzy frill of franco-Cowtown *je ne sais quoi,* the Three Yodeliers. "I Ain't Got Nobody" became one of Brown's favorite yodeling-falsetto performances, and he continued to sing it later as a member of the Light Crust Doughboys with Bob Wills.

Brown left the Doughboys in the fall of 1932, to be replaced by Tommy Duncan. When Duncan auditioned for the band, Wills asked him to sing "I Ain't Got Nobody." One contemporary Texas musician, Jimmy Thomason, recalled that, "about two days after he [Duncan] joined, he laid an Emmett Miller thing on them. And Bob and Tommy would do the talking deal at the front of 'I Ain't Got Nobody' and to me that's what sold the Doughboys to their audience." Later, in 1935, when Wills and the Texas Playboys recorded the song, Duncan imitated Miller's vocal performance as closely as he could. Conversely and perhaps significantly, Miller's version had no influence at all on the Monarch Jazz Quartet, a black vocal group who recorded "I Ain't Got Nobody" for Okeh in the fall of 1929.

Miller's recording of "I Ain't Got Nobody" opens with a brief prelude of blackface dialogue set against a musical background. Miller, addressed as Sam, is assisted by Dan Fitch, whose troupe Miller rejoined this summer. Fitch remarks that Sam looks kind of blue.

"Wuh-well, I'm a man, I'm a man what's in bad shape," says Sam. "T-to tell ya the truth, I-I just lost my wife."

"It must be hard to lose a wife," says Fitch with sympathy.

"I-it's almost impossible," reflects Sam.

Fitch goes on to inquire as to her estate: "Did she leave you much?"

"A-about twice a week."

The Dorsey Brothers Orchestra, with vocalist Scrappy Lambert, would record another version of "I Ain't Got Nobody" in October. Lambert was only one of several singers the Dorseys used on their own Okeh recordings throughout the period that they recorded with Miller. At the first Dorsey Brothers Orchestra session, four months before the first Crackers session, they had used Irving Kaufman, one of the most prolific and ubiquitous of the era's band singers. In March they had used Bill Dutton on "Coquette" and other songs. In April they had used Seger Ellis to record "My Melancholy Baby." Eight days before the first Crackers session, they had used Lambert. Over the course of the next year, Smith Ballew and Bing Crosby would also sing with the Dorsey Brothers Orchestra. Several of these recordings were moderately successful, beginning with "Coquette" in the month of the first Crackers session. The most successful was "Let's Do It (Let's Fall in Love)," with Crosby, in the spring of 1929.

I wonder if anyone — Miller himself, or Tommy or Jimmy Dorsey, or one of the other Crackers, or producer Justin Ring — ever entertained or broached the thought of Miller recording as a singer for the Dorsey Brothers Orchestra. I wonder what the Dorseys and the other Crackers really thought of Miller, how they felt about the anonymity and dissociation the veil of the Georgia Crackers afforded, or imposed on, them. The last session of the Dorsey Brothers Orchestra would be in 1935. The Dorseys then would pursue their separate paths. I wonder what Tommy Dorsey, recording with Frank Sinatra as his singer five years thence, would remember of the singer from Macon.

The third recording made by Miller and the Crackers this June day in 1928 was "Lovesick Blues," which Miller had first recorded in 1925. As on "I Ain't Got Nobody," Miller opens with a blackface prelude with Fitch. It is for a moment strangely evocative of the 1858 dialogue "The Blues," from *Christy and Fox's Complete Melodist and Joke-Book,* quoted above.

"Sam, you sure do look like you've got the miseries."

"Man, I-I ain't got no miseries. I-I'm got de blues, dat what's the matter wit' me."

"The birds singin' in the trees and the sun am shinin', you shouldn't have no blues."

"I know I-I shouldn't have 'em, buh-but I got every known indication of being in that condition."

"What's the matter, did they lock up your bootlegger?"

"No, it's worse than that. I went home this mornin' and peeped through the window: that sweet thing of mine had done caught air. So now I got them lovesick blues." (A singular expression: *done caught air.* Jimmie Rodgers, two years and some months later, in his "Travellin' Blues": "my good gal had done caught air.")

Then, to the slow vamping of the Crackers, Miller breaks into his song.

It was likely this version of "Lovesick Blues," coupled in its release with "I Ain't Got Nobody," that became the direct inspiration for the 1948 performance that twenty-five-year-old Hank Williams rode to fame.

By then Miller's "Lovesick Blues" had served as the inspiration for several straight country acts. Stylistically, down to its melody, looping licks, and wild blue yodels, the first Dixon Brothers recording, "Weave Room Blues" (Bluebird, 1936), was derived directly from it. The Alabama-born country singer Rex Griffin (1912–59) recorded "Lovesick Blues" for Decca in December 1939: a stripped-down replication of Miller's version, which he claimed to have gleaned from Miller's stage shows.

In his 1925 "Lovesick Blues," Miller sang "I'm nobody's purty papa now." In 1928, recording "I Ain't Got Nobody," he longed for a "sweet cracker mama." Then, in his new "Lovesick Blues," which followed it, the phrase "purty papa" became "cracker papa." Rex Griffin amended it to "cracker daddy"; and as sung by Hank Williams, it became "sugar daddy." As written and copyrighted, the lyric was simply "I'm nobody's baby now."

Williams was well acquainted with both Miller's version and Griffin's version. "Just got back from New York and have a hint regarding publisher on LOVESICK BLUES unless we can prove this tune is public domain," wrote Wesley Rose to Williams on March 28, 1949, six weeks after the Williams record was released, without composer credit. "You mentioned you had an old Decca record by Rex Griffin and also an old record by Emmett something or other on this tune. Please mail these to me at once."

A curious historical footnote is that Wesley Rose's father, Fred Rose (1897–1954), the guiding light of Williams's career, was a co-author, with George A. Little and Peter L. Frost, of the 1920 song "Sweet Mamma (Papa's Getting Mad)," recorded by Miller and the Crackers in 1929.

The fourth recording made on June 12, 1928, was devoted to blackface dialogue with musical background: a routine with Fitch called "The Lion Tamers." Elements of this blackface piece could be heard some years earlier on "Then I'll Go in That Lion's Cage," recorded for Okeh in 1923 by Shelton Brooks (1886–1975), the black author of "The Darktown Strutters' Ball" of 1917. Moran and Mack also had done a lion-taming bit in their 1927 two-part Columbia recording "All About Lions."

The second Crackers session was on August 9, 1928. Manny

Klein may have replaced Leo McConville on trumpet. The songs recorded were "Anytime," which Miller had previously recorded in 1924, and "St. Louis Blues," reckoned to be the most-recorded song in history except for "Silent Night."

On "Anytime" Miller opens once again with a blackface prelude with Fitch; but here Fitch addresses him as Emmett. And here, for a change, instead of complaining about wives, living and dead, Emmett is looking forward, albeit benightedly, to becoming a bridegroom.

The third session was on September 14, 1928, five days after the premiere of Al Jolson's *The Singing Fool:* "Take Your To-morrow" and "Dusky Stevedore." Miller appears to have traveled downstate for this session from Syracuse, where he was appearing in the Dan Fitch revue on September 13–15. Turk McBee, who was also appearing in the Fitch show, claimed to be the drummer at this session.

Both songs were the recent work of lyricist Andy Razaf and composer J. C. Johnson. "Take Your To-morrow," published as "Take Your Tomorrow (and Give Me Today)," was described on its sheet-music cover as "A Philosophical Song" and a "Fox-Trot Ballad."

"Eddie, you is killing me," Miller responds to the guitar work of Eddie Lang that blossoms from the ensemble opening of "Take Your To-morrow"; and the notes with which Lang later embellishes Miller's vocal flights are here especially attentive, especially imaginative.

Eddie Lang was the first great jazz guitarist, an originator whose influence altered the course of American music. His real name was Salvatore Massaro; he was born in South Philadelphia in 1902. Like many jazz musicians of Italian descent, he had a background of classical training, specifically the violin; and the only other guitarist whom he held in any esteem was Andres Segovia (1893–1987). It was with another South Philly violinist, his boyhood friend Joe

Venuti (1904–78), destined to become the first jazz master of his instrument, that Lang as a guitarist formed his earliest and most enduring musical alliance. Performers together since grammar school, they joined the Bert Estlow quintet in nearby Atlantic City in 1921. It was in Atlantic City in the summer of 1924 that Lang was hired by Red McKenzie, the leader of the Mound City Blue Blowers. McKenzie, a former jockey from St. Louis, was one of the notable white jazz singers of the day. His Mound City Blue Blowers were an outrageous group, part straight jazz, part hokum, part novelty act, and McKenzie was known to sing through a tissue-covered comb. Lang's affiliation with the group, which brought him to London, lasted about a year.

Lang's first studio work was in the summer of 1923, recording with Charlie Kerr for Edison. Since then he had become the most popular and prolific studio guitarist of the day. During the period that he worked with Emmett Miller, he also recorded with Texas Alexander, Louis Armstrong, Gladys Bentley, the Dorsey Brothers Orchestra, Cliff Edwards, Seger Ellis, Bessie Smith, Victoria Spivey, Eva Taylor, and many others.

Respected and sought by black artists as well as by white, Lang worked with more black performers than any other white musician of the twenties. He had recorded with Noble Sissle in 1927. His work with Clarence Williams was extensive: it was with Williams and King Oliver that he accompanied the eccentric bluesman Texas Alexander in the fall of 1928; with Williams that he accompanied Victoria Spivey and Eva Taylor in the summer of 1928, Bessie Smith in the spring of 1929.

He recorded guitar duets with bluesman Lonnie Johnson in 1928 and 1929, also during the period in which he worked with Miller. The two guitar virtuosi, both of whom were under contract to Okeh, had first worked together at a Texas Alexander session in New York on November 15, 1928. Two days later, Johnson and

Lang recorded the first of their duets, which, as the blues writer Chris Smith has noted, are considered to mark the first important interracial partnership in jazz. Their significantly titled "Two Tone Stomp" was followed that day by "Have to Change Keys to Play These Blues." Four more Okeh-Johnson-Lang duets followed in May of 1929: "Guitar Blues," "A Handful of Riffs," "Blue Guitars," and "Bull Frog Moan." In October of 1929, there were another four duets: "Deep Minor Rhythm Stomp," "Midnight Call," "Hot Fingers," and "Blue Room Blues." All of these remarkable duets, those of 1928 and those of 1929, were released as by Lonnie Johnson and Blind Willie Dunn (the order of the names was reversed on the last two releases), masking Lang's identity perhaps in apprehension — by Okeh, and possibly by Lang as well — of adverse reaction to their interracial aspect. In April of 1929, Johnson and Lang were joined in the Okeh studio by King Oliver on cornet, J. C. Johnson (the co-author of "Take Your To-morrow") on piano, and singer Hoagy Carmichael. These recordings, "Jet Black Blues" and "Blue Blood Blues," were released as by Blind Willie Dunn's Gin Bottle Four. It has been said that Lang appropriated the name of Willie Dunn from the blind New York newsboy from whom he bought his papers, and that he paid the newsboy for the use of his name.

Alonzo "Lonnie" Johnson (c. 1894–1970) is today generally recognized as the most extraordinary and progressive blues guitarist, and one of the most powerful and poetically gifted songwriters, of his time. Born in New Orleans, he began his recording career in 1925. Like Lang, he was a former violinist, and he frequently played the violin on his earliest recordings. His influence was pervasive and profound, notably on the legendary Robert Johnson, for whom Lonnie's many records were an object of study and emulation. He was a man of numerous and conflicting aspects, from kind-hearted and loving to bitter, brooding, and cruel, and his rare eloquence served them all. In late 1929 and early 1930, following his last session with Lang, Lonnie Johnson recorded some of his most cold-blooded, murderous, dark-spirited, and haunted songs, such as "She's Making Whoopee in Hell Tonight," "Another Woman Booked Out and Bound to Go," "Death Valley Is Just Half Way to My Home," and "Headed for Southland": songs that, as the writer Chris Smith has suggested, cannot but have spoken directly to the younger Johnson, whose own dark and often demonic songs became the stuff of legend. A rare example of demonic song done by white musicians is the fine, Faustian "Done Sold My Soul to the Devil," a composition credited to Harold Gray and originally recorded by Clara Smith in 1924. Recorded in Dallas in December 1937 by the Western-swing band of Dave Edwards & His Alabama Boys, it is, like Robert Johnson's satanic "Me and the Devil Blues," also recorded in Dallas, some months earlier, in June of 1937, a cool and rhythm-bound performance put forth without melodrama.

The influence of Lonnie Johnson extended further than is often perceived. Listening to "Hey Joe" by Jimi Hendrix anew in the light of Johnson's 1930 "Got the Blues for Murder Only" is to never hear it quite the same again. Bob Dylan, who met and performed with Lonnie Johnson, said of him plainly and straightforwardly, "I must say he greatly influenced me."

The blues for murder only. Pat Hare (1930–80) was a musician whose black-magic electric-guitar conjurings through overamplified distortion foreshadowed those of Hendrix, recorded "I'm Gonna Murder My Baby" in the spring of 1954, in the Sun Records studio in Memphis. Hare's recording would remain unissued for more than twenty years, long after he had been imprisoned for fulfilling the intention expressed in the song, having murdered not only his baby but, for good measure, a cop as well. It was a good time for murder music. In 1953, on the Herald label out of New York, had come what may have been Pat Hare's musical, though certainly not emotional, inspiration: the Rocketeers' astonishing "Gonna Feed My Baby Poison." This rare record by this obscure black vocal quartet was issued not only on black vinyl but as an even more rare bloodred-vinyl pressing as well.

Did Robert Johnson wonder at the identity of Blind Willie Dunn, the Italian-American kid known as Eddie Lang, who was the guitarist whom the elder Johnson most respected?

"He could play guitar better than anyone I know," Lonnie Johnson said of Lang. "The sides I made with Eddie Lang were my greatest experience."

Some of Lang's best work was with Joe Venuti. Over the years 1926–33 they collaborated on duet, small-group, and big-band recordings for a variety of labels — recordings that served as the inspiration for the team of Django Reinhardt and Stephane Grappelli.

Lang also recorded as a featured artist for Okeh, twenty-two recordings spread over the years 1927–32. Some of these, such as "Prelude" (1927), an adaptation of Rachmaninoff, op. 3, no. 2, were experimental in nature; others, such as "Rainbow Dreams" (1928), written for his wife, Kitty, were original compositions; all served to showcase a virtuosity that was as rare in imagination as in elegance. On three of his May 1929 recordings, released as by Eddie Lang and His Orchestra, the band was Jimmy and Tommy Dorsey, Stan King, Leo McConville, Arthur Schutt, and Joe Tarto — the Georgia Crackers without a singer.

Miller loved the way Lang played. It has been said that he would listen to Lang's records for hours, hushing those around him when any Lang record played. What seemed to make him most proud of his own records, it was said, was that Lang was on them. It has also been said that Miller claimed to have performed with Lang onstage.

Miller was not the only singer who loved Lang's work. Paul

Whiteman hired Lang and Venuti for five hundred dollars a week in May of 1929. Lang replaced Snoozer Quinn in the Whiteman orchestra, and on the day after the final Georgia Crackers session, Lang recorded with Whiteman for the first time. Bing Crosby was then still one of Whiteman's singers, and Lang was said to have become Crosby's "closest friend, his omnipresent attendant, his social and musical advisor." Lang left the Whiteman orchestra soon after appearing in *King of Jazz,* the semi-Technicolor musical that Whiteman made for Universal in 1930. Crosby, after his first solo hits of 1931, insisted on Lang as a studio accompanist for all his recordings; and Lang worked with Crosby in his radio broadcasts, theater shows, and his 1932 Paramount feature, *The Big Broadcast,* as well. On the sole, 1932 recording ("Lawd, You Made the Night Too Long") where Lang is absent, there is no replacement, no guitar.

There is no telling where Lang's gift would have taken him. But he did not live beyond his thirty-first year; did not live to see 1934, the year in which the era of the amplified guitar began. In late January 1933 he recorded with Crosby as part of a group that included Bunny Berrigan, Tommy Dorsey, Benny Goodman, Stan King, and the Mills Brothers. On February 28 the Joe Venuti–Eddie Lang Blue Five made four recordings for Columbia. Less than a month later, on March 26, 1933, Lang died in New York from complications following a routine tonsillectomy.

Two weeks after Miller's recording of "Take Your To-morrow," Lang played on another Okeh recording of the song, by Frankie Trumbauer and His Orchestra, with Smith Ballew singing and Bix Beiderbecke on cornet.

"Dusky Stevedore" had been recorded in June by Nat Shilkret and the Victor Orchestra and by the California Ramblers (Harmony), and in July by Frankie Trumbauer and His Orchestra (Okeh), with Beiderbecke but without Lang, and with Trumbauer himself singing. Later this month, it would be recorded for Columbia by Thelma Terry and Her Play-Boys, with Joe Davis as vocalist and Gene Krupa on drums.

In this autumn of 1928, had a citizen found his way to the right Manhattan speakeasy, he might have encountered not only Emmett Miller but William Faulkner as well. It was in New York in October of this year that Faulkner, sojourning from Mississippi, completed *The Sound and the Fury.* Faulkner, it is said, was once thrown out of a speakeasy for singing "I Can't Give You Anything but Love"; and this was the season of that song: Cliff Edwards's big hit record of it was in the air, and there was another by Seger Ellis.

I like to think of the two of them meeting, the singer with the trick voice and the singing author of *The Sound and the Fury,* lost in the after-hours haze, two visionary sons of a dying South.

The fourth Crackers session was on January 8, 1929, after the Fitch tour folded. "I Ain't Gonna Give Nobody None o' This Jelly Roll" was written by Spencer Williams and Clarence Willliams in 1916, published as a "jazz song" in 1919 ("This Number on All Phonograph Records and Music Rolls," the sheet music proclaimed), and recorded by Mamie Smith and Her Jazz Hounds for Okeh in 1922. Eight years after Miller's version, Cliff Bruner's Texas Wanderers recorded the song at their first session, in February 1937, for Decca. Bruner was a fiddling alumnus of the Musical Brownies, the group that Milton Brown had founded after leaving Bob Wills and the Light Crust Doughboys. Jimmie Davis, in a fleeting return to the risqué stuff of his early career, recorded it in the fall of 1951.

"(I Got a Woman Crazy for Me) She's Funny That Way" was a recent song by Richard A. Whiting and Charles N. Daniels, the latter writing under the pseudonym of Neil Morét. The Dorsey Brothers Orchestra, with vocalist Smith Ballew, had recorded it for Okeh on November 21, 1928. "You Lose" was a blackface crapshooting routine with Charles Chiles, who had worked with Miller in the Fitch troupe. Both their characters here are nameless.

The fifth session was on January 19, 1929, when Joe Tarto was added on bass: "Right or Wrong," written in 1921 by Haven Gillespie, Arthur Sizemore, and Paul Biese, and recorded in 1928 by Peggy English (Brunswick) and the California Ramblers (Pathé Actuelle and Perfect); "That's the Good Old Sunny South," a new song by Jack Yellen and Milton Ager, also recorded this winter by Harry Reser's Rounders (Edison), Joe Venuti (Okeh), and Benny Krueger (Victor), which would be laid aside, eventually to be coupled with the shelved "God's River"; and "You're the Cream in My Coffee." The latter, written by Bud DeSylva, Lew Brown, and Ray Henderson, had premiered the previous October in the show *Hold Everything* at the Broadhurst Theatre. Within ten days of its premiere it had been recorded by both the Ben Selvin orchestra with Jack Palmer (Columbia) and the Ted Weems orchestra with Parker Gibbs (Victor). The torch singer Ruth Etting had recorded it in December, for Columbia.

Vocally, this was Miller's most subdued and conservative session. Throughout "Right or Wrong," where we expect his voice to bolt and soar at every occurrence of the word "true," there is instead a noticeable reining, a sense of taut restraint. He forgoes flight until the song's end, and even that is tame and tepid. Of all Miller's recordings, "That's the Good Old Sunny South" and "You're the Cream in My Coffee" are his most straightforward and least eccentric. He sounds for all the world like a crooner, though that word was not yet in vogue.

But there is something else about these recordings, something jarringly uncharacteristic, the precise nature of which eluded me for quite some time. Then I realized what it was: *sincerity.* Not the real thing, of course, but the pretense of sincerity that is the stock-in-trade of most singers as we know them. Generally Miller eschews the very notion of sincerity; his performances treat love, loneliness, and life itself with wry, good-natured mockery — and his best performances are of songs that do the same. Sincerity is decidedly not his racket. Yet here he is sounding, well, *sincere.*

It may be that Okeh was here responding to disappointing sales by directing Miller to tone down his style; as there seemed to be no market for his singular manner of singing, it would be better to modify the singing to fit the market. The star of the day was Gene Austin (1900–71), the Texas-born Victor recording star whose easy, affable, and somewhat feminine voice had dominated popular taste since 1925. While we know nothing of Jimmie Rodgers's awareness of Emmett Miller, we do know that Rodgers idolized Gene Austin.

Born the same year as Miller, Austin had begun his recording career the same year as Miller as well. But Austin had thrived beyond the vaudeville stage. His "My Blue Heaven" of 1927 was the bestselling record of the decade, a decade that belonged to him and the manic-voiced Jolson. Austin, whose picture was on the cover of "She's Funny That Way," had recorded the song in November 1928; Miller had recorded it two months later, in January 1929. That recording, too, had been one of restraint. Austin's record, already released by then, became a hit; Miller's would barely catch hold of its coattails. But it was too soon to know that, and this session, eleven days after Miller's recording of "She's Funny That Way," seems a continuation of the attempt to recast Miller in the Gene Austin mold.

Austin, for all his immense success, was a transitional figure, a singer who represented the passage from the old-style vaudeville singing of the acoustic-recording era to the new era of the crooners. He, like Jolson, would fade in the thirties. Rudy Vallee, Bing Crosby, Russ Columbo: these were the singers, theirs was the style, that would define and dominate popular music in the thirties.

Vallee came first. He had a hit on Harmony less than a month after Miller's session of January 19, 1929, and by spring he would be one of Victor's biggest stars. But Crosby (1903–77) was the key: the first singer to work the microphone as if it were a woman — not only singing to it as if it were a woman, but taking it in his hands as such. Though overlooked and all but invisible to modern eyes, this was the most revolutionary move in the history of popular singing. Before Crosby, the microphone was regarded as an ill-favored object, a cold and ugly technological necessity whose presence was something to be overcome. He made of it a surrogate of desire, an instrument of physical as well as of vocal expression. When he caressed that microphone for the first time, it was a breakthrough; and the hands-on-mike stage presence of every singer, black and white, has been an ever intensifying reverberation of that breakthrough, from Sinatra and Dean Martin and Wynonie Harris to Elvis and Mick Jagger, Jim Morrison and Iggy Pop and beyond.

That Emmett Miller, pressed to emulate the likes of Gene Austin, emerged sounding more like a crooner than like Austin is an example of his being, let's not say ahead of his time, but hopelessly apart from it. Other singers of the day, such as Smith Ballew, fared well as crooners. Even Miller's old pal Cliff Edwards managed to keep his singing career alive by making records as a sort of whimsical crooner for Brunswick and Vocalion in the early thirties. By then, however, Edwards had a new career. No stranger to the movies, he had been one of the first Vitaphone performers, and had made his feature-film debut in *The Hollywood Revue of 1929,* following which he appeared in over sixty more films through 1945, eight of them in the year 1931 alone. He was in half a dozen Tim Holt Westerns, played a reminiscing soldier in *Gone with the Wind,* did the voice of Jiminy Cricket in *Pinocchio.* In the midst of all this, in 1933, he somehow found time to declare bankruptcy; and he was in fact practically destitute, and a solitary figure, when he died in a

Hollywood nursing home in the summer of 1971. "He had a trick voice," noted the *New York Daily News* in its obituary.

No matter how he sang, of course, bug-eyed Edwards never could have made it as a straight crooner, and Miller's chance of making it as such was even more remote. Even if he could have cultivated this style of singing, this sweetness of voice, with any depth and conviction, he lacked the look, the air, the appeal of the crooner.

The sensibilities of his songs were the least of his problem: as late as 1932, Bing Crosby crooned of "old Virginny and those pickaninny days" (in his Brunswick recording of "Cabin in the Cotton," with Eddie Lang on guitar). Had Miller sung the same, it would have emerged as perverse, antiquated. It was a matter of other sensibilities, of style and persona. The voice and song of Miller's day were mellifluous, romantic; and these are attributes to which he could not lay claim.

Yet one wonders at the possibilities. To hear Sinatra singing "Melancholy Mood" with Harry James and His Orchestra in 1939 is to hear and feel a certain beauty, a somber breezy power rarely possessed by song. Had Emmett Miller been given these same lyrics, this same arrangement, this same music, the result may have been nothing less than a song that terrified rather than mesmerized: breeze turned to gust, melancholy to madness, moonlit lovesickness to more dangerous and unspeakable feelings. It would have been something. But it was not meant to be, or else it would have been.

The lesser vaudeville recording stars of the twenties would share the fate of Austin and Jolson. The thirties would belong to the crooners, as it would belong to the Dorseys and to swing. Miller never was a star, lesser or otherwise, nor would he be. He missed the boat, both coming and going. For all his brilliance, he belonged, at best, to the sideshow of the age, where all that does not conform, all that lies beyond the range of the lowest common denominator, brilliant and bad alike, is relegated to curiosity and in the end left on the church steps of posterity.

More than seven months passed before the next session, which was on September 5, 1929. Leo McConville may have replaced Manny Klein on trumpet.

Enough time had elapsed for sales of his January recordings to suggest that Emmett was unlikely to be another Gene Austin. The die by now may have been cast; Okeh by now may have already given up on him. One thing is known: after this month, the Georgia Crackers would be no more. We cannot be sure of the circumstances, or of Miller's awareness of them, of whether or not he knew or felt that his days at Okeh were numbered. But we can hear that his voice once again was unleashed. Where a sense of restraint had been perceivable seven months ago, there seemed now to be a certain lackadaisical abandon, a spirit of true uncaring freedom.

Three songs were recorded. "Lovin' Sam (The Sheik of Alabam')" was written in 1922 by Jack Yellen and Milton Ager. It was introduced by Sophie Tucker; the song's sheet music declared it to be "Featured by Walters & Goold"; and Rufus Greenlee and Thaddeus Drayton, a tap-dancing team from the South, used it as a showcase number in their New York shows of 1922. The song was perhaps inspired by Perry Bradford's 1913 song "Loving Sam from Alabam," which Greenlee and Drayton are believed to have done later that year as a final-act specialty number in *Liza,* the most successful black musical comedy of the 1922–23 season. "Lovin' Sam (The Sheik of Alabam')" was recorded in 1922 by Margaret Young (Brunswick) and the Harry Reser Trio (Gennett); in 1923 by Nora Bayes (Columbia). Bayes (1880–1928), née Goldberg, was a New York stage star from Milwaukee; she had a theater named for her on Broadway. *Liza,* originating as *Bon Bon Buddy, Jr.* at the Lafayette in Harlem in September of 1922, had opened as *Liza* at Daly's Theatre on Broadway and Sixty-third Street in November, promoted as the successor to that theater's *Shuffle Along.* A few months later, when it moved into the Nora Bayes Theater on Forty-fourth Street, *Liza* became the first black show to play Broadway proper during the regular theatrical season. It was at this time that Bayes recorded "Lovin' Sam (The Sheik of Alabam')."

As Joe Laurie, Jr., tells it in his book *Vaudeville,* Bayes was one of several female headliners who "carried 'insurance' in the form of pickaninnies, or 'picks,' as they were called." Laurie explains that "After singing a few songs of their own, they would bring out the picks (a group of Negro kids that really could sing and dance) for a sock finish." He concludes, "I never saw any picks flop."

Yellen and Ager wrote their song at a time when the silent-flickering romance of Rudolph Valentino in *The Sheik* (1921) held America in the thrall of its seduction; "Lovin' Sam" lost not a whit of its edge with the passing of years. Its metaphors were purely American and still of the moment: the Sheik of Alabam' made those "high-brown babies" howl "like the babies cry for Castoria" — a reference to a popular over-the-counter children's calmative whose active ingredient was alcohol, and whose advertising motto was "Children Cry for Fletcher's Castoria." Here again Miller interpolates his "cracker papa," a phrase that evidently had grown to enrapture him:

> There ain't a high-brown gal in town
> who wouldn't throw her cracker papa down
> to be the bride of this colored Romeo.

In addition to its American release, "Lovin' Sam" was released in England, coupled with "St. Louis Blues," on the Parlophone label. British Parlophone here seems to have perceived Miller as black: the record bears the imprint "Race Series (The Negro and His Music)," with "St. Louis Blues" designated as Number 21 in this series, "Lovin' Sam" as Number 22.

"Big Bad Bill (Is Sweet William Now)," another Yellen-Ager song, had been previously recorded by Miller in 1925. Since then, the song's popularity had inspired the blackface act of Sweet William and Bad Bill, the names under which William LaMaire and John Swor, a brother of Bert Swor, recorded for Brunswick-Balke-Collender in 1927.

"The Ghost of the St. Louis Blues" was a new song by Billy Curtis and J. Russel Robinson, a former associate of W. C. Handy. Here Miller was joined by Phil Pavey, who had sung harmony with him in the Field Minstrels. Pavey in February of this year had made his own records for Okeh: "Utah Mormon Blues" and three other titles. On them, he may have been accompanied by the New Orleans–born pianist Spencer Williams (1889–1965), who was credited as the co-author of three songs in the Miller repertoire: "I Ain't Got Nobody," "I Ain't Gonna Give Nobody None o' This Jelly Roll," and "The Blues Singer (from Alabam')."

Williams was indicted and tried for murder following a deadly stabbing in Harlem in 1931. From the *New York Times,* November 18 of that year:

"Spencer Williams, a Negro songwriter whose compositions include 'I Ain't Got Nobody' and 'The Birth of the Blues,' was held without bail in Homicide Court yesterday for a hearing next Tuesday charged with homicide in connection with the fatal stabbing of Harold Bakay, a Harlem night club dancer, at 131st Street and Seventh Avenue on November 7. The stabbing, the police said, followed an altercation between the two men over a girl dancer. Williams is 38 [sic] years old and lives at 400 West 153d [sic] Street."

Upon his acquittal, Williams left America for Europe, where he lived, first for almost twenty years in London, then in Stockholm from 1951 until 1957. Returning to America, he made his home in

the black community of St. Albans, Queens, where the already for-
gotten R&B shouter Wynonie Harris then made his home. It was
eight years later, at Hillcrest Hospital in Flushing, Queens, that
Williams died in the summer of 1965, the summer of the Rolling
Stones' "(I Can't Get No) Satisfaction," the summer of Bob Dylan's
"Like a Rolling Stone."

"The Ghost of the St. Louis Blues" would have the most diverse
release of Miller's records: in addition to its original Okeh release,
it would be issued on the American and British Parlophone labels,
on the French and Australian Odeon labels.

The seventh session took place a week later, on September 12,
1929, when Gene Krupa replaced Stan King on drums. Born in
1909, Krupa was the youngest of the Georgia Crackers. He had begun his recording career in Chicago less than two years earlier, and
had done his first New York studio work a few months later. Six
days before this Georgia Crackers session, he had played with Jimmy
Dorsey and Joe Tarto at a Red Nichols session for Brunswick; on
the day after this session, he and Tarto would join other musicians
to record for Columbia under the name of the Midnight Airedales.

Three songs were recorded by Miller at this final Georgia
Crackers session: "Sweet Mama (Papa's Getting Mad)," copyrighted, with the substantive of maternal endearment spelled
Mamma, in 1920 by Fred Rose, George A. Little, and Peter L. Frost,
and recorded that year by Marion Harris (Columbia), Flo Bert
(Paramount), and the Original Dixieland Jazz Band (Victor), and in
1921 by Lucille Hegamin (Arto), the Southern Negro Quartette
(Columbia), and the Palmetto Jazz Quartet (Okeh); "The Pick-
aninny's Paradise," written in 1918 by Sam Ehrich and Nat Os-
borne, and previously recorded by Miller in 1924; and "The Blues
Singer (from Alabam')," copyrighted earlier this year, in April, by
Agnes Castelton and Spencer Williams, and first recorded, also in
April, by Bessie Brown (Brunswick).

Marion Harris had transposed the elements of "Sweet Mama (Papa's Getting Mad)," sung it from a woman's viewpoint, warning a "sweet papa" of her growing ire. Miller may have been unfamiliar with this earlier version, or he — or, more likely, Okeh — may have found its lyrics too rough. In either case, he deletes a deliciously threatening line, absent from the copyrighted lyrics, that Harris had sung with relish: "I've got a razor, boy, and you've got a throat." Instead he repeats a verse, almost as toothsome, about "flirting with the undertaker."

At the previous session, he had recorded "Lovin' Sam (The Sheik of Alabam')." Written four years after "The Pickaninny's Paradise," it represented the new coon song — hip, louche, sultry; a coon song that could no longer be called a coon song, that demanded to be called a jazz song — as surely as "The Pickaninny's Paradise" represented the mawkish and the old. But, of course, Miller in his mawkishness had never been sincere. Here again, as in 1924, the effect of his *"ain't that nice?"* is decidedly un-nice, subtly maniacal. For Miller, hip and louche are not attributes of context, but a transcendence of context. Born of the racket of poignancy and picks, his "Pickaninny's Paradise" is a triteness, tried and true, that tugs at the heartstrings; but the paradise itself of which he sings seems in the end not far from Nightmare Alley, and his singing as much a tug on the sleeve as on those strings.

In the world as colored by Miller's voice, we are never far from Nightmare Alley. That phrase: trick voice. Let it fall from the light into the darkness, and it, too, becomes sinister. The barker, after-hours, confiding to the geek: "Guy here, old timer, does the trick voice. Things he can't talk about. You know the story. A bottle every morning, place to sleep it off." A trick voice: like something one encounters in Burroughs; or like that line of Dickens's that Eliot transmuted into the macabre by placing it at the head of the original *Waste Land:* "He do the Police in different voices."

In "The Blues Singer (from Alabam')," Miller reverts to opening with a blackface-dialogue prelude, which he had not done since the second Crackers session, in August 1928. The manner of his partner here brings to mind Roy Cowan, with whom the first blackface-dialogue records were made, but the voice of this unknown partner is deeper, less expressive. Both characters in the routine are nameless, and the central joke is a drunk-driving Emmett running down an old man.

On this last Georgia Crackers recording, Miller reprises, with a slight variation, the surreal, high-swirling line with which he had opened "Thousand Frogs on a Log" back in January 1928, a mere twenty months ago, when the world still looked rosy: "*I don't want no more your greasy cabbage greens*" — a signature now as then, but here one that echoes with a certain finality.

The music that Miller made at these sessions was quite unlike anything else ever to be heard on record, then or since. Only one other, equally obscure singer approached, however remotely, this weird alchemy of black and white, hillbilly and jazz; and his recording career seems oddly akin to Miller's own.

His name was Roy Evans. He recorded from 1928 to 1931, making his first record, for Columbia, in Atlanta on April 11, 1928, two months before the first Crackers session. It was a two-part piece called "Weary Yodelin' Blues," accompanied by an unknown pianist. The record was released in both Columbia's 1300 pop and 15000 hillbilly series.

Little more than two months later, on June 15 (three days after Miller's first Georgia Crackers session) and June 18, Evans recorded again, also for Columbia, but now in New York, and also with lone pianists, but now no longer unknown pianists: James P. Johnson on June 15, J. C. Johnson on June 18. The former Johnson was a composer who had recorded under his own name since 1921 and accompanied Bessie Smith and many other blues singers; the latter, also a prolific composer and accompanist — he would record in the following year as part of the guitarists Lonnie Johnson and Eddie Lang's pseudonymous Blind Willie Dunn's Gin Bottle Four — was the co-author, with the lyricist Andy Razaf, of "Take Your Tomorrow" and "Dusky Stevedore."

At the session with J. C. Johnson, Evans recorded "I Ain't Got Nobody" and Johnson's "Dusky Stevedore," which were released in the hillbilly series. Miller had recorded the former less than a week before, at the first Crackers session, but he did not record the latter until the following September. In July 1928 Evans recorded with a group he called the Mississippi Maulers. This group included Tommy Dorsey, guitarist Eddie Lang, trumpeter Leo McConville, and drummer Stan King, all of whom were also then recording with Miller, as well as bassist Joe Tarto, who would become a Cracker early the following year. On September 4, 1928, with James P. Johnson, Evans recorded J. C. Johnson's "Take Your Tomorrow," which Miller recorded ten days later, while Columbia chose to reject Evans's version.

In October, with Eddie Lang, who had recorded the previous month with Miller, Evans recorded a two-part "Lonesome Yodelin' Blues." In early 1930 Evans sang on several Columbia recordings by Rube Bloom and His Bayou Boys, with Tommy Dorsey, Manny Klein, Benny Goodman, and others; and with the Dorseys, as the Charleston Chasers, also for Columbia.

Ultimately, Evans's singing comes up somewhat empty, its reality nondescript and disappointing beneath the veneer of its promise.

Like the singing of the age as whole, it lacks the range and force, the exuberant energy, the wild-mingling resonances of wicked absurdity and honest emotion, the irreverence to music, to expressiveness itself, that sets Miller's singing apart. Evans's yodeling and hard-edged trilling effects are old-fashioned: dull and theatrical lingerings of olden styles and olden days. While Columbia promoted him as "The Eccentric Voice," his eccentricity sounds more contrived than natural. At its best, Evans's music has feeling and a certain haunting quality. Miller's music goes further. It is an exorcism of feeling, a turning inside-out, a haunting unto itself. The more one listens to Evans, and to other singers of the time, the more one appreciates the astounding anomaly of Emmett Miller's style, spirit, and achievement.

At a Roy Evans session on June 20, 1928, Evans was joined by Garvin Bushell, the reed-and-woodwind master whose recording career spanned from 1921, when he accompanied Edith Wilson as a member of Johnny Dunn's Original Jazz Hounds, to his seminal recordings in 1961 and 1962 with John Coltrane, Eric Dolphy, and Miles Davis. Given the nature of the times, the industry, and the marketplace, it is very curious that the musicians with whom Roy Evans was associated at the outset of his recording career were all men of color: James P. Johnson, J. C. Johnson, Garvin Bushell. It further intrigues that Garvin Bushell (1902–91), in an interview late in his life, recalled Roy Evans as a "tall brownskin fellow." Bushell also recalled performing with Evans at Ed Smalls's Paradise, one of the most famous of the Harlem nightclubs to which white patrons were drawn uptown by black talent. One of Evans's records — "Syncopated Yodelin' Man" c/w "Jazbo Dan and His Yodelin' Band," was released, in the fall of 1928, in the Columbia 14000-D race series as well as in popular series.

Could it be, contrary to the auditory evidence, that Roy Evans was, indeed, a "tall brownskin fellow"? There are no known photographs of him, and Garvin Bushell's recollection, the only physical description that we have of Roy Evans, invites speculation. It is a fact that Roy Evans was featured in an MGM Movietone Act short film of 1929, but, while a copy of the sound-disc for this short was discovered, in France, in 1996, there seems to have survived not even a fragment of the film itself.

But enough of color. I tire of every race. I shall, however, here glance for a moment, in this context of color and auditory evidence and speculation, to the bellowed words of Big Joe Turner's "Tell Me, Pretty Baby" of 1948:

> *They say brown-skinned women are evil*
> *And yellow girls are worse.*
> *I got myself a mulatta, boy;*
> *I'm playin' it safety first.*

Or is there no comma intended between the penultimate and ultimate words of the third line of this quatrain? —

> *I got myself a mulatta boy*

Has the question of a solitary punctuation mark — Big Joe Turner vs. Big Hank Fowler vs. the ear of the beholder — ever before or since presented an ambiguity of momentousness such as this?

Get thee, then, a mulatto, regardless of gender, punctuation, or pronunciation; and proceed, then, behind me, together, as one.

It would appear that Columbia's interest in Roy Evans was spurred by Victor's great success with Jimmie Rodgers's first "Blue Yodel." The Rodgers record, rush-released in February 1928, was an immense hit in the weeks prior to the recording of Evans's "Weary Yodelin' Blues." (The sales of "Blue Yodel" would eventually be reckoned at an astonishing 454,586 copies.) Perhaps when the comparatively soulless blue-yodeling of Evans failed to capture the fancy of the market, Columbia then guided him to the same sort of material that by then, in June, was being recorded for its Okeh subsidiary by its new Southern singer Emmett Miller. It is possible that the company's renewed interest that spring in Miller as a singer had also derived in part from Victor's success with Rodgers. As it turned out, the best-known of Rodgers's imitators, Jimmie Davis and Gene Autry, would begin their recording careers at Victor the following year. Like Rodgers, Autry had also worked blackface in a medicine show. Other gifted emulators of Rodgers included Bill Cox and Cliff Carlisle.

Anyway, next time you're at a social gathering and the familiar subject arises — Miller versus Evans — you'll know what to say. Then shall you be the life of the party; loneliness and awkwardness shall be behind you; new friends, prospective employers, and the target sex shall flock unto you, as they have unto me.

Eddie Lang died in 1933, Stan King in 1949. Tommy Dorsey went in 1956, Jimmy in 1957. Arthur Schutt passed on in 1965, Leo McConville in 1968. Gene Krupa died in 1973. Manny Klein, born in 1908, was still alive. But Klein's involvement as a Cracker was uncertain, his name preceded by a question mark in the personnel listing of three of the Miller sessions detailed in the standard discographical reference, Brian Rust's *Jazz Records 1897–1942*.

Joe Tarto (1902–86) was a survivor of these sessions whom I tracked down in New Jersey in 1976.

"The only Miller I knew was Eddie Miller," said Joe Tarto.

"But you played at three of Emmett Miller's sessions, didn't you?"

"Glenn Miller?"

"No. *Emmett* Miller. You played on his records."

"To be honest with you, I don't recall. There were so many of them, I lost track. I really did."

Joe suggested I call Chauncey Morehouse, a popular jazz drummer of the 1920s and '30s who Tarto said had a good memory. Morehouse also lived in New Jersey.

Morehouse (1902–80) was able to give me some interesting information on the lesser-known musicians on Miller's sessions. He recalled that Stan King was celebrated for his unswayable beat, that Arthur Schutt was a heavy drinker, and that Manny Klein, a houseman in the NBC band with Chauncey, once played with Toscanini. But he had no memory of Emmett Miller.

"The only Emmett I ever knew was back in Chambersburg, Pennsylvania. Emmett Waugaman. His father ran a drugstore."

"And Emmett Kelly, the clown," added Mrs. Morehouse, who was listening on another line.

"When we were at NBC," said Chauncey, "the dates came so fast that we'd go out and do a date and come home and I'd be layin' in bed at night and I'd think, 'Who in the hell was the leader of that session?' We were always working. It's hard to remember. A lot of guys thought Chauncey was a fag name."

B y the last of the Georgia Crackers sessions, Miller's moment was over. He was not yet thirty.

The irony of his fate was that he had become a minstrel man during minstrelsy's final days. His season of glory with the Al G. Field Minstrels was the last barely successful season that the Field Minstrels would know. A tour schedule from 1908 shows the Al G.

Field Minstrels opening at Marion, Ohio, venturing as far east as Buffalo, on to Louisville via Indianapolis, then south through the Mississippi Valley to New Orleans, Galveston, San Antonio, Texarkana, and so on — some sixty-odd cities in all. The troupe's present itinerary was a skeletal remnant of what it once had been. The show was on the skids and had barely made it this far; had not even played Atlanta in '26. Even the reviews seemed to regard it as a dying thing.

Miller returned to the Dan Fitch troupe at about the time of the first Crackers session, when Fitch joined Miller for "The Lion Tamers." Rehearsals began that August. "The thousand frogs should go as big as ever for the young man from Macon," Fitch was quoted as saying in the July 21 *Billboard,* which misidentified Miller as "Emmet Mills." Realizing that the old days were over, Fitch billed his show with the promise of "Girls and Memories of Minstrels." No one, however, seemed interested in the memories.

In the Fitch tour of 1928–29, Miller was reunited as end-man with Leslie Berry, his old friend from the Field days, and with Billy Everett, from the old Fitch troupe of 1924. The show also featured Turk McBee.

Working the Keith-Albee-Orpheum circuit under Pat Casey, the Fitch tour opened on August 22, at the Carlton, in Red Bank, New Jersey. After three nights in Red Bank, there were three nights in Trenton, then three nights in Bridgeport, Connecticut. The troupe made its way in September through New York — Troy, Binghamton, Elmira, and Syracuse — then on to Grand Rapids, Michigan, then Toledo and Columbus, Ohio. Opening in Detroit on September 27, the show passed through Youngstown, Akron, Cleveland, Cincinnati, and Dayton, Ohio, and emerged in Louisville, Kentucky, on October 25. From Kentucky, the tour moved through Indiana and Illinois, and shut down in Milwaukee in the first week of 1929.

According to Turk McBee, it was in Evansville, Indiana, on the night of the Hoover-Smith presidential election, that Miller received his first royalty check from Okeh. The sum, said McBee, was about four thousand and five hundred dollars. "There was a gambling joint back of the theater, and he went there," McBee told Jeff Tarrer in an unpublished 1979 interview. "He stayed there gambling, and we went down to catch the train for Erie, Pennsylvania, and they paged me from the depot. Emmett: 'I'm coming down there in a few minutes.' I said, 'You'd better hurry, 'cause the train's gonna leave.' Emmett: 'Well, meet me at the door.' I said, 'For what?' 'You gotta pay the cab-driver. I ain't got a penny.'"

McBee told of the night, in Lexington, that "the city council sent somebody down to check to see if he [Miller] was a real nigger." Lasses White and Emmett, he said, would frequently go to the black area of a town to listen to "the colored people talk." But "when Emmett went down there, the niggers started talking like him."

Elsewhere in the course of Tarrer's interviews with him, McBee, in the way of defending blackface, explained of himself: "Never used that word, 'nigger.'"

It is in a disheveled scrapbook that McBee left behind upon his death many years later that the only known reviews of this show survive. One is undated, and there is no indication as to place, except for a mention of the show having been "at Keith's," which serves to date it between early September and late October of 1928. The latter part of the penultimate paragraph, the first part of the last:

"Then there is Turk McBee, Jr., one of the youngest members of the cast, at the xylophone. Turk is a wow with his mallets or whatever you call the things you pound the xylophone with.

"The Harmony Aces, who already proved their wares in the minstrel opening, again do noble work in singing popular hits. Their voices blend beautifully in familiar strains. Emmett Miller, one of the end men, assisted by Leslie Berry, the other end, amuses the audience with his brand of humor. And to show his versatility, he scores an instant hit with his 'I Ain't Got Nobody,' old but still popular since he was called on to sing it twice."

There is an advertisement, too, for the show's engagement at the Palace in Cincinnati, during the third week of October 1928:

DAN FITCH GIRLS

AND

MEMORIES OF MINSTRELS
Under Personal Management of Dan Fitch
SPEED-SPLENDOR-BEAUTY-PEP!

———————

EMMETT MILLER . . . .*Comedian and Recording Star*
TREVOR LEWIS . . . .*Radio's Lyric Tenor*
TURK McBEE, JR. . . . .*Boy Wonder*

SMIRNOVA DANCERS

JOHN & GEORGE HARDGROVE . . . .*Midshipmen*
HARMONY ACES . . . .*A Jazz Band of Voices*

BILLY EVERETT ? ? ?

A review of the Palace show mentioned "Turk McBee, juvenile xylophonist." As for Emmett Miller: "audiences demanded encore after encor[e]."

The Palace presentation also featured, as its photoplay, the new Buster Keaton eight-reeler, *The Cameraman:* a silent picture, another fading ray of a time gone by.

In the summer of 1928, the Neil O'Brien Minstrels, the Lasses White Minstrels, and other troupes abandoned production plans. "It looks as if vaude has the X on minstrel stars for the coming season," observed *Billboard*. The actual situation was bleaker than that. The stars of minstrelsy were fleeing a sinking ship, and only a few found sanctuary in vaudeville. Lasses White staged minstrel shows for the American Legion in Arkansas in 1929, for the Elks in Iowa in 1930.

As white minstrelsy died, black troupes in the South and Midwest fared somewhat better: the Alabama Minstrels, the Fashion Plate Minstrels, J. A. Coburn's Minstrels, J. F. Murphy's Georgia Minstrels, John Van Arnam's Minstrels, Jordan's Swiftfoot Minstrels, Pete Werley's Florida Cotton Blossom Minstrels, the Rabbit Foot Minstrels, Richard's and Pringle's Georgia Minstrels, the Royer Brothers' Great American Minstrels, Silas Green from New Orleans, S. J. Lincoln's Minstrels, Warner and Moorman's Famous Brown Derby Minstrels, and other black shows were still active in 1929–30. The fading Rabbit Foot Minstrels was the most venerable of these troupes. It had grown out of the Imperial Colored Minstrels, formed in 1899 by the Florida showman Patrick Henry "Pat" Chappelle (1869–1911). Chappelle had reorganized his outfit in 1900 as a musical-production troupe. In the following years, it had become a variety tent show, but retained the name of its first production, *A Rabbit's Foot*. Upon Pat Chappelle's death, the Rabbit Foot Company had been taken over by a carnival promoter named Fred S. Wolcott. Headquartered in Port Gibson, Mississippi, Wolcott had retained the name of the Rabbit Foot Company for several years — the troupe was still known as such in 1915, when Ma Rainey and Bessie Smith traveled with it — then changed it to the Rabbit Foot Minstrels, under which name the tent show survived until 1951.

Why did minstrelsy die? Lew Dockstader was asked in 1902 to explain the decline of minstrelsy's popularity. He said that minstrelsy was foundering because the essential black qualities had become dated and lost. Given the advantage of hindsight, the song-publisher Edward B. Marks would later offer his explanation: "When the leading minstrels entered the better-paid field of vaudeville, minstrelsy went with them."

In the end minstrelsy was eclipsed by vaudeville, which had grown in popularity since 1865, when Tony Pastor leased the Bowery Minstrel Hall, renamed it Tony Pastor's Opera House, and produced his first revisionist minstrel-variety shows. Pastor (1832–1908), an Italian-American born in New York, had worked in blackface minstrelsy as a teenager, and the vaudeville shows that he pioneered were derived as much from minstrelsy, particularly the olio segment, as from the European music-hall and burlesque traditions. Pastor moved his venue from 201 Bowery to 585 Broadway in 1875.

In 1868, when Tammany Hall under Boss Tweed had settled into its new headquarters on East Fourteenth Street, a ground-floor theater in the property was leased to Bryant's Minstrels. Pastor took over the theater in 1881. It was here, at Tony Pastor's Fourteenth Street Theatre, on the north side of the street between Third Avenue and Irving Place, that vaudeville entered its heyday.

Pastor's vaudeville monopoly on Fourteenth Street was broken in 1893, when Benjamin F. Keith and Edward Albee opened their Union Square Theatre a block to the west. Keith and Albee had similar backgrounds as circus grifters and sideshow spielers. They had met in Boston in 1883, formed a partnership two years later to open the Bijou Theatre in that city. They played the wholesome angle from the start: their acts, in Keith's words, "were free from vulgarity and innuendo." The Union Square Theatre was their first

New York venture. From it would bloom the most powerful of vaudeville empires east of Chicago.

Farther uptown, the Victoria Theatre, built by Oscar Hammerstein in Longacre Square in 1899, switched from legitimate theater to vaudeville in 1904, the year that Longacre Square became Times Square. It remained the premiere vaudeville house until its closing in 1915. It was surpassed by the Palace, built in early 1913, at Broadway and Forty-seventh Street, north of Times Square.

The Palace Theatre opened under the ownership of Martin Beck, the head of the Orpheum Circuit, which dominated vaudeville west of Chicago. It was soon taken over by B. F. Keith and E. F. Albee, whose Keith-Albee operation was the dominating force in the eastern states. B. F. Keith died in 1914, but the organization lived on. By the early twenties, working out of offices above the Palace, Keith-Albee booked some three hundred theaters east of Chicago. The Al G. Field Minstrels, the Dan Fitch Minstrels, and Emmett Miller worked theaters that were part of this Keith circuit. Even the colossal New York Hippodrome became a Keith-Albee property. Opened in 1905 by Frederick Thompson and Skip Dundy, the creators of Coney Island's Luna Park, the Hippodrome occupied a full block of Sixth Avenue between Forty-third and Forty-fourth streets. It was the world's largest theater. Flashing electrical signs advertised its opening with the slogan ENTERTAINMENT FOR THE MASSES. *Panem et circenses.*

The Jazz Singer of 1927 may have sent something of a chill through the Keith-Albee and Orpheum outfits. In 1928, the year that Miller rejoined Dan Fitch, the Keith-Albee and Orpheum organizations merged; and in 1929, the year before Albee's death, the Radio Corporation of America (RCA), the parent of Victor, obtained control of Keith-Albee-Orpheum, and thus was born Radio-Keith-Orpheum (RKO), consolidated by Joseph Kennedy. For

Victor stars such as Jimmie Rodgers, tours of the RKO circuit were forthcoming. In the spring and summer of 1929, supported by an acrobatic act, a comedy act, and a dance revue, Rodgers headlined an RKO package tour of Southwestern and Southern movie theaters at a reported salary of a thousand dollars a week. Struggling old-time Keith acts such as Fitch and Miller were not so fortunate.

As vaudeville moved uptown, Tin Pan Alley followed it. By 1880 the music-publishers' row was Fourteenth Street, where Pastor had his theater. In the 1890s it gravitated north to West Twenty-eighth Street, accruing the name of Tin Pan Alley along the way. One of those who took credit for the phrase was the songwriter and publisher Harry Von Tilzer, a Jew from Indiana whose real name was Harry Gumm (and one of whose four brothers was a co-author of "You're Just the Girl for Me," recorded by Emmett Miller in 1925). By 1910 Tin Pan Alley was located near Herald and Greeley squares at Thirty-fourth Street. In the 1920s it settled into the environs of the Palace, West Forty-sixth and Forty-seventh streets.

Between 1880 and 1900 — the decade that saw the rise of the recording industry and Tin Pan Alley, the rise of ragtime, jazz, and the blues — the urban population of America more than doubled; and as America grew more urban, vaudeville grew increasingly pervasive, and it became the heart of her lowbrow culture, which is to say her culture.

"The beauties of Ethiopian Minstrelsy, it may be said, are now looked upon as the wonders of the progressive age in which we live." Thus the introductory words of *George Christy's Ethiopian Joke Book, No. 3,* penned in 1858. (This introductory "Critique," going on to bemoan the departures from canonical negrisimilitude that had begun to degrade minstrelsy, closed with a cry of praise for the enduring artistic integrity of the celebrated minstrel whose name the book bears: "*He looked every inch a Negro.*") In the succeeding "progressive age," the same might be said of vaudeville.

Blackface had its place in vaudeville — Ziegfeld's *Follies,* publicized as "Glorifying the American Girl," was described by the black entertainer Noble Sissle as "glorified minstrelsy with girls" — but that place was not within the context of minstrelsy's nostalgia for a past that never was. And while Emmett Miller worked vaudeville as well as minstrelsy, by the time of his season of glory, it too was doomed.

In the summer of 1896, the moving-picture marvels of the Lumière Cinématographe had opened at Keith's Union Square Theater, the Kineopticon at Tony Pastor's. By the summer of 1899, Vitagraph pictures were a part of Pastor's daily bills.

Adolph Zukor had opened his Automatic Vaudeville theater in New York in 1903. Located on East Fourteenth Street, the thoroughfare of Tony Pastor's theater, Automatic Vaudeville dispensed of the human element, offered no living, breathing entertainment. With its peep-box shows of flittering, sputtering film, Automatic Vaudeville was a sublimely named auguring of things to come, as urban culture became electronic culture. In the summer of 1915, the old Victoria vaudeville house was demolished and another theater erected on its site. The new theater, the Rialto, was an omen: the first movie house built without a stage.

In the twenties radio and then talking pictures — phantom voices, phantom players; ethereal waves and flickerings of magic light — brought the golden age of vaudeville to a close, just as vaudeville had brought to its end that of minstrelsy. Florenz Ziegfeld suspended his annual *Follies* after 1927, the year of *The Jazz Singer.* There would be only one more season, in 1931. Ziegfeld died bankrupt in 1932, the year the great Palace became a movie house.

Radio had been the first blow. Talking pictures, the fatal blow. What dead and dying remnants lingered, the Great Depression blew away. Talking pictures were the only form of entertainment to prosper in the years of that depression. In the thirties, low burlesque took vaudeville's place, to offer what the moving pictures, after the Hays Production Code of 1930, no longer could: smut. But the cheap-gilt heyday of burlesque was short-lived. It was banned in New York in the spring of 1937, and by 1942 it was gone.

Minstrel movies were not unknown. Indeed it has been argued by Michael Rogin in *Blackface, White Noise* that the American movie industry was born of blackface. Edison Kinetoscope had made films of black minstrelsy dance bits as early as 1894, and one of the Edison synchronized-sound experiments had been a minstrelsy film of November 1914, featuring a hand-colored finale. *Al Jolson in a Plantation Act,* a one-reel, three-song Vitaphone short, had been made in April of 1926, the very month that the Vitaphone partnership of Warner Brothers and Western Electric came into being; and in 1928–29, as blackface stage shows faded, blackface talkies came to the screens above those stages. *Billboard* reported in the summer of 1928: "A minstrel performance is to be produced in sound pictures by Universal — comedians, singers, interlocutor, hoofers and specialty artistes appearing in the conventional first part, olio and afterpiece, just as the bill was presented in the days of Barlow, Wilson, Primrose and West. The picture will be titled *The Minstrel Show.* The scenario was written from the story, *The Mystery Man,* by George Rogan and Norman L. Spur. The end men and interlocutor have not yet been selected, but it is likely that names will weigh heavily in the casting."

In 1929 came *The Grand Parade* from Pathé, *The Rainbow Man* from Paramount, and the Fox Movietone production of *New Orleans Frolic,* which claimed for its finale "the biggest minstrel show ever staged," featuring almost every Fox player. *Why Bring That Up?* was an "all-talking, singing, dancing" Paramount feature of 1929 that starred the blackface vaudeville team of Moran and Mack, the Two Black Crows. Bert Swor, the veteran Field minstrel, who appeared in the 1929 Paramount picture *The Carnation Kid,* also had a role in *Why Bring That Up?,* and afterward teamed awhile with his old partner Charles "Mack" Sellers as George "Moran" Searey's replacement. Working together back in the teens, they had been Swor and Mack, but now Swor became Moran. As such he would star in 1930 in Paramount's subsequent Moran-and-Mack picture, *Anybody's War;* but he would star, too, that year, on his own and as himself, in two Vitaphone shorts for Warner Bros. Charlie Mack, whose persona had sustained Moran and Mack through various Morans, died four years later in an automobile accident.

There were Amos-'n'-Andy pictures as well, such as *Check and Double Check* of 1930. But the future of blackface was as doomed in pictures as on the stage, even if actual blacks in pictures were occasionally further blackened, presumably so that audiences could be assured that they were getting the real thing. An example of this perfect Hollywood logic was the makeup applied by Paramount to Cab Calloway in *The Big Broadcast* of 1932, a film that also featured Eddie Lang. And, while the blackface comedy of Amos 'n' Andy proved immensely popular on radio, *Mr. Bones and Company,* a Monday-night minstrel program broadcast by the NBC-WJZ network in the summer of 1931, achieved no such success.

Al Jolson, however, would not lay down the cork. We see in him Meachum's law fully operative: "A Nigger singer will always be a Nigger singer. You can put any kind of makeup on them, but they'll always come back for the cork." Jolson, over the hill and still frothing, considered "the greatest production number ever done" the Busby Berkeley sequence he filmed in 1934 for *Wonder Bar,* in which he sang "Goin' to Heaven on a Mule" in blackface while the dancer Hal LeRoy, also blackened, cavorted amid watermelon sections. Jolson appeared blacked-up again, in the role of E. P. Christy, in *Swanee River,* the fanciful 1939 Hollywood biography of Stephen

Foster. His faded recording career ended three months before his death in 1950, with "Massa's in de Cold, Cold Ground" and "De Camptown Races."

In the late summer of 1929, the Al G. Field Minstrels disbanded in mid-season. It was the summer that NBC began broadcasting *Amos 'n' Andy* nationally, sponsored by Pepsodent. Did minstrelsy die? Or did it simply, or subtly, undergo a metamorphosis?

It is interesting to note that, as the quaint fantasy of the happy antebellum coon, the figment on which minstrelsy was predicated, lost its currency, the parallel fantasy of the whimsical and picturesque hillbilly simultaneously rose to take its place in the subculture of Southern show business.

In the early years of the country-music industry, this masquerade of dress and manner, the artful pose of comical rusticity and folksy backwoods charm caricatured by urbane performers — as can be seen in photographs of the cast of any country radio troupe of the twenties, and heard in many recordings — was the equivalent, if not quite of blacking up by white minstrels, then surely of the sham of the darky persona adopted by sophisticated black performers such as Bert Williams and George Walker, who in 1895 billed themselves as the Two Real Coons, just as wily white performers would later present themselves as the Hillbillies or the Mountaineers, the Fruit Jar Drinkers or the Possum Hunters. Chester Lauck and Norris Goff's popular radio act, Lum and Abner, was less the counterpart of Gosden and Correll's Amos 'n' Andy than of Williams and Walker's Two Real Coons, for Lauck and Goff's hillbilly act was essentially one of white men in whiteface. Bert Williams, professional coon and Mason, was a student of Aristotle; Chester Lauck, professional rube, a banker.

The country-music masquerade would spread to an imagined, stage-set West, to the singing cowboys beloved of country music and Hollywood in turn. "If the Man in the Moon Were a Coon," a minstrel song posited; Roy Rogers, crooning astride Trigger, would voice nothing of hypothesis: "The Man in the Moon Is a Cowhand."

And country music became the last bastion of the coon song, too. One of the earliest records in the Okeh 45000 hillbilly series, inaugurated in 1925, was Fisher Hendley's "Nigger, Will You Work?"

In 1927–29, as minstrelsy went to its grave, country records included Uncle Dave Macon's "The Coon That Had the Razor" (Brunswick), Charlie Parker and Mack Woolbright's "Give That Nigger Ham" (Columbia), Dr. Smith's Champion Hoss Hair Pullers' "Nigger Baby" (Victor), Earl Johnson's Dixie Entertainers' "Nigger in the Cotton Patch" (Okeh), the Carolina Twins' "I Want My Black Baby Back" (Victor), Bill Cox's "Nigger Loves a Watermelon" (Supertone). String-band instrumentals bore titles such as the Stripling Brothers' "Big Footed Nigger in the Sandy Lot" (Vocalion), the Mississippi Possum Hunters' "Rufus Rastus" (Victor). "Run, Nigger, Run" was recorded in at least three country-music versions: by Fiddlin' John Carson (Okeh, 1924), Uncle Dave Macon (Brunswick, 1925), and Dr. Humphrey Bate's Possum Hunters (Brunswick, 1928); Cox's "Nigger Loves a Watermelon" (1929) echoes "Run, Nigger, Run" and other old songs.

Though its title may today elicit reflexive interpretation, "Run, Nigger, Run" is a good example of the essentially non-racist nature of many such songs. In this case the song's refrain voiced encouragement for escape. The folklorist Dorothy Scarborough found "Run, Nigger, Run" to be popular among Southern black singers. In her 1925 book, *On the Trail of Negro Folk-Songs,* she claimed the song had its true origin among black slaves in the antebellum South.

The influence of minstrelsy in country music lingered well into the following decade and beyond, though its manifestations grew decidedly more polite, as in the Stripling Brothers' "Negro Supper Time" of 1937.

Concurrently the Grand Ole Opry became the last mainstream venue for blackface. Lasses White joined WSM in the fall of 1930: three shows weekly beginning October 1. Joining him was Lee Davis "Big Fat" Wilds, who had worked with White in his All-Star Minstrels and performed with him on WRR in Dallas in the summer of 1927. On WSM they were known as Lasses White and Honey Wilds. Together, Lasses singing, Honey on guitar, they recorded Lasses's old "Nigger Blues" in 1935. It was a title that Victor prudently chose not to release. In 1936 they moved to California, where they performed at KEHE for a year. White appeared in the 1939 Gene Autry picture *Rovin' Tumbleweeds,* and he remained in Hollywood until his death in December 1949. Wilds returned to Nashville, teamed with Bunny Biggs. Together Wilds and Biggs performed on the Opry, as Jamup and Honey, into the 1940s. They recorded a blackface venture into "De Lion's Cage" for Bullet Records of Nashville in 1946.

Al Tint, who was Jewish, also went the country route. In the spring of 1934, he sent a postcard to *Billboard* saying "that he is getting to be a real 'hillbilly,' using dialect and all that goes with it." By the spring of the following year, he was touring with one of the Grand Ole Opry's road companies. In the summer of 1937 he joined the WLS National Barn Dance of Chicago.

A salient observation reported in the *Billboard* of March 4, 1939, seems here somehow relevant: "Real hillbillies rarely have good night club acts, says Meyer Horowitz, who ought to know. Jewish and Italian hillbillies usually outshine all others on showmanship, he says." Horowitz was the owner of the Village Barn, "New York's most successful night club using the homespun motif."

It is interesting to note that the phrase "cork opry" was applied to minstrelsy at least as early as January 1927, several months before the Grand Ole Opry had its name.

As we have seen, Miller as a singer vanished into the abyss between two times, that of the vaudeville singer, for which he arrived too late and too unsuccessfully, and that of the crooner, in which he was lost. But if he could not prevail in the music industry, why then could he not at least have survived?

His was a twilight time, and the abyss toward which he traveled could not be perceived. The boy of ten who dreamed of becoming a minstrel, the young man who became one, could not see that minstrelsy, even then, was dying, or that vaudeville was doomed. Today, peering into that twilight, we can see what those who moved in it could not.

The syncopated coon song, born of minstrelsy, had died out in popular music by Miller's time. As a genre of lyric grotesquing black sensibilities, the coon song dated to the work of George Washington Dixon, Thomas Dartmouth Rice, and other blackface entertainers of the 1820s and 1830s; but the song that gave the genre its name did not come along until the century neared its end, and it was a different sort of coon song, imbued with the new musical spirit and style of syncopation: "All Coons Look Alike to Me," written by Ernest Hogan, a black comedian from Kentucky who called himself the Unbleached American. Hogan's real name was Reuben Crowder; he changed it because Irish comedians were popular at the time. Many old-timers considered him the best dancing comedian that ever lived, better even than Bert Williams, the most celebrated of the day.

The foremost coon shouter in the years before Jolson was a white vaudeville singer named May Irwin. In 1895 Irwin used Hogan's dance song "La Pas Ma La" in *By the Sad Sea Waves,* a show set in a lunatic asylum; and in 1896 she incorporated "All Coons Look Alike to Me" into her new show, *Courted into Court.* As published that year by M. Witmark & Sons, "All Coons Look Alike to Me" was a sheet-music bestseller; as recorded that year by Len Spencer for Columbia, it was a bestselling record.

The song, which Hogan later "expressed regret" at having written, was based on a song he picked up from a saloon-singer in Chicago: "All Pimps Look Alike to Me." The Harlem Renaissance author James Weldon Johnson wrote in his classic *Black Manhattan* (1930): "The melody of the song was beautiful and the words quite innocuous, but the title became a byword and an epithet of derision."

George Washington Dixon popularized "Zip Coon" in 1834. The word "coon" was in use as a racial epithet by the time of the Civil War. One of Billy Kersand's best-known songs was "Mary's Gone with a Coon." *The Lantern* of New Orleans published a reference to "coon songs" in January 1887, nearly a decade before "All Coons Look Alike to Me." But it was Hogan's song that captured the public imagination, and it was Hogan and his song that took the rap.

It is a shame and a sorrow that the song became a bane to Hogan's later life. In a different age, Maya Angelou, a lesser writer than Hogan, was able to live down the disgrace of her 1957 album *Miss Calypso,* which included her original composition "Mambo in Africa." One might perhaps have been tempted to give her credence as a poet had she laid down her laurels in advancing age to resume her singing career with a mambo version of Hogan's suppressed classic.

Hogan died in Lakewood, New Jersey, in 1909, "haunted," in the words of E. B. Marks, "by the awful crime he had unwittingly committed against the race." Isidore Witmark, the eldest of the Witmark sons, claimed to have contributed to the writing of the song. He, too, saw its effect on Hogan: "his own people took offense; his tune became for him a source of unending misery, and he died regretting that he had written it."

The house of M. Witmark & Sons seemed perfectly suited to be in the coon-song racket. Marcus Witmark was a Prussian immigrant who settled in Fort Gaines, Georgia, served in the Confederate army, and ended up in Hell's Kitchen after the Civil War. His freed but faithful slaves, it is said, followed him all the way, only to be driven back by the hostility of New Yorkers, who resisted the post-bellum influx of migrating blacks.

Three of Marcus Witmark's five sons entered minstrelsy in their youth: Julie, a blackface singer, joined the troupe of Thatcher, Primrose & West in 1885, the year that the firm of M. Witmark & Sons was founded; Frank and Eddie worked as a team in vaudeville and with Lew Dockstader's Minstrels. Father and sons were Masons all; Marcus and his bride, Henrietta, were referred to by all as Daddy and Queen Witmark.

The Witmark firm's involvement in minstrelsy went beyond publishing. In addition to songs, the Witmarks offered a full line of black-dialect joke books, and was a supplier of high collars and ties for end-men, costumes, props, and burnt cork. In 1899 they issued *The First Minstrel Encyclopaedia* and *The First Minstrel Catalogue.* As late as 1939, Isidore Witmark expressed the hope that "the minstrel show, in altered form, will return."

At the same time, the Witmark company's involvement with black writers was not restricted to the authors of coon songs. The baritone and composer Harry Thacker Burleigh, Will Marion Cook and Paul Laurence Dunbar, the brothers J. Rosamond and James Weldon Johnson all did business with the Witmarks. Burleigh, who, like Cook, was a student of Dvořák, also collected and arranged a collection of *Negro Minstrel Melodies,* published by Schirmer in 1909. The collection included the works of Stephen Foster and other white composers.

From the coon song, around the time its name gained wide currency, in the late 1890s, there evolved another genre: ragtime song, a corollary of classic, or piano, rag. The October 1897 issue of the magazine *Étude* introduced its readers to the new music by explaining that "'Rag time' is a term applied to the peculiar, broken rhythmic features of the popular 'coon song.' . . . Unfortunately, the words to which it is allied are usually decidedly vulgar, so that its present great favor is somewhat to be deplored." This evolutionary period is illustrated by a 1900 ragtime contest in New York at which the semifinalists were weeded out by having to rag two minutes of "All Coons Look Alike to Me," which had been adapted as a part of Max Hoffman's "Rag Medley" in 1897. The Metropolitan Orchestra, which recorded "Coon Town Capers" in 1897 and "Who Dat Say Chicken in Dis Crowd?" in 1900, recorded "Rag Time Society" in 1901. James Weldon Johnson, perceiving these musical developments as they unfolded, published *The Evolution of Ragtime: A Musical Suite of Six Songs Tracing and Illustrating Negro Music* in 1903. As noted above, "I've Got a Gal for Ev'ry Day in the Week" was a 1900 ragtime coon song that survived as a 1944 boogie piece by Big Joe Turner and pianist Pete Johnson.

Though the name of Scott Joplin would emerge foremost, and rightly so, in the history of ragtime, it was young Ben Harney (1871–1938), a former minstrel from Kentucky, whose performances at Tony Pastor's Music Hall led to the ragtime raptus that seized Broadway and Tin Pan Alley in 1896. Harney's music was not true ragtime. His appropriation of the term to describe his semisyncopated coon songs was, like the *Étude* definition of ragtime, an aspect of the blur of the age, a foreshadowing of the confusion and misuse that would soon surround terms like jazz and blues. Harney, who maintained that he was white, was believed by his black contemporaries to be adroitly passing. In fact, he was a mulatto. He worked at Pastor's with a black "stooge" named Strap Hill.

"The Mississippi Rag," the first published rag, again not technically a ragtime composition, appeared in 1897, the work of W. H. Krell, a white bandleader in Chicago. Isidore Witmark appeared astute when he later referred to songs such as "All Coons Look Alike to Me" not as ragtime but as "early symptoms of ragtime." However, in 1897 he let no such distinction stand in the way of commerce. His firm's "Rag Medley" of that year consisted of syncopated arrangements by Max Hoffman of seven songs in the Witmark catalogue, including "All Coons Look Alike to Me." The cover of "Rag Medley" proclaimed "The Present Day Fad." It was also in 1897 that Witmark published *Ben Harney's Rag-Time Instructor,* promoted as "the only work published giving full instructions how to play ragtime music on the piano."

The first publication of true ragtime composition came in October of that year: Theodore Northrup's "Louisiana Rag." It is ironic and another instance of the blur of the age that the song's publisher, Thompson Music of Chicago, seemed unsure how to sell it: the sheet-music bore the title "Louisiana Rag Two Step," above it the words "Description of Louisiana Niggers Dancing," and in parentheses, perhaps by arrangement with Witmark, the phrase "Pas Mas La," an evocation of "La Pas Ma La," the popular Ernest Hogan dance song of 1895. Northrup, who later composed a march for Isidore Witmark's wedding, was in fact the author of the syncopated arrangements published by Witmark under Harney's name in the *Rag-Time Instructor.* Another true rag, Thomas Turpin's "Harlem Rag," followed in December 1897. The first ragtime hit, Scott Joplin's "Maple Leaf Rag," came in September of 1899.

It was during this same period that the coon song, as written by blacks such as Hogan, entered a new domain beyond minstrelsy. The first black show to break from the minstrelsy tradition was *The Creole Show* of 1890. Organized in New York by the white vaudeville entrepreneur Sam Jack, it featured Sam Lucas and other black minstrels of the day, plus a female chorus line and mistress of ceremonies. Its existence was primarily that of a road show: it played Boston and Chicago, closed in New York after a brief off-Broadway run. *The Octoroons* followed in 1895, financed by John Isham, who had been a booking agent for *The Creole Show.* Billed as a musical farce rather than a minstrel show, the production of *The Octoroons* in New York brought true black musical theater into being. Three years later, in 1898, Will Marion Cook's *Clorindy, or the Origin of the Cakewalk* and Bob Cole's *A Trip to Coontown* brought black musical comedy to a new domain as well.

As to the true origin of the cakewalk, it is believed to have begun at about the same time as minstrelsy, around 1840, with slaves parodying the formal dances of their masters. These burlesques came to be mimicked in minstrel shows. After the Civil War, when blacks entered minstrelsy, they assumed parts in the minstrels' cakewalk. As Terry Waldo puts it in his book *This Is Ragtime:* "By the time the ragtime era began in 1896, the cakewalk was being performed by blacks imitating whites who were imitating blacks who were imitating whites." I'm sure that the gist of this wonderful little observation can, with not much squinting, be applied to the whole of popular culture.

All-black productions thrived on Broadway through the first decade of the new century. By 1910, when most of its guiding stars, like Hogan and Bob Cole, were dead, or, like Will Cook, had gone on to other things, there began, in James Weldon Johnson's words, a "term of exile of the Negro from the downtown theatres of New York." Uptown in Harlem, however, there grew "a real Negro theatre" and music of a different rhythm, a different soul. Meanwhile in 1910, as that "exile" began, the most famous black star of the day, Bert Williams, became a member of the *Ziegfeld Follies,* breaking the color barrier in vaudeville's grandest show. Four years later, in 1914, Williams would appear in a moving picture, *Darktown Jubilee.*

Al Jolson, meanwhile, took the coon song to its limits. More than a singer of syncopated coon songs, he was the most manic and forceful of the latter-day coon shouters. As the critic Gilbert Seldes noted of him, Jolson was driven by an almost "demonic" intensity, an urgent spirit of catharsis that seemed at times like a form of bizarre possession. Overbearing and repellent as a man, as a daimon of theatricality he was mesmerizing; and the success of his vocal flamboyance and eccentricities freed the way for every singer that followed. As Jolson the stylist overtook the song, he was beheld no longer as merely a minstrel or a blackface showman, but as an embodiment of the age, a jazz singer.

With the demise, or transformation, of the coon song, Tin Pan Alley ragged its way toward the brewings of the Jazz Age and big-city blues; and as it did, minstrelsy began to rock within its long-tail blue. W. C. Handy's "Memphis Blues" was in the repertoire of the Al G. Field Minstrels by 1915.

But if we can peer into that twilight with something of perspective, the real nature of its sound escapes us. Neither archaic recordings of the day nor modern recreations can give us a true sense of the spirit and excitement of this music, which suffered both creatively and technically within the constraints of the recording industry's conservatism and pre-electrical technology, and which suffers today from the effete and archival sentimentality of those who would interpret or revive its untelling notes.

An exception perhaps were the controversial minstrel-show revivals staged in New York in the mid-sixties. Written and produced by Noble Sissle (1889–1975) and Eubie Blake (1883–1973), with Sissle as interlocutor, the programs, produced in Harlem and elsewhere, were re-creations of the black, Georgia-Minstrels type of show.

Some years earlier, in October of 1939, W. C. Handy had produced an all-black symphony-to-swing concert at Carnegie Hall. The first half of the program included among its classical presentations an excerpt from James P. Johnson's symphony *From Harlem;* the second was a minstrelsy program, featuring members of the

Crescendo Club, a songwriters' fraternity of which J. C. Johnson was then president. The former Johnson, amid more illustrious achievements, had made blackface-dialogue records with Andy Razaf as the Two Watermelon Seeds in 1926. The latter Johnson was the author, with Razaf, of "Take Your To-morrow," which Emmett Miller had recorded in 1928. The program ranged from early minstrel songs to the songs of the great black stage shows of the early twenties. Handy described the evening's "minstrel grand finale": "*'Way Down Yonder in New Orleans,* thrillingly sung by the entire company, followed by a wild orgy of blues, jazz, jitterbug and jive, now called swing, in which the following bands participated: Cab Calloway, Noble Sissle, Louis Armstrong and Claude Hopkins. Although they were unable to be there in person, Duke Ellington, Thomas 'Fats' Waller, Andy Razaf, Benny Carter and Jimmie Lunceford were represented by the playing of some of their noted compositions." This must have been something, this "wild orgy," this acknowledgement and illumination of the condemned and deserted ground, the breeding ground and dumping ground, of minstrelsy.

A rare opportunity to experience an errant wisp of the spirit and excitement of late-teens twilight minstrelsy exists, I think, in the 1979 recording by Jerry Lee Lewis of "Alabama Jubilee," a song by Jack Yellen and George A. Cobb that dates to 1915 and exemplifies rag song at its peak, replete with vestigial coon-song sensibilities.

Biblical law decreed that every fifty years a Jubilee year was to be proclaimed. The twenty-fifth chapter of Leviticus, where that law is laid down, makes specific reference to the redemption of slaves. The Alabama Sacred Harp Singers recorded "Jubilee" for the Library of Congress in 1938; the following year, also for the Library of Congress, the black singer Uncle James Archer, born into slavery, recorded a fragment of a piece called "Year of Jubilee." A fragment. Fragments all, of those unwritten Mississippi Delta Dead Sea Scrolls.

In America, 1915 was the fiftieth year following the abolition of slavery. Alabama, however, was one of the Southern states whose legislatures refused to ratify the Fourteenth Amendment to the Constitution of the United States, which formally granted citizenship and civil rights to blacks; and subsequently, in 1867, Alabama was placed under military rule.

This is not to tie together Leviticus, American slavery, Emancipation, the history of Alabama, and the Tin Pan Alley team of Yellen and Cobb. It is merely to glance at the endless and endlessly enticing confluences of fragment and fractal.

The team of Arthur Collins and Byron Harlan recorded "Alabama Jubilee" for Columbia and for Victor in the summer of 1915; the Victor Military Band also recorded it in 1915, as part of a one-step "Alabama Jubilee Medley." The Collin-Harlan record was a hit, and Al Bernard and Ernest Hare covered it. Bill Helms and His Upson County Band recorded it for Victor in Atlanta in 1928; accompanied by his Happy Five, Herschel Brown, he of "Talking Nigger Blues" ignominy, did a kick-out-the jams instrumental version under the title of "Alabama Breakdown" for Okeh; the Cherokee Ramblers, a jug band, recorded it for Decca in 1935; the Rice Brothers' Gang recorded it for Decca in 1939, at the same New York session that brought forth the original version of "You Are My Sunshine," to be appropriated a few months later by Jimmie Davis; Atlantic Records released a recording of it by the Howington Brothers in 1950; an ersatz-Dixieland version recorded by Red Foley for Decca was a top-ten country hit in 1951; Jerry Reed recorded it for RCA in 1976. An echo of "Alabama Jubilee" can be heard in Bessie Smith's 1933 recording "Gimme a Pigfoot (and a Bottle of Beer)," whose authorship is credited to the vaudeville performer Wesley "Sox" Wilson. Here, Alabama becomes Harlem, Parson Brown becomes Hannah Brown, but the echo of the old spirit is strong; and, ironically, it is stronger still in the version of the song that Smith's devotee Billie Holiday later recorded, in 1949. (Smith recorded "Gimme a Pigfoot" at her last session. Billie Holiday was the next singer booked into the same studio: she was seventeen years old and making her recording debut, as a vocalist for Benny Goodman, who had played clarinet behind Smith on "Gimme a Pigfoot.") The stock comic figures of the sinful preachers Parson Brown and Deacon Jones — both of whom appear in "Alabama Jubilee," the one dancing round "like a clown," the other rattling "them old bones" — were a part of the black songster tradition since the nineteenth century, with Parson Brown appearing in published sheet music as early as the 1900 cakewalk "Foggy Jones." (The word "Levite," as in the Levitical law-making priests of Leviticus, was used in the seventeenth century as a contemptuous term for the clergy, as in Congreve's "wanton young Levite." The use of the word in this sense lingered into the nineteenth century, close in time and spirit to the appearance of Parson Brown and Deacon Jones, as well as to that of the echoes of the Levitical year of Jubilee in the evolving black-gospel tradition. Fragment, fractal, and Funky Chicken. Canaanite and cakewalk. Rolling them bones: dice, the oldest of gambling devices, older than the Bible, found in tombs of ancient Egypt. Snake eyes and gematria. Herodotus said that Ramses III descended alive into the realm of the dead, where he played dice with Isis. Seven the hard way, and the number of the beast. As the Good Book tells, if you wanted to talk to God, you had to roll them bones: you could put one or more *yes* or *no* questions to Yahweh. The mediator of Yahweh's response was a priest who rolled the sacred dice known as the Urim and the Thummim, one of which represented a positive answer, the other a negative one — it's in the first book of Samuel 14:41; check it out. The officiating priest, the Deacon Jones of the Old Testament, carried these dice in the pouch of a vestment called the ephod — it's in Exodus 28:30; check it out. It was the granddaddy of all rigged games, for Yahweh remained free, presumably by causing the repeated rolls of the dice to produce inconsistent results, not to answer the inquiry in a particular case — 1 Samuel again, 14:37 and 28:6.) These stock figures survived into the rock-'n'-roll era. One of the birth-cries of that era was Wynonie Harris's version of Roy Brown's "Good Rockin' Tonight." Recorded in 1947, "Good Rockin' Tonight," which became one of the great R&B hits of 1948, invoked the names of both Elder Brown and Deacon Jones. Earlier, in 1944, as a vocalist with Lucky Millinder and His Orchestra, Elder Brown and Deacon Jones were also invoked in Millinder's "Who Threw the Whiskey in the Well?"

These comical personifications of preacherly hypocrisy, having endured from the late nineteenth century to the dawn of rock 'n' roll, were exiled from Elvis Presley's 1954 recording of "Good Rockin' Tonight." As with the line, "You may get religion, baby," that was expurgated from Presley's 1955 version of Arthur Gunter's 1954 R&B record "Baby Let's Play House," any hint of irreverence toward religion was deemed too controversial for the great mediocrator of rock 'n' roll, which Presley — Levi, Elvi, Levite; Elvis Aron; Aaron, seditious, he of the budding rod, sign that the priestly tribe of Levites were divinely appointed; Elvis Aron Presley, born the year that Jerry Lee was born, cold and in the ground (cause of death: lack of gumption) by the year of Jerry Lee's "Alabama Jubilee" — was from the very outset: the mediocrator who made of the fine crude bread of real rock 'n' roll a sterile and insipid Wonder Bread for the masses. This was the tradition, more so than the rock-'n'-roll tradition, of which Presley truly was born. "Blue Moon of Kentucky," the flip side of Elvis Presley's first record, was a version of a song originally recorded in 1945 by Bill Monroe and His Blue Grass Boys. Monroe himself proved an expurgator of lyrics. Recording Jimmie Rodgers's 1930 "Blue Yodel No. 8" as "Mule Skinner Blues" in 1940, Monroe altered Rodgers's innocent-enough "I can pop my initials on a mule's behind" to "I can pop my initials on a mule any old time." In any event, the song, as rendered, wildly and freakishly, by the Fendermen, ended up as a rock-'n'-roll hit of 1960, thirty years after Rodgers's original — a hit reputed to have slipped the word "fuck" amid its frenetic repeated gabbling of the word "bucket," which reputation may, in that callower day, have been responsible to some extent for the record's popular success.

What a paragraph. But, as the man said, παντα ρει. And that's a fack, Jack. Παντα ρει–ει–ο–de–lay–ει–ο–de–lay–ει–ο–de–lay–ει–ει–οοοο. Back now to where it began, to that old and haunted jubilation ground, to tumbling dice over unmarked graves, to Deacon Jones and Parson Brown and the double first cousin of the Reverend Jimmy Lee Swaggart.

Jerry Lee interprets "Alabama Jubilee," but he does so viscerally, as one to whom this lost music appeals and communicates as vibrantly today as it did to others in a bygone age; and he revives as well, but in a magical and Lazarus-rising sort of way. That he sounds at times as if he might lapse from stupor to coma does not really detract from his performance. It is that kind of song, one whose languidly rollicking evocation of good times secretly seems as lost and undone, as desultory, as melancholy, as desperately forlorn, and as fatal as a debilitated drunken laugh at the end of a two-week bender. Or maybe it's just Jerry Lee. Or me. In any event, it's something real, a glimpse into a music, into a world, whose soul has been shut off to us.

Lewis has said that there have been only three great song stylists besides himself: Al Jolson, Jimmie Rodgers, and Hank Williams. There is certainly no other performer whose music has been so timeless and brilliant an alchemy of theirs; and the deep-sprawling roots of that music includes songs from nineteenth-century minstrelsy: among his Sun recordings are versions of "Dixie," Stephen Foster's "Old Black Joe," and James A. Bland's "Carry Me Back to

Old Virginny." The only other performers in Lewis's lifetime to treat such songs with similar imagination were the Mills Brothers, in their recordings of "Old Folks at Home" (1937) and "Old Black Joe" (1940).

If Emmett Miller can be seen as a missing link, Jerry Lee Lewis, at his incendiary best, can be seen as a melting-down of the chain itself.

By the late teens, the stylized jazz-blues distilled by men such as the former minstrel W. C. Handy were impelling the spirit of America. Mamie Smith made her first records in 1920; Bessie Smith would make hers in 1923.

Johnson, in *Black Manhattan,* discerns the end of black theatrical exile in the production at the downtown Garden Theatre of three dramatic plays by the Coloured Players: "April 5, 1917," he writes, "is the date of the most important single event in the entire history of the Negro in the American theatre." Even here, the pervasive shadow of minstrelsy was present, in the person of actor Jesse Shipp, who portrayed Barabbas in the main play, *Simon the Cyrenian.* Shipp, a featured performer some years before in *A Trip to Coontown,* had begun his professional career as a member of the minstrel show known as Forty Whites and Thirty Blacks, organized in 1893 by George H. Primrose and William West.

Though the Coloured Players premiere very well may have been, as Johnson has it, "the first time anywhere in the United States for Negro actors in the dramatic theatre to command the serious attention of the critics and of the general press and public," the spring of 1921 could be seen as a landmark of equal importance to low culture as the spring of 1917 was to high.

In that spring of 1921, the black musical *Shuffle Along* opened at the Sixty-third Street Music Hall, later refashioned as Daly's Theatre. Its more than five hundred performances gave the big-time white shows a run for their money. Written, produced, and performed by blacks, *Shuffle Along* was largely the combined inspiration of two partnerships: the ragtime pianist and composer Eubie Blake and the lyricist and singer Noble Sissle; and the team of Flournoy Miller and Aubrey Lyles, whose blackface routine "The Mayor of Dixie," discussed above, served as the show's core. With the success of *Shuffle Along,* black musicals became the rage, even if the behind-the-scenes creative talent was sometimes white, as with *Plantation Revue* of 1922.

Gilda Gray, a star of the *Ziegfeld Follies* whom Edmund Wilson described as "the semi-bacchante of Main Street," started a national dance craze that year when she introduced Ziegfeld's audiences to her version of the Shimmy, a black dance that had been around under that name since at least 1909. (Gray's real name was Maryanna Michalska, and she was from Wisconsin. Sophie Tucker had discovered her, given her a new name, and brought her and her Shimmy to New York in 1919, the year Mae West did the Shimmy in Arthur Hammerstein's *Someday.* Gray denied that blacks had anything to do with the origin of her dance, which she claimed to have invented in a saloon in Cudahy, Wisconsin, in 1916; West, who brought it to Broadway several months before Gray, claimed to have refined it from a crude dance called the Shimmy-Sha-Wabble encountered on Chicago's South Side. Shimmy, Shimmy Shewobble, and other variants were names for the same dance; and "Shim-Me-Sha-Wabble" was a 1929 record by Miff Mole's Molers. West's claim was made in her 1959 autobiography.) In that same *Follies* of 1922, Gray sang a new fox-trot called "It's Getting Dark on Old Broadway":

> *Just like an eclipse on the moon,*
> *ev'ry cafe now has the dancing coon.*
> *Pretty choc'late babies*
> *shake and shimmie ev'rywhere.*

Real dark-town entertainers hold the stage;
you must black up to be the latest rage.

Yes, the great white way is white no more;
it's just like a street on the Swanee shore.
It's getting very dark on old Broadway.

Indeed, Broadway would never be the same, and Tin Pan Alley, vaudeville, and, in its desperation, minstrelsy would have to heed ever more closely the vanguard of black music. Minstrelsy by then could see the writing on the wall: vaudeville was killing it. Vaudeville was blind to its own fate; but the dream of sound pictures would soon become a reality, and vaudeville would topple as well into the grave it had dug for minstrelsy.

A song such as "The Darktown Strutters' Ball" of 1917 can be seen as representative of the shift in music that occurred in those twilight years. Written by a black vaudevillian, Shelton Brooks, incorporating both the lingering sensibilities of coon-song and rag-song minstrelsy and the nascent sensibilities of the Jazz Age, it was the first song to be recorded by the Original Dixieland Jazz Band, and became an immense pop hit.

A few years later, when this band recorded W. C. Handy's "St. Louis Blues," the vocalist would be Al Bernard, who had recorded the song for Aeolian-Vocalion and Emerson in 1919, and would record it again and again: for Edison and for Victor; twice in 1927, for Brunswick and for Okeh; as a blackface monologue, under the pseudonym John Bennett, for Madison in 1928, the year that Emmett Miller recorded it. (This blackface-monologue version would be reworked into a dialogue between Bob Wills and Tommy Duncan on Wills's 1935 recording of the song.)

Bernard was born in New Orleans on November 23, 1887; he

died in New York on March 6, 1949. His roots were in minstrelsy and vaudeville: roots whose influences he shared with some of the black musical luminaries from that same time and place: Papa Charlie Jackson, born in New Orleans in 1885; Spencer Williams, born in New Orleans in 1889; Clarence Williams (who was no relation), born in Plaquemine in 1893; Lonnie Johnson, born in New Orleans in 1894 or 1899. Like Clarence and Spencer Williams, he was an associate of W. C. Handy. Be it the raw and rough-hewn but chordally advanced sound of Papa Charlie Jackson, or the sophisticated jazz-blues of Spencer Williams or of Clarence Williams (or of his protégée Bessie Smith) or of Lonnie Johnson, or the minstrelsy-pop of Bernard, their music, like Handy's, was the common legacy, the holy, shameless thievery, the many-tongued hydra of what had come before.

To hear Papa Charlie Jackson — the first solo male blues star — is to draw back the veils of mystery. When he sings playfully, in "The Cat's Got the Measles" (1925), of "a rumblin' deep down in the ground" that "must've been the Devil chainin' my good gal down," we feel for a moment that we have found the source of Van and Pete's more ominous "rumble down in the ground" that "was only the Devil chainin' his sweet mama down," in their 1928 "Yodel Blues" — until, that is, we find that Jackson's song is credited to the team of Murphy and Smiley, who lie, like their source in turn, beyond the light shed by those drawn veils. (Similarly, we hesitate to draw conclusions when another element of "Yodel Blues" — the pelagic majesty of the "change in the ocean," the "change in the deep blue sea" — reappears in 1929 in the obscure bluesman Eli Framer's only released recordings, "Framer's Blues" and "God Didn't Make Me No Monkey Man.") And when Papa Charlie Jackson sings, also from 1925, "Hot Papa Blues" and "Take Me Back Blues," we cannot but help think of the sound and songs of Jimmie Rodgers to come. Of all the mysteries of origins suggested by the repertoire of Papa Charlie Jackson — seventy-odd recordings made between 1924 and 1935 — perhaps the most singular is "No Need of Knockin' on the Blind," which he recorded in Chicago in the spring of 1928. Here is a variant of a song that can be traced through the Anglo-American tradition back at least as far as one of the tales in Boccaccio's *Decameron,* more than half a millenium before.

"I can get more men than a passenger train can haul," sings Bessie Smith in "Ticket Agent, Ease Your Window Down," a composition credited to Spencer Williams and recorded by Bessie in the spring of 1924. A year later, in the spring of 1925, Papa Charlie Jackson, in "The Faking Blues," switches the target sex and sings, "I can get more women than a passenger train can haul": a line that would forever be associated with Rodgers after his first "Blue Yodel," recorded two and a half years later, in the fall of 1927. And surely it was through Rodgers's "Blue Yodel" that the black bluesman Oscar "Buddy" Woods, an associate, accompanist, and fellow Louisianan of Rodgers's white idolater Jimmie Davis, in turn appropriated the line in his recordings, in 1936 and 1937, of "Don't Sell It (Don't Give It Away)," the authorship of which was credited to Woods and Davis.

In that same, wonderful "Blue Yodel," we encounter the couplet, "I'm gonna buy me a pistol just as long as I'm tall; I'm gonna shoot poor Thelma just to see her jump and fall." (It is the "jump" — the graphic descriptive blow, in one perfect monosyllabic jolt, of that savored gun-blast, that delivers the line to the realm of poetry: the Flaubertian ideal of *le mot juste,* the precise and luminous word, that Ezra Pound embraced and which at this very time — the fall of 1927 — was laying as the cornerstone of the melopoeia and phanopoeia that marked and elevated the most musical of the Cantos, XXV–XXX. *Le mot juste.* Melopoeia: the music and sound of poetry. Phanopoeia: the evocation of the powers of mood through imagery. Pound, in a piece published in the *New York Herald Tribune,*

January 20, 1929, the day after Emmett Miller's fifth Georgia Crackers session: "In phanopoeia we find the greatest drive toward the utter precision of word." Many years later, toward the end of his life, in Canto CXX, Pound in wisdom waved away all that he had wrought: "I have tried to write Paradise," he said plainly. Then in three lines, he brought forth the wisdom he had gained:

> *Do not move*
>> *Let the wind speak*
>>> *that is paradise.*

That wordless wind, in which the true power of poetry moves, lies beyond erudition and the artful invocations of the muses. What Ezra Pound did in his Roman-numeral'd Cantos, what Jimmie Rodgers did in his arabic-numeral'd Blue Yodels: it is all part of that wind, that melopoeia, that phanopoeis. That Pound knew to give names to such things, that Rodgers did not: it did not matter, and it does not matter. It is all part of that wind, that American grain, that poetry — from the Greek, ποίεον, *poieon,* "make"; a poet is a maker — to which we are heir. Jimmie Rodgers, at his best, is as fine and fitting a musical background as the chansons of Arnnaut Daniel, the *ballate* of Francesco Landini. They were, after all, both makers, stealing from the wind, at the same time, each in his own way. In a private letter to his father, who appealed to Pound to unlock the mysteries that might render his son's work comprehensible to him, Pound answered: "There ain't no key. Simplest parallel I can give is radio where you tell who is talking by the noise they make." *And then went down to the ship, set keel to breakers, forth on the godly sea.* Is that Pound? Is it Homer? Is it Andreas Divus's 1538 rendering of Homer into Latin, found and Englished by Pound in the first decade of the twentieth century, emerging, in 1925, as the opening of the final version of the much-worked and re-worked Canto I? From the eighth century B.C., through a Latinized text in the sixteenth century A.D., to an Englishing in the twentieth — the wonder and accruing power of this transmission, this transformation, the wind of its endless making: as much as the provenance and providence of it beguile, more beguiling still is the ultimate and unknowable provenance and providence of it. That is to say, from whom did that beautiful thief of the wind, that maker we know as Homer steal it, sensing its force and taking it unto himself, like Pound from him millennia later, as the stuff of good making?

"Dozens of these stories," wrote Robert Fitzgerald in the postscript to his translation of *The Odyssey*, "had been told, or sung, among Aegean people for generations before Homer." Of that figure known as Homer: "Our poet came late and had supremely gifted predecessors."

While it was from Homer that Pound in his magisterial erudition drew the inspiration for his own vast undertaking, his own setting forth on the godly sea, the fact remains that the world of that source was not one of erudition. As Fitzgerald bluntly states: "the world of Homer was illiterate. During the eighth century B.C. the people of the Greek mainland and islands imported a Semitic alphabet and began using it, at least for brief inscriptions. If Homer lived to see this, he probably thought of it as a new magic or amusement, almost certainly not as the medium of his work. We can surmise that we owe our text of *Iliad* and *Odyssey* not to Homer but to the importunity of some technician who 'took them down,' as nowadays a man would do with a tape recorder."

Fitzgerald refers to Homer as a "singer," and explains that "the telling of the story, and the incidental acting of roles, should be called 'singing.'" By all accounts, he says, the Homeric singer used and depended on an instrument besides his voice: "the ἀοιδός, an affair of a few gut strings with some kind of resonator, possibly a tortoise shell, like the later lyre. It would be anachronistic to think

of it as a guitar or lute, so I call it a 'gittern harp' and sometimes refer to the performer as a harper. Homer describes him more than
once as plucking or strumming an overture to a given tale or song,
and he must have used the instrument not only for accompaniment
but for pitch, and to fill pauses while he took thought for the next
turn. No doubt the instrument marked rhythm, too." The origin of
the instrument is lost in the dust and silenced melodies before history: our first glimpse of stringed-instrument players in the West is
a group of small seated marble figures from islands in the Cyclades,
dating to a period as far back as 2700 B.C. Like most early bluesmen,
the Cycladic figures are seated as they hold their instruments.

The Cyclades were a part of the southern Aegean region, the
cradle of Greek civilization, dominated by the Minoan culture of
Crete, which emerged from its long Neolithic dawn and began to
flourish at about the time those stone Cycladic figures were hewn.
It was in Crete, about a thousand years later, that the earliest form
of the archaic Greek language came into being. The first clay tablets
containing this script, which came to be called Linear B, were discovered in Knossos in 1900, the year of Emmett Miller's birth. It
was fifty-two years until the script was successfully deciphered, by
Michael Ventris and John Chadwick. In *The Times Literary Supplement*
of June 30, 2000, in an essay occasioned by the publication in full
of the four-volume corpus of Linear B inscriptions from Knossos,
John Ray, the Herbert Thompson Reader in Egyptology at the University of Cambridge, pondered the Linear B sign of the consonant
l, and its lack of differentiation from *d.*

"An explanation for this may well be that the original language
for which this script was devised contained a 'dark' *l*-sound, something like *ld.* A similar change can be seen in the probably non-
Greek name Odysseus, which appears in Latin as Ulixes or Ulysses.
The dark *l*-sound is characteristic of the languages of Anatolia."

Like the Cyclades, southwestern Anatolia was part of the

southern-Aegean cradle-realm. As for Odysseus/Ulysses, there are those who believe that the *Odyssey* was originally written in Linear B, as its tentative dating to the eighth century B.C. may place its origin at a time before the full development, in that century, of the Greek alphabet.

The dark-*l* sound. It permeates the blues of the Delta. Upon first encountering Ray's musings on the beautiful dark-*l,* I heard it inside me: Jimmy Rogers, known as Chicago Jimmy Rodgers but born of the Delta — James Lane (1924–97) of Rulesville, Mississippi — singing his deep-brewing "Luedella" of 1950. The dark lady of the Sonnets. The dark lady of the Delta. The dark lady of the Dark *L.* Luedella. Those mute stone figures of the Cyclades. The Minoan Snake Goddess, her faience figurine discovered at Knossos by Sir Arthur Evans, the discoverer of those clay tablets. Odysseus/ Ulysses reaching through the *l*-dark sea of poetry for Penelope; Jimmy Rogers, through the *l*-dark Delta of the same for cruel Luedella. To hear those mute figures play and sing, to hear the bare-breasted Snake Goddess sigh. To hear the dark *l* of it all.

Like the Homeric singers, Papa Charlie Jackson of the dark-*l* land played a "gittern" thing: a mongrel six-stringed banjo-guitar. Ragtime Henry Thomas, born in Texas in 1874, and closer in time even than Jackson to the lost sources of America's musical prehistory, played not only the guitar but panpipes, too, which he fashioned from bamboo. An even earlier example of a bluesman's panpipes is found in the mysterious Big Boy Cleveland's mesmerizing instrumental, "Quill Blues," recorded in the spring of 1927, about ten weeks before Thomas's first recordings. Panpipes, the syrinx of the ancient Greeks, were older than the music that Homer made and knew. Thomas's recordings, made in 1927–29, are the oldest form of blues captured by a record company's greed: old but not primitive, for they are as much a part of that nineteenth-century show-business tradition as they are of the dirt roads and outback through which the gathering wind blew, through Texas as through the Delta, through New Orleans as through New York, through the juke joints and the vaudeville halls and the minstrel tents alike.

From one illiterate world to another. *"As nowadays a man would do with a tape recorder."* From Homer to Ragtime Henry Thomas, from their respective lost, dark-*l* sources to them. From the sound of the panpipes that Homer mentioned in *The Iliad,* to the sound of the panpipes in the open Texas fields.

All the railroad men just drink up your blood like wine. And the wine-dark sea. The wind above, the chthonic rumble deep down in the ground. And that railroad. *I can get more women than a passenger train can haul.* And the train kept a-rolling, all night long. From Fred Moody in 1901 to Bascom Lamar Lunsford in 1928 to Bob Dylan in 1966; from Murphy and Smiley to Papa Charlie Jackson to Van and Pete; from Papa Charlie Jackson to Jimmie Rodgers to Buddy Woods. *"There ain't no key."* To look behind, with eyes that are right, is to look ahead. To listen to the wind of this moment is to hear the wind of every moment. Did Emmett Miller, in Manhattan, glance at those words of Pound in the *Herald Tribune* that day? Did Ezra Pound smile at the sound of Jimmie Rodgers, perhaps even of Emmett Miller? Did William Faulkner have the slightest bit more of an idea than either Rodgers or Miller of what "phanopoeia" meant? I think not. And yet I think, too, that they all understood it, and that they all made it. Winds don't need names, any more than Thelma did.

In "Low Land Moan," recorded by Lonnie Johnson for Okeh in Chicago twelve days after Jimmie Rodgers recorded his first "Blue Yodel" for Victor in Camden, Johnson sang, "I'm going to buy me a shotgun just as long as I am tall; I'm going to shoot my woman just to see her fall." This virtually simultaneous rendering of the couplet — ultimate origin unknown — by Johnson, whose poetic sensibilities are usually astoundingly unerring, lacks the *coup de grâce* of Rodgers's "just to see her *jump* and fall." Little more than a year later, in "Got the Blues (Can't Be Satisfied)," Mississippi John Hurt didn't threaten, he stated: "Took my gun and broke the barrel down; put my baby six feet underground."

The phrase " 'T' for Texas, 'T' for Tennessee," also from Rodgers's first "Blue Yodel," appears in Johnson's "Kansas City Blues," recorded three days after "Low Land Moan." But Johnson's "Kansas City Blues" was essentially a takeoff on Jim Jackson's currently successful "Jim Jackson's Kansas City Blues," which also contained the phrase and, recorded well over a month before Rodgers recorded his first "Blue Yodel," also very likely may have been the immediate source of the first words — " 'T' for Texas, 'T' for Tennessee" — of Rodgers's first "Blue Yodel." The phrase " 'T' for Texas, 'T' for Tennessee" would come forth again in "Future Blues," a 1930 recording by Willie Brown (1900–52), who is considered, with Charley Patton (1891–1934) and Son House (1902–88), to be one of the triumvirate of "primitive" Delta blues masters associated with the Will Dockery plantation of Dockery, Mississippi.

More than a quarter of a century after Jimmie Rodgers, in his first "Blue Yodel," raised his vision — appropriated or otherwise — of that gun as long as he was tall, and his vision — appropriated or otherwise — of getting more women than a passenger train could haul, Big Joe Turner, in his "Midnight Cannonball," conflated the passenger train with the pistol: "I'm gonna buy me a ticket long as I am tall." Luke Jordan's "My Gal's Done Quit Me," recorded for Rodgers's label, Victor, in 1929, somewhat melodically echoed the 1927 Rodgers song while evoking a train ticket "as long as my right arm," a piece of hyperbole that predated the Rodgers song: "Gonna buy me a ticket just as long as my right arm," sang the Pullman Porters Quartette, a black vocal group, in "Pullman Passenger Train," believed to have been recorded in November 1927, the month on the last day of which Rodgers's "Blue Yodel" was recorded.

Iliad and *Odyssey.* Wrath, heartbreak, wandering. Big Joe Turner,

A.D. 1974: "I can't read, can't write; gonna buy me a telephone." Homer, c. 750 B.C.: Can't read, can't write; gonna get me a gittern thing.

"All I Want Is a Spoonful," sang Papa Charlie Jackson in 1925, bringing to mind "A Spoonful Blues," recorded in 1929 by that paradigm of "authentic" deep-Delta blues, Charley Patton, and Charley Jordan's "Just a Spoonful" of 1930, not to mention the "Spoonful," infused with metaphorical ambiguities anew, that Willie Dixon "wrote" and Howlin' Wolf recorded in 1960. All of them leading to, all of them blown away by the intravenous Gnosticism of Bob Dylan's "Shot of Love" of 1981: "Don't need a shot of heroin to cure my disease." (Gnosis, from the Greek γνῶσις, knowledge, or seeking; from γνω–, the root of γιγνώσκειν, to know. Intravenous Gnosticism? Charles Olson, *The Maximus Poems,* "Maximus, from Dogtown — I," 1959:

> *We drink*
> *or break open*
> *our veins solely*
> *to know.*

These lines themselves turned to song, projective-verse doo-wop, through Ed Sanders, the Fugs, "I Want to Know," 1966.)

Above all, especially in his earliest recordings, of 1924, we are struck by how Papa Charlie Jackson's singing is not so very different, in sound or in spirit, from Al Bernard's.

And all those who have bought wholesale into the romance of the preternatural, *ex-nihilo* originality and brilliance of Robert Johnson (1911–38), the fabled master poet of the Delta blues, would be well served, as was Robert Johnson himself, by listening to the records of Lonnie Johnson, the beginning of whose recording career, in 1925, predated that of the younger Johnson by more than a decade. Describing Robert Johnson as "both the most influential and most demonstrably influenced blues guitarist of his time," the writer Stephen Calt astutely observed: "Though posthumous white appreciation of [Robert] Johnson has hinged largely on his lyrics, his influence on black musicians rested almost solely on the novelty of his guitar work."

That posthumous white appreciation discerned in Robert Johnson's songs a brilliance of lyrical originality that was often in truth a brilliance of lyrical theft or variation. It is one thing to be moved by the somber fatalistic imagery of Robert Johnson's "Love in Vain," recorded at his final session, on a Sunday in Dallas in June of 1937; it is another thing to know that the essence and most moving stroke of that imagery had been recorded, also in Dallas, almost five years earlier, in "Flying Crow Blues" by Eddie and Oscar, the singing black slide-guitarists, Eddie Schaffer and Oscar Woods, who played on several early Victor recordings by the white country singer Jimmie Davis, under whose aegis they also recorded on their own for Victor, first as the Shreveport Home Wreckers, then as Eddie and Oscar.

In the end, I believe, it was not the music of Robert Johnson, but the mystery of him — the legends that grew around his vanishing and fate, a vanishing and fate that remained unsolved for more than thirty years after his death; legends, involving a horrid end through evil spell or demonic possession, attributed to blacks but loved by whites — that made of Robert Johnson the most mythic of bluesmen. In this sense, Robert Johnson has a lot in common with Emmett Miller: it was for long the mystery of them that overshadowed and lent magic to what they had left behind. In a related sense, the big difference between them is not that Robert Johnson was greater, more gifted than Emmett Miller. Of course he was. The big difference is that Miller's ghost never entered the salon of white vogue.

When the brilliance of Charley Patton, the brooding Son House (another influence on Robert Johnson), and other Delta bluesmen are reverenced and regarded in terms of primitive purity and un-compromising individuality of expressiveness, it must be kept in mind that their own regard for these rare qualities, aside from matters of the soul, was directly in proportion to the effective commerciality of these qualities. When the primitive-sounding Blind Lemon Jefferson (1893–1929) began his career, destined to be one of the most successful in the pre-war blues industry, it was with a hip sensibility that belied his sound, with phrases such as "jump and jive," as in his "Long Lonesome Blues" of early 1926, two years before the earliest evidence of the existence of the word "jive" as traced by *The Oxford English Dictionary,* thirty years before Louis Prima's hipster recording of "Jump, Jive an' Wail." Even Henry Thomas, with his panpipes and lost-root rhymes; even Henry Thomas, whose music could with some justification be called primitive, was hip enough to prefix a moniker of modernity to his name: Ragtime Henry Thomas.

These men, contrary to the circumstances into which they were born, were not rubes. Papa Charlie Jackson had sung of "Gay Cattin'," of living high and cool and hip, in 1926. Charley Patton, Willie Brown, and Son House, the triumvirate of "primitive" Delta blues masters, were, in the black parlance of the day, gay cats. Just listen to them verbally jive and wail on the second take of Louise Johnson's "All Night Long Blues," a take that remained unissued for more than half a century. It was recorded, at the Paramount studio in Grafton, Wisconsin, on May 28, 1930 — the same time and place that Brown and House also made their first records. (Patton had begun recording, also for Paramount, not quite a year earlier.) Louise Johnson, a rough-handed Delta piano-player, is supposed to have been eighteen at the time and a mistress to both Brown and House, if not to Patton as well.

As for the phrase "gay cat," its use in this sense seems to have been short-lived and exclusively black. In white hobo slang, going back to the late nineteenth century, the words denoted a lesser, inexperienced member of the tramp community, and in time came to imply homosexuality as well: a "gay cat" being the punk-queer companion of an older, veteran hobo, synonymous with "gunsel," a Yiddish-derived pejorative epithet of like meaning — ultimately from the German *gänslein,* a gosling or little goose — that had been a part of white criminal slang since the early years of the twentieth century. The queer connotations of the word "gay" itself were withstood in black music for at least twenty years after the word had come to commonly denote homosexuality: the Midnighters, Ruth Brown, and Louis Brooks all had minor R&B hits in 1955 with "It's Love Baby (24 Hours of the Day)," a song that proclaimed, with no trace of double entendre, "I need your love to keep me gay."

But back to the Delta, back to when gay cats were gay cats and sissy men were sissy men. Ma Rainey sang of her man's male lover — "my man says sissies got good jelly roll" — in her 1926 "Sissy Blues." The little-known bluesman George Hannah, in a voice befitting his complaint, recorded his bold "Freakish Man Blues" in 1930.

The pianist, composer, and erstwhile blackface performer James P. Johnson sang of "The Bull Diker's Dream" in 1938. (Johnson had accompanied Rosa Henderson on her 1927 "Gay Catin' [*sic*] Daddy," done several months before Viola McCoy's "Gay-Catin [and *sic* again] Daddy.") Lucille Bogan had abbreviated the matter to "B.D. Woman's Blues," in 1935. The origin of this term for an exaggeratedly masculine Lesbian remains a mystery. Its earliest known appearance is in *Nigger Heaven,* the 1926 novel by Carl Van Vechten, the white New York dandy and *Vanity Fair* columnist whom the black writer James Weldon Johnson credited, in 1930, as the man "who first pointed out that the blues-singers were artists."

But, again, back to the Delta.

The simple and irrefutable truth is that no human being would rather break his back in the cotton fields than take in good folding money by making records. Any primitive-sounding artist, no matter how great his gift or integrity, would gladly, if he could, refine that primitivism and adulterate the truth of himself and his voice, to increase the prospect of sales whenever possible. Looking at the rare photographs of the likes of Charley Patton, Son House, and Robert Johnson, we see men who appear far from primitive. In the recording studio, the blues, like everything else, was *ad captandam vulgus,* calculated to take the fancy of the marketplace.

Papa Charlie Jackson, the first commercially successful male blues singer, an archaic voice from another age, presented himself with subdued pride and dignity in a fashionable three-piece suit. He, like Patton, House, and Johnson, are the equivalent of Jimmie Rodgers of Mississippi in his tuxedo or his fine cocked hat, rather than in his Singing Brakeman get-up. The blues, to all who knew and loved them, were far less a god than was money. In this sense, a man such as Furry Lewis (1893–1981) was far more truly representative than Charley Patton or Son House of the true nature of the big river of the Delta blues. From his roots in the Delta, Lewis followed the river to Memphis, a course that involved him in the music jug bands, medicine shows, and the W. C. Handy orchestra. As a true voice of the Delta, as a black man who worked in blackface, as a figure in the urban and urbane music of jazz and the big-city, as well as the big-river, blues, Lewis is an illumination unto himself, just as his 1928 "Kassie Jones" is a flowing unto itself, beyond place or time. "I believe I'll buy me a graveyard of my own," he sang in "Furry's Blues" of that same year. "I'm gonna shoot my woman just to see her fall," he sang in that same song. Furry's song followed Jim Jackson's "I'm Gonna Start Me a Graveyard of My Own" by seven months. Both Lonnie Johnson and Jimmie Rodgers had sung the year before of shooting their women just to see them fall. Like Jackson — like Johnson and Rodgers, too — Lewis was indeed graveyard as well as illumination unto himself: a graveyard where the dead voices of the past lay buried, unmarked, and unknown, to be hoodooed forth in illumination both of that past and of its powers anew. An awareness of that illumination and those powers was evinced by the Rolling Stones, who twice during the seventies insisted that Lewis open their concerts in Memphis. It was evinced as well by James Luther Dickinson, a modern voice of Mississippi and of Memphis who has been called upon as a musician by the Rolling Stones (*Sticky Fingers,* 1969; released 1971) as well as by Bob Dylan (*Time out of Mind,* 1997): a resurrected "Kassie Jones" was amid the wondrous conjurings of Dickinson's 1971 *Dixie Fried,* most of which was recorded in the fall of 1970 at Criteria in North Miami Beach, Florida, the same studio at which *Time out of Mind* was recorded more than a quarter of a century later. Nearly thirty years later, the North Mississippi All Stars, led by Dickinson's sons, Luther and Cody, would come forth with their own reworking of "Kassie Jones," melding it with ostraka of Jesse James's 1936 "Southern Casey Jones," in their *Shake Hands with Shorty,* released in the spring of 2000. Jim Dickinson's version bore the title "Cassie Jones (On the Road Again)"; his sons', the title "K.C. Jones." Among variations of "Casey Jones" that predated Furry Lewis's were those of white performers such as Fiddlin' John Carson (1923), Riley Puckett (1924), Gid Tanner (1927), Prince Albert Hunt (as "Katy on Time," 1928). Other black variations included the Memphis Jug Band's "On the Road Again," recorded in Memphis for Victor in September 1928, two weeks after Furry Lewis made his "Kassie Jones" in Memphis for Victor. Elements and versions of the song were to be found in published sources within the decade following the death of the real-life John Luther (Cayce) Jones (1863–1900), who crashed his Illinois Central locomotive into another train early in the morning of April 30, 1900, near Vaughn, Mississippi. The first hit version of "Casey Jones," published by the Southern California Music Company of Los Angeles, was copyrighted in 1909 by the lyricist T. Lawrence Seibert and the composer Eddie Newton. Various popular white mainstream performers recorded the song in 1910, among them Billy Murray's American Quartet, whose 1910 Victor record is believed to have sold well over a million copies. According to tradition, Seibert and Newton took the song from Wallace Saunders, a black Canton, Mississippi, engine-wiper who knew Jones and composed the song soon after Jones's death.

"When I was in Missouri, would not let me be," sang Furry Lewis in "I Will Turn Your Money Green" of 1928.

"When I was in Missouri, they would not let me be," sang Bob Dylan in "Tryin' to Get to Heaven," on *Time out of Mind*, almost seventy years later.

I thought Jim Dickinson might have been the connection; but, no, he says: "I can take no credit for any of Bob's lyrics."

Dickinson remembers Dylan reading through lyrics he had written on notebook pages. "Though we talked about Furry," says Dickinson, Dylan seemed more interested in Sleepy John Estes, a Memphis-based contemporary of Furry Lewis who made his first recordings in 1929 and had passed away in 1977. Estes, with whom Dickinson had performed, had said of Dickinson, "I like the way this man plays. He lays back on the changes and waits for me. I'm an old man. I knows where I'm going."

The playing-surface of the Columbia compact disc of *Time out of Mind*, designed to evoke the look of a Columbia 78-rpm record from fifty years before, bears the phrases "Electrical Process" and "Viva-tonal," which Columbia introduced to its labels in late 1926, and which became a familiar feature of its labels in early 1927: the year that Furry Lewis, Jimmie Rodgers, and so many other luminous voices came to be heard; the year of Emmett Miller's glory; the year that the great flood of the Mississippi, the great flood of the Delta, the great flood, ignivomous and exundant, which seemed to sunder the chthonic sacrarium, κτύπησε Ζεύς χθόνιος, and bring forth the *tombaroli,* the holy grave-robbers and thieves; to loose the cestus of Mystis, sweet tectonic mama, and raise, in skirl and sigh and yodel and moan, in epiclesis, in *aestus,* in quietus — *stile vecchio, stile duro, stile nuovo* — the tessitura of it all, the dark and myriad-voiced antediluvian song and resurrection in the light of new morning, *matutina lux,* Viva-tonal and electric, wild-souled and endlessly rocking. "In me the tiger sniffs the rose," said Siegfried Sassoon. Amazing the scents, amazing the stirrings of nature in the balmy breeze after the flood. William Faulkner of Mississippi, born the same year as Charley Patton of Mississippi, got his best book, *The Wild Palms,* out of that flood of 1927. Theophany, like trouble, is everywhere.

"I do not know much about gods; but I think that the river / Is a strong brown god," wrote T. S. Eliot. And, some lines later: "The river is within us."

Plotinus spoke of being alone with the Alone: "the soul must see before it neither evil nor good nor anything else, that alone it may receive the Alone." It is that long, endlessly resonant bent theophanic and fatal blue note of a journey, that drifting and drifting, of the alone to the Alone, that defines what has come, in rill and in torrent, in the wake of the flood. The real and literal flood itself, of course, had nothing to do with it: a reverberation of Shango, a paraph of the elements, nothing more. It serves only as a marker, an awful and terrible serendipity, and no meaning should be read into it or sought.

Empedocles, fifth century B.C.: "The blood around men's hearts is their thought." Little Willie Littlefield, A.D. 1952: "Blood is redder than wine." Even Henry James, whose façade was that of thought itself, embraced the wisdom that transcended the ascot: "Wherever we go," he wrote, "we carry with us this heavy burden of our personal consciousness and wherever we stop we open it out over our heads like a great baleful cotton umbrella, to obstruct the prospect and obscure the light of heaven."

Keep your thought in your heart, and get you a pint if you must let go to your head what don't belong there. Forget about neurons and the firings of synapses being the sum of soul and spirit. If the pre-Socratics or Little Willie Littlefield or Henry James or all of Ch'an can't drive it home, go back to that year of the flood, 1927, turn up the volume and listen to Blind Willie Johnson's "Dark Was the Night." Follow him from there to "John the Revelator," three years later. And from there — other voices, other years — follow that fatal, beauteous, and theophanic drifting. With the grace of God, a shot of love, a wisp of wisdom, and a fine black-on-black silk jacquard shirt, you may be fortunate enough to live, feel, and never think again.

The so-called primitive Delta bluesmen were victims, not devotees, of the deprivation of a wide-ranging musical sophistication. Their achievement in the face of this is immense; their willingness, indeed their eagerness, to purloin from beyond their realm what they could is more than understandable: it is admirable. Muddy Waters's prison-break from the Delta blues, his transformation of those blues following his move to Chicago, culminating in his taking up his first solid-body electric guitar, in 1954, was a cultural revolution — a creation through destruction — whose equal would be found only in Bob Dylan's thunderous assault on, and deliverance of, rock 'n' roll little more than a decade later, in 1965.

These were the culmination in cataclysm, Muddy Waters in 1954, Dylan in 1965, of that rumbling deep down in the ground, that change in the ocean, that change in the deep blue sea; the breaking forth in violence and in glory from the grave, the secret place where the shades and dead voices gathered.

Highway 61. Just as the Mississippi runs from Lake Itasca in Minnesota to the Delta, so Highway 61 ran from the Delta to the north country of Bob Dylan's Minnesota youth. "Where I lived," he maundered in early 1966, three days after finishing *Blonde on Blonde,* "it's all hillbilly stations." These, as he said, were "stations on a direct route from Louisiana." It all came "right down the Mississippi River," and "that's all there is to it." It was as simple as that. "It was all there." Heraclitus again: the flowing of the all. "I didn't know any individual songs."

In his sundering, with *Highway 61 Revisited,* of the seventh seal of all that remained unrevealed, Dylan fulfilled the prophecy of rock 'n' roll — that is to say, the prophecy of voices dead and long forgotten, out of time. In the wrath-rhythmed imagery of the Eidophusikon of "Highway 61 Revisited," a song whose secondary referential geography, after that of the *mappa mundi* of the plague-lands of the soul, is the Greenwich Village netherworld rather than the lands of Highway 61 itself, Dylan nevertheless ignites the combustive blast of the song's opening with the white-heat of the Spirit-driven black music of the 1920s and earlier: "God said to Abraham," the opening line of that blast is taken directly from the Old Testament, where it occurs three times, in Genesis 17:9, 17:15, and 21:12, leading, as in "Highway 61 Revisited," to God's commanding Abraham, in Genesis 22, to kill his son, Isaac. It is, amid the cataclysm of *Highway 61 Revisited,* a harkening in thunder and in lightning to the primal sanctified bedrock of the blood and hellfire of that olden music and its olden powers. Recorded in New York, April 18, 1929: "Abraham Offers His Son Isaac" by Rev. Beaumont and His Congregation, released on Paramount as by Rev C. H. Welsh and Congregation.

In Genesis, God orders the sacrifice to take place at Moriah, a site that remains a mystery to biblical scholars. In Dylan's song, the killing is to be done down on Highway 61, the fabled road of origin, of mystery, the road from Moriah to Memphis. The name Abraham means son of Abraham, the name of the man to whom Bob Dylan was first-born, as Robert Zimmerman, in Minnesota; and the name of the wife of Abraham was changed to Sara — "And God said unto Abraham, As for Sarai thy wife, thou shalt not call her name Sarai, but Sarah *shall* her name *be*" (Genesis 17:15); Sarah: in Hebrew, *śārâ* (שָׂרָה) — and Sara, whose name was changed from Shirley, was the name of the woman whom Dylan took as wife in the season following *Highway 61 Revisited.* From Moriah to Memphis to Minnesota to Manhattan: origin and mystery.

That root, γνω-, of γιγνώσκειν, to know, and of γνῶσις: its own ultimate root is the Indo-European *gn,* whence *gen.* In *The Origins of English Words: A Discursive Dictionary of Indo-European Roots,* Dr. Joseph T. Shipley begins his extensive, several-paged entry for *gn, gen* with the words: "This root is so prolific that some scholars divide it in two. It defies partition. For its two meanings, to know and to beget, continue to entwine through the linguistic changes." Through the Germanic consonantal *k* shift, came, among a myriad, both "knowledge" and "cunt," the latter no less a begetter, a generatrix, a vessel of genesis than, in its Gnostic, spiritual sense, the former.

We know nothing. This is the only knowledge allowed us, the only knowledge in which wisdom lies. Again, Charles Olson, writing in 1954, the year that Elvis killed what had been real, the year that the electric hoodoo of Muddy Waters and others resurrected what Elvis killed: "Against Wisdom as Such." The title of Olson's essay could be taken to say it all, were it not for the words that therein overpower:

He who controls rhythm / controls

U.S. Highway 61 began in that city of origin and of source, New Orleans, the city of Louis Vasnier, of Al Bernard, of Papa Charlie Jackson, of Spencer Williams and Clarence Williams, of Lonnie Johnson, of so many more. It ran north along the course of the Mississippi, through the fertile Delta of the blues, through the homeland of Muddy Waters and those who came before him; through Memphis, through St. Louis, and beyond. Songs such as Roosevelt Sykes's "Highway 61 Blues" of 1932 had given it vague, mythic stature as bloodstream and as symbol, of freedom and of fate.

Dylan, in the notes to *Highway 61 Revisited*: "The songs on this specific record are not so much songs but rather exercises in tonal breath control. . . . [*ellipsis points his*] the subject matter — tho meaningless as it is — has something to do with the beautiful strangers . . . [*ellipsis mine*] & the holy slow train."

For a man whose métier has never been prose, these are remarkable words. "The beautiful strangers" — the ghosts of those who have come before, the gathering of the voices and stirrings of the dead — is a wisp of evocative lyricism befitting the movement of a pen held by fingers that bear both the dust of the recently broken seventh seal and the gunpowder from of a recently fired blast, fingers unclenching in the calm perception after tumult. But "the holy slow train" is nothing less than melopoeia and rhythmus unto itself.

If the Delta bluesmen are to be considered the great, illiterate Homeric voices of the blues, we must bear in mind the words of the great and literate Homeric translator and scholar Robert Fitzgerald: "Our poet came late and had supremely gifted predecessors." We must bear in mind the unknown ghosts behind Charley Patton and Son House; the ghosts behind Lonnie Johnson and others; those from whom these men afterwards took as they grew, as all who grow take, as Robert Johnson took from them. To praise the primitive for its own sake is to patronize and to embrace in arrogance the "purity," the "naturalness," the "beauty" of downtroddenness and misery.

Charley Patton's best shirt and tie, Son House's white shirt and black tie, Robert Johnson's sharp chalk-stripe suit, fancy necktie, and snap-brim hat: such was the image, far from primitive, that these men wanted to project. (Similarly, but perversely, while adopting and selling a pose of the visionary and the revolutionary, the triumvirate — Burroughs, Kerouac, and Ginsberg — of the so-called Beat culture was a product of the Ivy League. If much good can be said of them — Burroughs's adherence to conservative dress throughout his long-lived and successful con game of packaging second-rate science fiction as literature of the ages; Kerouac's affinity for the true music of his age, such as that of Wynonie Harris; Ginsberg's flashes of true poetic brilliance amid the con game of his own stage-show mysticism — far more good can be said of the one true writer of that age, Hubert Selby, Jr., who dressed no part and joined no movement and truly did make literature of the ages. But no good at all can be said of those, the great deluded consumer generation, the children of the Beats, who replaced the truth of substance with the lie of posture, who refused to accept reality without masquerade.

The demeaning coon show of the celebration of the primitive, the romance of *rusticitas* — the donning of overalls and tattered caps — came only later, when young, "liberal," white America, seeking escape from vacuousness through the delusive pseudonegritude of the "raw, hard truth" of the blues, brought about the grossest and most degrading of all minstrelsies. A few old and long-forgotten black guys made a few bucks by putting on the required act; and in those few dollars, at least something good, if low, came of it. But what came of it, above all and most devastating, was the lie of a picture of the blues as they never were. It was a fine thing that Mississippi John Hurt (1893–1966) was able to have revived a career that had been stillborn in 1928; a shame that, in doing so, he was compelled to assume the persona of a backwards cottonfield coon imposed upon him by a young white America that saw itself as a force for racial equality and brotherhood. It is this same America, a few years older, balder, and more ridden with the scabies of academic nonsense, that now seeks to find psychosociological meaning in the minstrelsy of another era. The truth is that it is those who damn, those who seek the answer to the chimerical question of racism in minstrelsy, who are themselves both the damnable and the answer; they who themselves are the purveyors and consumers of a truly insidious minstrelsy that they refuse or are unable even to recognize as such. If the new minstrelsy, the white folks in the black folks' yard, can be viewed as an outgrowth of the so-called folk-music "movement" — which began with the Almanac Singers of 1941, approached its commercial heyday in the late fifties, with pop hits such as the Kingston Trio's "Tom Dooley" (1958), and reached its apogee in the mid-sixties, when Bob Dylan, who had ridden its wave rather artfully and disingenuously, made his brilliant leap from the comfortably fraudulent to the devastatingly real — it is fitting that one of the most popular of the so-called folk-music, the New Christy Minstrels, took their name from a blackface minstrelsy troupe, the Christy Minstrels, of nearly a hundred and twenty years before.

There are no academic blues. There are no academic truths. There are no academics in really sharp suits or fine snap-brim hats.

Academic studies, the pus of the cerebrum in captivity, are nothing more than what Big Joe Turner, in a song title and lyric of 1941, referred to as "Chewed Up Grass": that is to say, bullshit.

This somehow brings to mind, and tempts me to maunder a bit about Samuel Beckett and Nicholas of Cusa. But perhaps it is better that we return to Al Bernard, who at least is almost as little known — or these days, maybe equally as little known — as the noble fifteenth-century philosopher of Cusa who, like Beckett, knew that Scholasticism, like scholasticism, was and always will be the enemy and ruin of all wisdom.

Bernard — who took no explicit side in the above issue — made one of the first sound-film shorts, worked in radio as early as 1923, and had a prolific and intriguing recording career, which began in 1916 and which today is largely terra incognita. He is known to have recorded for at least two dozen companies, with releases on at least thirty-five labels: blackface routines with Billy Beard for Okeh, with Lasses White for Columbia; duets with Ernest Hare for Edison and other labels, with Vernon Dalhart for Columbia, with guitarist Frank Ferera for Victor and Puritan. Among his Puritan recordings with Ferera was the 1923 Italian-dialect fox-trot "Me No Speaka Good English," written by Harry Pease, Ed Nelson, and Moe Scheneck, who rhyme "open a barber shop" with a "marry a wop." The song was also recorded by Billy Jones and Ernest Hare, the popular Happiness Boys.

The root of the word "wop" is as ancient, and as benign, as that of the word "nigger," which, like its cognate "negro," descends from the Latin *niger*, meaning simply "black" or "dark in color." The probable root of "wop" is the Latin *uappu*, which was used literally to describe wine gone bad, but which was also used figuratively as early as the first century B.C., by Horace, to describe a good-for-nothing, a worthless character. From *uappu* came the Sicilian *vappu* and *guappu*, which connoted arrogance, bluster, and maleficence entwined. It was these Sicilian words that were commonly used to describe the work-bosses who lured their greenhorn *paesani* into servitude in New York City in the early years of the twentieth century.

In New York and other American seaports, the lowly labor of the Italian immigrants' servitude — the dockside toil and offal-hauling that others shunned — came to be called, after the work-bosses, *guappu* work; and eventually the laborer himself, and not the boss, was known as *guappu*. The peasant immigrants' tendency to clip the final vowels from standard Italian and Sicilian — as in *paesan'* for *paesano* — rendered *guappu* as *guapp'*, which was pronounced, more or less, as *wop*.

Jack London, who gave us the first appearance of the word in print, wrote in 1913, in *John Barleycorn,* of a financial desperation that had driven him years earlier to seek "work as a wop, lumper and roustabout." But the word settled on the Italians from whose tongue it had come, and in time all of them came to bear its malison.

In their *Vocabulary of Criminal Slang,* Louis Jackson and C. E. Hellyer include the entry: "Wop, noun. Used primarily in the East. An ignorant person; a foreigner; an impossible character." But not just any foreigner. "He's a wop," wrote P. G. Wodehouse in 1915. "A wop, a dago." And lest there be any misunderstanding, "An Italian." That was the year that Irving Berlin wrote the stereotypical "Hey, Wop," recorded by Rhoda Bernard for Pathé, and by George Thompson for Edison.

It was with a wop song that the Russian-born Jew Irving Berlin began his illustrious career, in 1906. Berlin — he was still Israel Baline then — was eighteen years old, working as a singing waiter at the Pelham Café, a saloon with an upstairs brothel. Located at 12 Pell Street in Chinatown, the Pelham was run by a shady Russian whose swarthy complexion had led him to be known as Nigger Mike Salter. The waiter and piano-player of another joint, Callahan's Dance Hall at Chatham Square and Doyers Street, had come up with a hit of sorts, an Italian-dialect number called "My Mariuccia (Take a Steamboat)." While many of the most caricatured of coon songs of this period were actually written by blacks, "My Mariuccia" was the only wop song whose author bore an Italian name: Al Piantadosi, who shared the copyright with George Ronklin, and who would later collaborate with Berlin on songs such as "Just Like a Rose" (1909).

Billy Murray recorded "My Mariuccia (Take a Steamboat)" for Victor, which released it coupled with a recording by the team of Jones and Spencer. (Murray, who also recorded as a team with Len Spencer, had discovered Ada Jones; and it has been said that his own recordings with her, in 1907–22, were the most popular male-female duets in history.) "Pedro, the Hand-Organ Man," the Jones-Spencer recording coupled with Murray's recording of "My Mariuccia" was also done in ersatz Italian dialect. That Pedro was not an Italian name seemed to have escaped the attention of all involved.

At Salter's urging, Izzy and the Pelham pianist, Nick Michaelson, came up with a wop song of their own. It was called "Marie from Sunny Italy," and it was with the sheet-music publication of this song that Izzy Baline became Irving Berlin, a name which he fancied to have far more class. Soon Berlin had a classier job as well, uptown at Jimmy Kelly's on Union Square, in the neighborhood of Tony Pastor's theater, where Izzy had once worked for Harry Von Tilzer as a lowly boomer, a shill paid to applaud and enthuse wildly at the performance of any song published by the house of Von Tilzer. Harry himself, meanwhile, had not let Mariuccia pass unnoticed. His own composition "Mariutch Down at Coney Isle" appeared in 1907.

"Dorando," another wop song, followed from Berlin's pen in 1908; and in 1910 came "Sweet Italian Love," the most successful of them all.

When you kiss-a your pet,
And it's-a like-a spaghett',
Dat's Italian love.

Berlin's song, which seems to be the simile-borne forebear of "That's Amore," was featured in the show *Up and Down Broadway,* recorded by Byron G. Harlan for Columbia, Billy Murray for Edison. Murray, who had also recorded "My Mariuccia (Take a Steamboat)," followed "Sweet Italian Love" with "That Italian Rag" for Victor. His rendition of "My Mariuccia" was still listed in the Victor catalogue of 1920, under Italian Dialect Songs and Specialties, along with the likes of Collins and Harlan's "Nighttime in Little Italy," not to be confused with their "Down in Jungle Town" or "Nigger Loves His Possum."

Indeed, the origins of the coon song and the wop song were closely related. The earliest of the wop songs — George Austin Morrison's "The Organ Grinder's Song" of 1882, Frank Dumont's "The Dagoe Banana Peddlar" of 1888 — were from the heyday of minstrelsy and the coon song, that decade that saw the rise of the recording industry and Tin Pan Alley, the rise of ragtime, jazz, and the blues. While many blacks, however, prospered from minstrelsy, blackface, and the coon song, few if any Italians reaped the rewards of caricaturing themselves. In many ways, wop-face endured longer than blackface: for, just as many of the classic wop songs were written by Jews and performed by Jews and Irishmen, so the classic Italian movie gangsters were portrayed by Jews as well: Edward G. Robinson in *Little Caesar* (1931), Paul Muni in *Scarface* (1932). Only George Raft among them could boast an authentic tributary of dago red in his hereditary bloodstream. Such was America, where the blackest blacks were white and the most Italianate of Italians were Jews. After real blacks had come to portray Amos 'n' Andy, the lead character of the radio and television show *Life with Luigi* was still being portrayed by a J. Carrol Naish.

Meanwhile, real blacks and real Italians had together rocked the cradle of jazz. The first that America heard of what it would later call the Mafia was in newspaper accounts of certain happenings in New Orleans in the spring of 1869, when the *Times* of that city noted that the Second District had become infested by "well-known and notorious Sicilian murderers, counterfeiters and burglars, who, in the last months, have formed a sort of general co-partnership or stock company for the plunder and disturbance of the city." Emigration from Sicily and southern Italy was then still largely to Brazil and the Argentine. New Orleans, with its busy port traffic to and from South America, was a natural destination for many Sicilians, maverick mafiosi among them. From that time through the golden era of Storyville jazz, 1898–1917, many of the joints where jazz evolved were owned by members or allies of that "general co-partnership," and many of the musicians involved in that evolution were of Sicilian or southern-Italian descent. The Original Dixieland Jazz Band, which first recorded in 1917, had been founded by Nick LaRocca, who was born to Sicilian parents in New Orleans in 1889; and the Little Palermo section of the French Quarter continued to be an important breeding-ground of white jazz players through the 1920s. Louis Prima, who was born in that neighborhood in 1910, began making records in 1933 and gave America her first *real* wopsong recordings little more than a decade later, beginning with "Angelina" of 1944. (Angelina was the name of Prima's mother, who sang in local blackface shows in New Orleans.)

Vestiges of the wop song endured well into the rock-'n'-roll era. Blackie Crawford, a Beaumont, Texas, disc-jockey and country singer, recorded an Italian-dialect "Mariuch" for Starday in June of 1953. The song is credited to Crawford and someone named Romano, and the parenthetical southern-Italian hillbilly pronunciation guide "(Mottie-Ooch)" appears beneath the title on the label. It was the second record released by Starday of Beaumont, which would soon fare better with another local singer, George Jones. It seems poetically just that the musical steamboat journey of Mariuccia, begun in a Chinatown dive in 1906, involving a Jewish kid named Izzy and a Russian named Nigger Mike, should end forty-seven years later with a hillbilly disc-jockey singing in feigned broken English in a makeshift studio in Beaumont, Texas, a town known as the redneck capital of the world. It can do no harm to note in passing, that Mariuccia appears as well in the cosmogony of Louis Prima, who recorded "For Mari-Yootch" for RCA-Victor in 1949.

An even more curious latter-day wop song is "Hello Maria," recorded for Peacock in December of 1955 by Big Walter Price and His Thunderbirds, a rare instance of a wop song by a black singer. Price, who sings "Hello Maria" in a forthright Italianate broken English, is credited as the author of the song, which was released in 1956 as the flip side of his R&B classic "Pack Fair and Square." References to the names Luigi and Pasquale in "Hello Maria" suggest an inspiration in the radio and television show *Life with Luigi,* whose two main characters were so named.

But back to Al Bernard, whose ghost suffers our digression, or perhaps finds diversion in it. Let us resume without the artifice of transition, which dignifies neither author, reader, nor ghost.

His Edison work included intriguing titles such as "O-Le-O-Lady," "Prancin' Dancin' Yodelin' Man," and a version of "Stavin' Chain." And let us not overlook what may be the finest of Bernard titles: "I Got Horses and Got Numbers on My Mind." He collaborated on several songs with J. Russel Robinson (1892–1963), the pianist whom Spencer Williams called "the white man with the colored fingers." Bernard and Robinson worked as a vaudeville team, the Dixie Stars, and recorded together for several companies, including Okeh. A pianist for the Original Dixieland Jazz Band and the Macon-born blues singer Lucille Hegamin (1894–1970), Robinson also accompanied Marion Harris in vaudeville. He was a co-author of the 1920 hit "Margie" and "The Ghost of the St. Louis Blues," which Miller recorded in 1929. Among Robinson's early compositions was "The Minstrel Man," a 1911 piano rag published by John Stark, the publisher of Joplin's "Maple Leaf Rag." Robinson dedicated it to "the Minstrel Boys of America."

In March of 1919 Bernard copyrighted an original composition called "Shake, Rattle and Roll," which he recorded for Edison several weeks later, on April 29. (Edison released the recording as a Blue Amberol cylinder, but not as a disc.) Bernard's publisher, the ever appropriative W. C. Handy, chiseled in on the copyright as arranger, but in June of that year a new copyright amended authorship to Alfred Bernard alone.

Bernard also recorded his "Shake, Rattle and Roll" for Okeh prior to Okeh becoming the label of the General Phonograph Corporation in 1919, and then again for Aeolian-Vocalion in 1919. (The Aeolian-Vocalion label, founded in New York in 1918, became simply Vocalian in 1921, when Brunswick-Balke-Collender took it over from the Aeolian Company.) Jesse Stone (1901–99), who some years later, under the name of Charles Calhoun, would write the 1954 hit "Shake, Rattle and Roll" for Big Joe Turner, was in his late teens and already in show business, involved in minstrelsy as well as in vaudeville, at the time of Bernard's record. The original "Shake, Rattle and Roll" was about shooting craps, and Bernard echoed it in "Plantation Scene," a two-part Columbia recording he made with Lasses White and Company in 1923, in which he utters the cry "Shake, rattle, and roll!" in reference to a throw of the dice during a crapshooting bit. The same phrase can be heard in the Excelsior Quartette's "Roll Them Bones" of 1922.

At the time of Bernard's "Shake, Rattle and Roll," Okeh was the record label of the Otto Heineman Phonograph Supply Company in New York; its logo featured, within the *O* of Okeh, the crude image of an American Indian in profile, remindful of the more aesthetic image that had been appearing on the face of American five-cent pieces since 1913.

The Talking Machine World, May 15, 1918: "Otto Heineman, president of the Otto Heineman Phonograph Supply Co., New York, announced this week that the company is now ready to place on the market the Heineman record, which will be known as the 'OkeH' record. This name is derived from the original Indian spelling of the term colloquially known as O.K., standing for 'all right.'" (This predates the *Oxford English Dictionary*'s earliest citation of *okay, okey,* or *okeh,* which is from H. L. Mencken's *The American Language,* published by Knopf in 1919: "Dr. Woodrow Wilson is said . . . to use *okeh* in endorsing government papers." Though the theory of a derivation from the Choctaw *oke,* or *okeh* according to the Heineman transliteration system, is discounted, *O.K.* itself is traced to 1839.)

The label of Bernard's "Shake, Rattle and Roll" also bears the description "Baritone with Xylophone Orchestra." When I first saw it, I thought of Turk McBee, the minstrel xylophonist who worked with our baritone, Emmett Miller.

The more I learn of Bernard, and the more I hear Bernard, the more it seems — more importantly, sounds — that Bernard was almost certainly an influence on Miller as a singer. Both singers recorded for Okeh in New York in 1928, when Bernard was part of a regular Tuesday-night radio minstrel show broadcast over WJZ. They may have known one another; they had at least one associate, Lasses White, in common.

As for other antecedents, one contemporary reviewer wrote that, "with his unusual voice, Miller will revive memories of J.K. Emmett and Nat Krefe [Matt Keefe?]." The first of these, Joseph Kline Emmett, whose real name was Kleinfelter, was a German-dialect musical-stage entertainer known for his yodeling "Lullaby"

(1878), from the show *Fritz, Our German Cousin.* So closely associated was J. K. Emmett with his lead role in this show that he came to be known as Fritz, and so closely associated was his song with him that it came to be known as "Emmett's Lullaby," under which name it was recorded for Edison by the yodeling singer George P. Watson in 1899. J. K. Emmett was born in St. Louis in 1841 and died in 1891. We have no way of knowing what he sounded like, and neither did Miller. As for Matt Keefe, we know little more than that he was an old-fashioned, Tyrolean-style yodeler active in minstrelsy in the first decade of the twentieth century.

The minstrelsy of the coon-song era was dead by the time Miller left Macon. There were still interlocutors and end-men, still a Tambo to the right and a Bones to left; but the olio, the musical miscellany at the heart of the show, had become a sort of vaudeville in blackface, a showcase of the newer sensibilities and songs of the day — and not always in blackface at that: minstrel-show acts such as the Kings of Harmony, the Dan Fitch vocal quartet in which Miller sang in 1924, performed *au naturel,* in full Caucasian splendor. Bessie Smith and other entertainers in the black minstrel troupes no longer blacked-up like their forebears.

Miller entered minstrelsy in the midst of its twilight, the midst of its desperate embrace of the changing currents of Tin Pan Alley and the Jazz Age, currents whose ultimate sources had included, perhaps foremost, minstrelsy itself. Even if he did perceive it as a dying embrace, he was flush with the excitement of it. It was the only minstrelsy he ever knew. Besides, it was not his death; it could not be. For he rose and he flourished. Those reviews in the fall of 1927: bemoaning minstrelsy's demise and hailing him. It was as if, for one glorious and electric moment, he was the phoenix born of minstrelsy's ashes.

Exceeding the ken of any influence or contemporary, Miller was the most singular emanation of that bizarre twilight fusion of blackface minstrelsy, Tin Pan Alley, and jazz — an emanation through which the forces of country music and the blues swirled as well.

But popular taste did not take widely to his brilliance, and attempts to make a more conventional singer of him — at the sessions of January 1929 — had proved unsuccessful. His records sold poorly, and it was not a time for poor-selling singers to be tolerated or sustained. If there was any question of his future in the autumn of 1929, it was settled by the events of Black Tuesday, October 29.

In September 1929, following the last Georgia Crackers session, Miller traveled south to Atlanta. The fifteenth annual convention of the Georgia Old-Time Fiddlers' Association would take place there at the city auditorium on the last Friday and Saturday of the month. The Okeh recording star Fiddlin' John Carson, a former champion, would compete against Gid Tanner, the present champion, and a slew of comers. Midweek before the convention, Miller joined Carson and others in recording a three-record Okeh release called "The Medicine Show." Aside from his 1931 comedy release "Sam's New Job," these were the only Miller recordings to be released in the Okeh 45000 hillbilly series.

The others involved in "The Medicine Show" were: Moonshine Kate (Rosa Lee Carson, Fiddlin' John's guitar-playing daughter); Narmour and Smith; Frank Hutchison; the Black Brothers; a piano-player here referred to as Bud Blue; and a hayseed-hokum master of ceremonies by the name of Martin Malloy, of whom nothing is known.

In the second of the records' six parts, Miller, introduced by the spieler Malloy as "that great blackface comedian," performs a brief comic monologue and sings a snatch of "I Ain't Got Nobody," accompanied by a pianist referred to as Bud Blue; in the fourth he does a routine with Blue.

In reality, Bud Blue was Seger Ellis (1906–95), who had recorded "Prairie Blues" for Victor in 1925, and would record it again, for Okeh, in 1930, the year in which Okeh honored Ellis with custom-label status: the words "exclusive artist" curved beneath the spindle-hole, his name in art-deco lettering to the left, a photographic portrait of him to the right. Here on "The Medicine Show," when "that famous piano-player Bud Blue" plays "part of his famous 'Prairie Blues,'" Miller interjects a bit of in-character gibber.

In his routine with Miller, Ellis as Blue adopts a minstrelsy voice. In an exchange with Moonshine Kate, he uses his straight voice to portray a peeved candy vendor threatening to spank a conniving young customer.

"Don't you know it don't do any good to spank a girl over sixteen?" teases Kate.

"I know, but it'd be a lot of fun."

In the fourth part, Ellis as Blue joins Miller in another little routine, an early version of the joke — punchline: "What time will your wife be at home?" — that would be told half a century later by Robert De Niro as Jake LaMotta onstage in Miami in *Raging Bull*.

Miller does a brief routine in the fifth part, and, near the end of the sixth and final part, a comic exchange with Moonshine Kate is followed by an abbreviated rendition of "I Ain't Got Nobody" with Ellis as Blue on piano.

For one of their numbers, the Black Brothers, Jim and Joe, do "Oh, Dem Golden Slippers," the James A. Bland minstrel song from 1879.

These recordings may be considered epoch-making in that they seem to represent the first known use of canned laughter. In fact, the whole affair sounds sort of canned, as if pieced together to simulate the seamless gathering that it pretends to be. "The Medicine Show" is believed to have been recorded in Atlanta on September 24. It seems right for John Carson to have been in Atlanta, where the fiddlers' convention was to begin on the 27th; and there is no doubt as to the reality of his interaction here with Frank Hutchison or with Moonshine Kate, or of Kate's interaction with Miller or with Ellis, for whom no other recording activity is known between his New York sessions of August 26–27 (accompanied by Louis Armstrong, the Dorseys, Stan King, Eddie Lang, Arthur Schutt, and Joe Venuti) and October 11 (accompanied by Lang, Hoagy Carmichael, and others).

But the Okeh files also indicate that Narmour and Smith were recording in New York on the very next day, September 25. If their participation in "The Medicine Show" was indeed recorded in Atlanta, why then would they have undertaken a long train journey just to record again in New York the following day, rather than remain in Atlanta, where recording facilities were in place? On that day in New York, they recorded the breakdown "Sweet Milk and Peaches," also featured in "The Medicine Show."

In the way of a cursory glance at the tenuously mingled mists of Bud Blue, Seger Ellis, and the Georgia Crackers: Buddy Blue, Bud Blue and His Orchestra, and Bud, or Buddy, Blue and His Texans were pseudonyms employed in 1929–30 by both Okeh and the American Record Corporation family of budget labels for various releases by diverse New York studio groups, usually led by pianist Fred Rich and featuring singer Smith Ballew. Several musicians who recorded with Emmett Miller — the Dorseys, Stan King, Leo McConville, and Arthur Schutt — played on records Ballew made under his own name in 1929–30; the Dorseys and Lang accompanied Ballew on 1930 recordings by Ballew released under the names of the Embassy Dance Orchestra and Buddy Blue and His Texans; and Ballew sang on records made by the Dorsey Brothers' Orchestra in 1928–29. During the summer of 1929, the Dorseys and two other musicians who played as Georgia Crackers, Leo McConville and Joe Tarto, were under contract to Fred Rich, the director of the CBS house band. Seger Ellis, under contract to Okeh from the fall of 1926 to the fall of 1930, sang with Rich in 1927 and with the

Dorsey Brothers' Orchestra in 1928. The Dorseys, King, Schutt, and Lang, played with Ellis on recordings made for Okeh under his own name in 1928–29, as for example his New York sessions of August 1929, mentioned above; and they appeared with him, too, in a 1929 Vitaphone short. As a vocalist, Ellis sang in the high, sweet, almost ladylike style of Gene Austin.

I talked to Ellis in 1976, trying to elicit what memories of Miller I could.

"I was under contract to Okeh at the time he recorded," he told me. "He used to do a lot of yodeling, right? He was probably in his late twenties or maybe early thirties then. I think he was about a medium-sized man, a little on the plump side, if I remember correctly. I think he was balding. He'd lost most of his hair, or a lot of it. And he was definitely from the South, either Texas or Arkansas, I believe. I'm not sure. I only met him the one time. He had a big seller. I can't remember the name of it. He was no kid at the time; he'd been battling around for a long time. He happened to make this one record for Okeh and it sold real big and they got him back for another one, and the next session he didn't have anything that moved at all. And that was sort of the end of him. I think he played some guitar, but not on record.

"He was a fun-loving guy, it seems. He was also sort of a loner, as far as I know. I don't know anybody who knew him real well. They didn't even know him real well around Okeh, I don't believe."

Referring to the Dorseys, Ellis assured me that Miller's music "wasn't the kind of stuff they wanted to play. It was just a record date to them. It would've been Justin Ring's idea. He was musical director down at Okeh, and he practically A&R'd everybody's dates. He's dead now."

I asked Seger if Miller was considered a jazz singer or a country singer. "Oh, definitely country."

As far as memories of Emmett Miller went, this was about as fruitful and as illuminating as it got.

"The Medicine Show" represented something different for Miller. Perhaps he could have gained further entrée into country music, where coon songs were still current and parameters still inchoate. In an advertisement for the first disc of "The Medicine Show" in the November 1929 *Talking Machine World & Radio-Music Merchant,* Okeh gave Miller lead billing over the other acts. But any further venturing by Okeh regarding Miller's musical career would not be forthcoming. In October 1929, the month after the Atlanta sessions, the month that Jonathan Cape and Harrison Smith published *The Sound and the Fury,* the stock market suffered its worst crash since the fall of 1869. During the course of the depression that followed, even the biggest stars of the day would suffer. Paul Whiteman, the most popular bandleader of the era, could no longer meet his nine-grand weekly payroll; *King of Jazz* in 1930 showed a trimmed-down Whiteman orchestra, and further attrition led to the departure of Eddie Lang and others. Record sales, which had reached a hundred and four million in 1927, would fall to six million in 1932.

By then Emmett Miller was a fading memory. In March 1930 — the month that Okeh released "The Pickaninnies [*sic*] Paradise" c/w "The Blues Singer (from Alabam')" — he appeared at the Metropolitan in Atlanta, in a small vaudeville program that was given bottom billing beneath the "all-talking feature" *The Great Divide,* starring Myrna Loy, and a musical stage comedy called *Pardon Me,* starring local player Att "Skinny" Candler: four shows daily, with a top ticket price of fifty cents for the evening shows. Miller was not even mentioned in the theater's ads, which featured Candler's name and the promise of "Girls! Girls! Snappiest Girl Show in Town."

The music for the Metropolitan shows was provided by the band of Rudy Brown, who was associated with radio station WSB. Candler's "miniature musical comedy troupe" at this time also had a WSB program, a half hour every Monday night; and it is likely that Miller, whom Candler's business manager, Jim Eviston, considered "an added attraction," joined them on radio as a guest. The other added attraction with Miller was Sid Snap, billed as the Dancing Flash.

Little more than three years before, the Atlanta papers had praised Miller's blackface. Now they praised real black faces. King Vidor's "sensational all-negro drama," *Hallelujah,* premiered at the Loew's Grand in April 1930, while Miller was scuffling at the Metropolitan. The *Atlanta Journal* described the picture as offering "a barbaric rhythmic symphony of soul-touching spirituals and captivating blues," and declared it to be "amazing."

On October 17, 1930, Miller made his final Okeh recordings, four last blackface-dialogue sides, this time with Pick Maloney: "Sam and Bill at the Graveyard," "The Licker Taster," and a two-part routine called "Sam's New Job." The first of these, the graveyard bit, was a variation of an old medicine-show skit known as "Over the River, Charlie," an echo of which could be heard as well in "Next Week, Sometime," a 1905 song by Bert Williams and Chris Smith.

"We are now outside the cemetery," says Bill.

"Do you mean where the dead folk live?" says Sam.

As Bill explains, Sadie Dolittle's grandpappy was buried a few weeks ago without the benefit of baptism. Sam and Bill have been enlisted to exhume the corpse and set it right with God.

"I ain't gonna mess around inside no skull orchard," Sam objects.

Bill reminds him of the twenty-five dollars and quart of gin that they are to be paid. Sam is willing to forfeit the money, but the booze is tempting.

"You know the po' man cain't go to heaven till you dig him up and baptize him," says Bill, who plans to wait outside the cemetery walls while Sam does the job. But in the end, even the lure of the booze may not be great enough to overwhelm Sam's fear, and the deed remains undone.

The dark comic sensibility of "Sam and Bill at the Graveyard" is not so far removed from that of Faulkner, whose dialect humor often bears no little affinity to blackface. Faulkner was a man for a punchline: *As I Lay Dying* and *The Wild Palms* are great punchlines as well as great literature. At the heart of *The Reivers* is an element — the "sour dean" bit — cut from the cloth of blackface dialogue. Published in 1962, a month before his death, it makes of him one of the last, certainly one of the greatest, purveyors of such.

Amid the turbulent crosscurrents of *The Sound and the Fury,* there lies a statement that says much about the far murkier and more turbulent crosscurrents of white men in blackface, of black men in blackface, of white men in whiteface, of black men in whiteface; of black and of white, and of the common night they were born into, of the domain of that night, that deadly delusion called human nature, that man-made designation by which man sets himself apart from nature itself. The line: "That was when I realised that a nigger is not a person so much as a form of behaviour; a sort of obverse reflection of the white people he lives among."

Faulkner was no stranger to minstrelsy, jazz, the blues, or blackface comedy. Ford's Minstrels and W. C. Handy were as much a part of his youth as the canon of Western literature (which for him, as we have seen, may have included *Eneas Africanus* as well as the *Aeneid*); and he himself was a singer both of "Carry Me Back to Old Virginny" and "I Can't Give You Anything but Love."

The Sound and the Fury of 1929, the Georgia Crackers recordings of 1928–29: they are strange and wonderful cries, no matter how disparate, of the same strange and wonderful day, of a dying South and of things to come. It is said that Faulkner played over and over again a record of "Rhapsody in Blue" as he churned out *Sanctuary.* Maybe the Georgia Crackers provided the background for something else.

I remember rummaging through Faulkner's house in Oxford, Mississippi, many years ago, before it had been gussied up, entrusted to curators, and given the full landmark treatment. I remember finding there, lying in a dusty corner, a 45-rpm copy of the 1950 RCA-Victor recording of "Rudolph the Red-Nosed Reindeer" by Spike Jones and His City Slickers.

It was in *Flags in the Dust,* written in 1927 — *that year:* the year that Furry Lewis, Jimmie Rodgers, and so many other luminous voices came to be heard; the year of Emmett Miller's glory; the year of the great flood of the Mississippi, the great flood of the Delta, the great flood, ignivomous and exundant, which seemed to sunder the chthonic sacrarium, κτύπησε Ζευς χθόνιος, and bring forth the *tombaroli,* the holy grave-robbers and thieves; to loose the cestus of Mystis, sweet tectonic mama, and raise, in skirl and sigh and yodel and moan, in epiclesis, in *aestus,* in quietus — *stile vecchio, stile duro, stile nuovo* — the tessitura of it all, the dark and myriad-voiced antediluvian song and resurrection in the light of new morning, *matutina lux,* Viva-tonal and electric, wild-souled and endlessly rocking — in that year that William Faulkner of Mississippi, now, after two terrible novels, writing at last in his own true voice, saw it, heard it, captured it:

"Against the wall squatting a blind negro beggar with a guitar and a wire frame holding a mouthorgan to his lips, patterned the background of smells and sounds with a plaintive reiteration of rich monotonous chords, rhythmic as a mathematical formula but without music. He was a man of at least forty and his was the patient resignation of many sightless years, yet he too wore filthy khaki with a corporal's stripes on one sleeve and a crookedly sewn Boy Scout emblem on the other, and on his breast a button commemorating the fourth Liberty Loan and a small metal brooch bearing two gold stars, obviously intended for female adornment. His weathered derby was encircled by an officer's hat cord, and on the pavement between his feet sat a tin cup containing a dime and three pennies."

But Faulkner knew that it was all as nothing before the ineffable, without beginning or end: "then once more the guitar and mouth-organ resumed their blended pattern."

And there is the monkey-gland connection.

In the spring of 1929, working toward the end of *Sanctuary,* Faulkner had his character Miss Myrtle say: "Maybe he went off and got fixed with one of these glands, these monkey glands, and it quit on him."

Surely all but a sheltered few who read *Sanctuary* upon its first publication, in 1931, understood Miss Myrtle's remark. But, with the passing of many years, the meaning of her allusion lapsed into obscurity, as the ingestion of animal glands, and the implanting of them in the human scrotum, lapsed likewise into obscurity as a method of treating impotence.

The U.S. Food and Drug Administration and the American Medical Association began cracking down in earnest on animal-gland quackery in 1935, when, in June of that year, Dr. John R. Brinkley, the goat-gland king, lost his license to practice medicine. But for more than a dozen years, the curative powers of goat and monkey glands had been widely and firmly held to be effective. As stately a source as the fourteenth edition of the *Encyclopaedia Britannica* declared, in 1929, that "The grafting into men of testicles from apes (the so-called 'monkey glands') has been practiced by Voronoff and others with resulting rejuvenation." Through the medical practice of Serge Voronoff, a Russian emigrant to France, the African possessions of France, Britain, and Belgium were largely depleted of anthropoids, which he used to perform his gland-transplantation operations on a wealthy European clientele.

Faulkner was not the first literary man to mention monkey glands. In the 1924 introduction to his play *Saint Joan,* George Bernard Shaw spoke of "weekly doses of monkey gland" as a fortification against old age, and posed the question, "Which is the healthier mind? the saintly mind or the monkey gland mind?"

One of the most interesting references to monkey glands was made by Jimmie Davis. Born in Jackson Parish, northern Louisiana, in 1902, Davis was a city-slick country singer who performed somewhat in the style of Jimmie Rodgers. Davis eventually made his mark and his fortune with his 1939 recording of "You Are My Sunshine," and went on to serve two terms as the governor of Louisiana. He was, however, still relatively unknown when, in November 1932, at the Victor studio in Camden, New Jersey, he recorded his "Organ-Grinder Blues":

> *Gonna get me some monkey glands,*
> *Be like I used to was;*
> *Gonna run these mamas down*
> *Like a Dominicker rooster does.*

(As pertains to the smiting grammatical construction "used to was," the smitten are directed to the 1923 edition of Edward Gepp's *Essex Dialect Dictionary,* which alone treats of it. An American literary antecedent to Davis's usage is to be found in *Major Jones's Sketches of Travel,* the 1847 collection of Southern-dialect tales by William Tappan Thompson, who, like his associate and elder A. B. Longstreet, was known for his portrayals of the Georgia cracker: "Augusty's a monstrous pretty city; but it ain't the place it used to was." The construction is also to be found in the surviving letter of a freed slave, one Jourdan Anderson, writing from Dayton, Ohio, to his former master, Colonel P. H. Anderson, in Big Spring, Tennessee. This quite literate letter, dated August 7, 1865, is in reply to an invitation to return to work on the old plantation: "Sometimes we overhear others saying, 'The colored people were slaves' down in Tennessee. The children feel hurt when they hear such remarks, but I tell them it was no disgrace in Tennessee to belong to Col. Anderson. Many darkies would have been proud, as I used to was, to call you master. Now, if you will write and say what wages you will give me, I will be better able to decide whether it would be to my advantage to move back again. . . .")

In his 1935 "Good Liquor Gonna Carry Me Down," Big Bill Broonzy tells of "a little girl 'bout sixteen years old" who promises to satisfy his soul if only he quits drinking. Big Bill continues to "wake up in the mornin' holdin' a bottle tight."

> *Yes, I went to the doctor with my head in my hands,*
> *The doctor said, "Big Bill, I think I'll have to give*
> *you monkey glands."*

The age of monkey glands lingered dimly on. Headlined FOR MEN ONLY, a full-page advertisement in the *New York Daily News* of July 8, 1983, proclaimed the wondrous powers of Testorex-35. "In many cultures around the world," the advertisement explained, "the male sex glands of certain animals are consumed to enhance the stamina and potency for men who do not perform satisfactorily."

From William Cuthbert Faulkner (1897–1962) to William Lee Conley Broonzy (1893–1958), born in Mississippi a few years and a few counties apart.

"Then once more the guitar and mouthorgan resumed their blended pattern."

Elective glandular affinities. Booze, monkey glands, chords of words, chords of sound.

From Sara Martin and Clarence Williams's 1923 duet "Monkey Man Blues" to the Rolling Stones' 1969 "Monkey Man." Chords of words and sound. Iggy Pop, "Corruption," 1999: "Speak, monkey, speak."

It is the monkey man that seeketh the monkey gland. It is the every man of every race that seeketh monkey-juice.

In "The Licker Taster," a slick-talking Pick Maloney encounters a benighted Emmett Miller.

"Whatchoo got in that box?" he asks.

"Licker."

"Well, where'd you git it?"

"From the man down to the bootleg sto'."

Maloney explains that the booze "might contain poison." He raises the specters of death and blindness, says that folks all over have been falling victim to bad Prohibition rotgut. "Last week down at *At*-lanta, fifteen men died from drinkin' wood alcohol"; another twenty-four died "right here today." He explains that he is a government-paid liquor-taster, whose job it is to test for the presence of wood alcohol. In addition to his salary, he is paid fifty cents per sip. Thus he cons his hapless victim into paying him to guzzle away his booze.

In "Sam's New Job," the protagonist — at one point addressed fully as Samuel Johnson Jackson Lee — is asked by an employment interviewer where he was born.

"Georgia, captain, Georgia," Sam says.

Where in Georgia?

Sam garbles a muddle of phonemes that brings to mind the town name of Chattahoochee but is not: "Calliepousa." The blackface Yoknapatawpha.

"How do you spell that?"

"Just put down 'Rome.'"

One joke centers on a misunderstanding of the word "forefathers" as "four fathers" — an old routine that had already turned up in "Evolution," a Cameo recording by the Charcoal Twins.

The second part of "Sam's New Job" echoes the dead-wife bit from "Sam and His Family."

In November *Billboard* reported that Miller and Maloney had been "sighted and spoken on Broadway," and that "Miller was walking with a cane, just out of an auto wreck."

It was at this time that Okeh issued the last of the Georgia Crackers records, "God's River" c/w "That's the Good Old Sunny South," followed on November 25 by "Sam and Bill at the Graveyard" c/w "The Licker Taster."

In 1931 — the year that Louis Armstrong recorded the old minstrel song "Shine" (he would perform it the following year dressed in a tribal leopard skin in the Paramount short *Rhapsody in Black and Blue*) — two Columbus, Ohio, businessmen, Walter J. Redhill and G. C. Bradford, leased from Al G. Field's widow the rights to the name of the defunct Al G. Field Minstrels. In June of that year, Miller joined the troupe, with rehearsals scheduled to begin in Cincinnati in July.

The Honey Boy Minstrels had shut down in the spring. "I am not licked," declared John W. Vogel, who ran the Honey Boy outfit. "I am going to organize a big colored minstrel show, John W. Vogel's Afro-American Mastadon Minstrel Festival, and will give the public an old-fashioned colored minstrel show, such as they had in the days of Hicks & Sawyers, Callender and the Original Georgia Minstrels under the management of Richards and Pringle."

Vogel's determination notwithstanding, the only remaining major minstrel troupe still touring in the summer of 1931 was the John R. Van Arnam Minstrels, then in its twelfth year and travelling at this time through upstate New York and New England. The youngest member of the show was Turk McBee, Jr., whom Van Arnam praised as one of the company's most versatile performers. "Not at all surprising to see the kid spreading himself all over the stage," commented *Billboard.* "Turk Jr. is a natural born 'nigger singer.' He was born in a minstrel family. His father and his uncle were drummers 'way back in the days when the biggest road troupes vied with each other in featuring a star drummer." Billed as "The Latest Sensation on the Xylophone," McBee also performed as a partner with a comedian named Jimmy Leamy.

Minstrelsy was in such dire straits by this time that a preservation society of sorts, the National Minstrel Players and Fans Association, had been formed to uphold its remains. Organized in the summer of 1930, the association was part fraternity and part public-relations coalition. Its secretary, Robert Reed, helped to fill the space of *Billboard*'s ailing and shrinking "Minstrelsy" column with a complementary column called "NMP&FA Notes," which consisted largely of the past and halfhearted shorings of optimism for the future.

"Welcome into membership greetings last week went to our good friends Emmett Miller and Blackface Eddie Ross, both of whom will shortly be found trouping under the new Al G. Field Minstrels banner," reported Reed in July.

An intriguing item in *Billboard* states that on July 12, four days before his first rehearsal with the revived Field troupe, Miller traveled from Cincinnati to New York, "to make another song record." The item also states that "Emmett has two previous phonograph records (Victor) to his credit." According to a subsequent item, published in *Billboard* two weeks later: "Emmett Miller celebrated the opening of his tour with the Al G. Field Minstrels by making two more phonograph records for Columbia and Okeh. Titles of the numbers are *Don't Worry About Me* and *Lone, Sick Blues.*"

What is to be made of these reports? The references to "two

previous phonograph records" on Victor can be explained as simple error; but what of these alleged new recordings themselves? The first title suggests "Don't Worry 'bout Me," a song by Ted Koehler and Rube Bloom that would not be copyrighted until 1939; the second suggests yet another recording of "Lovesick Blues." But no other evidence of these recordings has been found.

The *Billboard* of July 25 contains an item captioned "Funny Country, I Tella Ya." It reads: "Signors Antonio Baglioni and Enrico Casazza, Italian businessmen visiting Cincinnati, stood in the lobby of the Fort Washington Hotel the other day surveying with curious eyes about 30 members of the Al G. Field outfit, who were about to start out for rehearsal.

"Signor Casazza approached Walter Redhill. 'Deesa gentlemen, who they are, please you tella me?' he inquired."

Redhill explains that the gentlemen are minstrels: "Talk, sing, dance, all sorts of nigger tricks."

Casazza conveys this explanation to Baglioni, who says: "Whatta I tell you? Damma funny country."

This somehow brings to mind James Bevacqua, the son of Calabrian immigrants, who performed in blackface as Jimmy Vee; somehow brings to mind Frank Mazziotta's 1902 Columbia recording of "Nigger Fever"; somehow brings to mind Lou Monte's 1954 version of "The Darktown Strutters' Ball," or Louis Prima's Italo-Yiddish rendition of same. Or maybe Big Walter's "Hello Maria." Or old Aunt Jemima herself, one of the rare female blackface acts of vaudeville: her real name was Tess Gardella; she was born in Wilkes Barre, Pennsylvania, in 1898, died in Brooklyn in 1950.

Aunt Jemima, like Parson Brown and Deacon Jones, with whom she cavorts in "Alabama Jubilee," was a stock figure of the black songster tradition dating to the nineteenth century; and she entered popular iconography and pancake mythology through a song, "Old Aunt Jemima," written and first performed in 1875 by the black minstrel Billy Kersands, who, it has been suggested, adapted it from an actual slave song of the antebellum work-fields.

"Adapted" may not be quite the proper word. Kersands, after all, though black, was a young New Yorker whose firsthand knowledge of the work-songs of slaves was likely less than that of many of the older, Southern minstrels, white as well as black, with whom he worked. Thus, if the song was indeed "adapted," it was probably done so indirectly, from a source, either black or white, among his fellow minstrels, or from an encounter with a workaday black unwise to the ways of show business or to the sort of money that Kersands was pulling down. Whatever the truth, the song became one of Kersands's more popular pieces, and it was taken up by other entertainers.

In the fall of 1889 in St. Joseph, Missouri, the song was being performed by the blackface vaudeville team of Baker and Farrell — one of them in proto-Jemima drag — when it was heard by Chris Rutt, a man in search of a name for his new self-rising pancake mix. Within a few months, Rutt sold out his Aunt Jemima pancake mix to the R. T. Davis Milling Company; and at the 1893 World's Columbian Exposition in Chicago, Davis brought Aunt Jemima to life in the person of one Nancy Green, a Kentucky woman who was then working in Chicago as a domestic cook. As Aunt Jemima, Green toured the country promoting the pancake flour of that name until 1923, when she was killed in an automobile accident at the age of eighty-nine. The Standard Quartette, one of the early black vocal groups, recorded a Columbia cylinder of "Old Aunt Jemima" in about 1895.

The Jemima bandanna was a raiment of sloth as well as of industry of hearth. The bluesman known as Peetie Wheatstraw (1902–41) complained in "Doin' the Best I Can" (1934) of the lazy, non-self-rising mate, the Anti-Jemima, who lay abed with a rag tied round her head: a complaint echoed more than forty years later, in

"Sick and Tired," a minor R&B hit for Chris Kenner in 1957 and for Fats Domino in 1958.

Following rehearsals at the Cincinnati Eagles Hall on Walnut Street and preliminary shows on July 30–31 in the suburb of Norwood, the 45th edition of the Field Minstrels opened in Dayton, the first stop in what was envisioned as a truck tour of twenty-three states east of the Mississippi.

The cast of forty-eight starred Miller and Eddie Ross, included twenty-seven instrumentalists, a female impersonator, and the yodeler Al Tint ("Novelty Surprise"). With an eighty-minute first part, a battery of ten end-men, a vocal quartet, and a twelve-act olio, the lengthy production, according to *Billboard,* inspired one troupe member to remark during rehearsal, "I'm telling you boys, this is the only minstrel production of Eugene O'Neill's *Strange Interlude* ever attempted." A featured element was the afterpiece produced by Miller, whom the *Cincinnati Post* described as "the clarinet-voiced comedian." This afterpiece was "The Abode of the Spirits," from the Field show of 1927.

There exists a transcribed shard of Miller's end-man performance this summer with interlocutor Leslie Berry, the sixteen-year veteran of the Field Minstrels who had previously worked with Miller in the 1926–27 Field shows:

L.B.: "You look like ten dollars."

E.M.: "Who? Me?"

L.B.: "Certainly. I am referring to you. Bright as a gold piece. And an Eagle is a gold piece. Don't you remember the table you learned at school? Ten mills, one cent; 10 cents, one dime; 10 dimes, $1; $10, one eagle."

E.M.: "Well, hush my mouf. But that ain't the way we learned it in my school, Mr. Berry. 'Ten mills, one cent; 10 cents, one drink; 10 drinks, one drunk; one drunk, 10 days.'"

Another:

L.B: "I suppose you read in todays's papers about the big robbery on Main Street, Emmett?"

E.M.: "Says which?"

L.B.: "The big robbery. You don't mean to admit that you don't read the newspapers?"

E.M.: "I don't read 'em. Robberies don't mean nothin' to me, Mr. Berry. I can see a robbery every Saturday just by lookin' at you drawin' your salary."

And another:

L.B.: "Emmett, what has become of our old friend, Mose Stein, who used to lead the orchestra in the Southern country?"

E.M.: "I haven't lost any orchestra leaders, Mr. Berry, and I ain't lookin' for any. But if you've got to find this one Pharaoh's daughter might hand you a bit of info."

L.B.: "Now what in the world has Pharaoh's daughter got to do with the simple question I asked you? I am asking where is Moses Stein? Do you know?"

E.M.: "No, but I got my suspicions."

L.B.: "Ridiculous! You've got your suspicions!"

E.M.: "Yeah. I read in *The Billboard* that Bob Reed has been throwin' parties for minstrel men at his home in Cleveland and I noticed that Charlie Rush and his missus was among those present."

L.B.: "Nonsense, man. What has Bob Reed's parties in Cleveland to do with the whereabouts of Moses Stein?"

E.M.: "Well, Mr. Berry, that's where Pharaoh's daughter found her Moses — among the Reeds and Rushes."

It could not get much worse than this: a humor of stillborn lines and rictus grins.

Before the tour was under way, *Billboard* had optimistically declared, "Minstrel boys show plenty of pep. All enthusiastic and rarin' to go"; and at its outset Robert Reed of the National Minstrel Players and Fans Association foresaw a new day, with the Field tour affording "the American people the first opportunity in many years to witness the presentation of minstrelsy on a scale established by Primrose & West, Dockstader, Neil O'Brien, Honeyboy Evans and others of yesteryear." Reed urged that "Minstrel Association members everywhere are requested to extend every possible co-operation in this reviving of minstrelsy interest by assisting the management of all minstrel productions which may visit their respective communities to the end that their visit may be successful."

In his following column, Reed observed, "Certainly, minstrelsy is on the upward climb. With John R. Van Arnam's Minstrels touring New England and the Field outfit now launched on its 45th tour of the nation, who is there that can offer dispute when we state that minstrelsy is coming back?" He concluded with a note of triumphant optimism: "Minstrels of 1931 — Al G. Field, John R. Van Arnam, Byron Gosh, all touring; who next? Yes, there will be more."

That note of optimism was struck in the *Billboard* of August 29. By then the Field revival was dead. Its obituary appeared in the magazine's next issue:

"Echoes of the flop of Bradford and Redhill's edition of the Al G. Field Minstrels are coming in from many points. Some of the boys who paid fares to join and suffered physical discomforts, as well as the loss of salary, are very bitter in denunciation of the managers who attempted to float the show without sufficient funds to justify the venture. Others, among them the heaviest salary losers, are inclined to laugh it off and charge their losses to experience."

Leaving Cincinnati on August 1, the troupe had made it intact as far as Toledo, where the show fell apart. Remnants of the troupe, after the parting of the owners, had organized an impromptu show at Defiance, Ohio, on August 26, then took refuge as a straggling band at Luna Park, Michigan.

A week after its report of the Field show's demise, *Billboard,* in its issue of September 12, observed that "Emmett Miller, star comedian of the late Al G. Field Minstrels has been a conspicuous figure in the Cincinnati theatrical colony since the closing of the Field show. He will probably play the picture houses in the South this fall. Last report he was negotiating a season in the Publix theaters in Georgia and Florida."

And in its next issue: "Emmett Miller, featured comedian and endman of the last and least edition of the Al G. Field Minstrels, was in Lexington, Ky., last week, where he met with several other veterans of the memorable minstrel campaign of last August. The conference ended with the singing of the old minstrel song, *The Ghost That Couldn't Learn To Talk.*"

On October 25, 1931, Okeh released, in its hillbilly series, the last of its Emmett Miller records, "Sam's New Job," a two-part routine with Pick Maloney. In mid-November Miller met in Lexington, Kentucky, with other performers from the recent Field fiasco: a gathering of shades.

On November 20 and 21 he performed at the State Theater in Winston-Salem, three shows a day, sharing the bill with a low-budget horse-racing picture called *Sweepstakes* and an episode of a serial called *Danger Island.*

This was the fate of many minstrel men. In 1930 Al Tint, the Yodeling Minstrel, had written to *Billboard:* "Had the pleasure of working on the same bill with Jimmie Rodgers, blues yodeler, in his act on the screen, *The Singing Brakeman.* . . . I followed right on after his picture in person and duplicated some of my yodeling. . . ." Not long after, Rodgers himself wrote to *Billboard,* from Houston: "I spent last night over in Lufkin and ran into my old friend, Lasses White, this morning. . . . Just bought myself a new seven-passenger car, and have all my recording for Victor finished until next February. . . . Hello, to the minstrel gang."

Continuing to play movie houses, Miller organized his own revue. In early 1932 *Emmett Miller and His Varieties of 1932* wound its way through the South on a tour of the Publix circuit. It was a company of twenty, also featuring Bobby Dyer, who worked as Miller's comedy partner, the dancers Lucille and Sterberg, and Chet Robinson and his Southern Syncopators. There were two days, February 10–11, at the Baker-Grand in Natchez. By early March, in Jackson, the five-piece Robertson band were being billed as Chet Robertson and his Georgia Crackers, an echo of Miller's glory days a few short years and a total eclipse of fortune ago. Within a month, they would become the Southern Syncopators once again.

In Biloxi, Miller was photographed at an exhibition baseball game between the Brooklyn Dodgers and the Washington Senators. The picture was published in the *Billboard* of April 16: "Left to right: Emmett Miller; Casey Stengel, Brooklyn Coach; Mayor Kennedy of Biloxi; Bobby Dyer; Walter Johnson, manager Washington Senators; Clark Griffith, owner Washington Senators; Al Schacht, baseballdom's chief funmaker (reclining); Judge Landis; Melvin Trayler; Max Carey, manager Brooklyn Dodgers, and Commissioner Swancey of Biloxi."

On April 9, Miller and his *Varieties* opened at the Majestic Theater in Shreveport.

Robert Reed, secretary of the National Minstrel Players and

Fans Association, closed his column in the *Billboard* of April 23, 1932, with a prediction: "Before we know it half a dozen minstrel shows will be trouping again."

The same issue published a dispatch from Lasses White in Shreveport, where he was putting on a show for the Shrine Temple: "I had the pleasure of seeing Emmett Miller and his *Varieties of 1932* show here last night. I enjoyed it very much. Miller is working fine and dandy, also Bobby Dyer, Chet Robinson and all the whole cast. The show opened here to capacity business and everyone here seemed pleased. I went backstage to see Miller and the bunch and we, of course, had a long talk about minstrelsy, and some of our experiences in same. The flesh shows seem to be taking a good foothold down in this section. No doubt next season will see more of them."

Lasses White was more fortunate than his fellow Field alumnus, more fortunate indeed than many blackface performers. As noted above, he had found radio work on WSM, Nashville, in the fall of 1930, and he would remain at WSM through 1936, when he moved to Hollywood. But he was not alone in his survival. As also noted above, Bert Swor, another star who preceded Miller in the Field troupe, made several movies. He worked on Broadway in 1931, on NBC radio in 1937. He even worked in blackface as late as 1941, onstage in Dallas, where he lived. He was still working two years later, when he was found dead in a Tulsa hotel room.

In the *Billboard* of June 18, 1932 — by this time Robert Reed and his voice of optimism had vanished, along with the National Minstrel Players and Fans Association — it was reported that "Emmett Miller turned up in Chicago about a week ago, where he encountered Al Tint, Roy Francis and other survivors of the Al G. Field Minstrels. Miller was looking for hoofers for his latest unit. Tint and Francis piloted him to the minstrel men's rendezvous and gave him the pick of the at liberty army. Miller has been working thru the winter and early spring months in Dixieland with units playing the picture houses."

The demise of blackface minstrelsy coincided with the growth of a more pernicious phenomenon, as the white aristocracy's patronizing vogue for negritude bloomed into a new and different minstrelsy in which "real" blacks became the "picks" of high society. Carl Van Vechten, the *Vanity Fair* dandy whom James Weldon Johnson described as the cultural commentator "who first pointed out that the blues-singers were artists," can be seen as a pioneer of the new, deadpan minstrelsy through *Vanity Fair* articles that he wrote on the blues in 1925 and 1926: highfalutin metaphrasing from on high of *Variety*'s earlier, laconic observation that "only a Negro can do justice to the native indigo ditties." It is interesting that James Weldon Johnson, a black man born in 1871, sees minstrelsy through benevolent eyes, while Van Vechten, a white man born in 1870, embraces and delights in the suffering of blacks, which he perceives as true and deep in the artifice of the commercially-calculated compositions and performances of black, urban jazz-blues. "It was the real thing," Van Vechten said of a performance by Bessie Smith: "a woman cutting her heart open with a knife." Her extraordinary skills as a sophisticated entertainer, honed as a performer with the Rabbit Foot minstrelsy troupe, are invisible to Van Vechten, whose willful eyes see only the "real" pain of a real black singer baring her soul as if cutting open her heart with a knife. A delight in the farce of blackface minstrelsy has given way to a delight in the sufferings of black souls. From delight in the caricature of the happy darky of bygone days to delight in the caricature of the suffering Negro — which is the more perverse?

There is a glimpse that tells much. On a spring night in 1928, Van Vechten pressured Bessie Smith to perform at his fancy Fifty-eighth Street apartment for a party of his upper-crust whitebread society friends. Smith, who could buy or sell anyone there, and who could outclass them all, knew very well why she was there: to play the nigger for these dilettantes. When her command performance was done, she made for her freedom from the "real" to the real. On her way out, Van Vechten's wife, the actress Fania Marinoff, attempted to give Bessie a tepid embrace.

"Get the fuck away from me! I never heard of such shit!" Bessie snarled, then knocked the haughty little lily-white bitch to the floor.

Bessie clearly was not offended by the notion of one woman embracing another; she had chased down and had her way with almost as many women as she had men.

Van Vechten aided his wife to her feet, then followed Bessie to the door. "It's all right, Miss Smith," he said timidly, "you were magnificent tonight."

The Ivy League teacher and cultural historian Ann Douglas includes an account of this night in her 1995 book, *Terrible Honesty: Mongrel Manhattan in the 1920s.* "White manners were on the occasion, I think, more impressive," she commented, "than black rudeness."

White manners? Black rudeness? What about human dignity, the real versus the "real," and a lead pipe up the ass of condescending hypocrisy? As Bessie told the story: "You should have seen them ofays lookin' at me like I was some kind of singin' monkey."

Negro: An Anthology Collected and Edited by Nancy Cunard was a milestone in, and monument to, the new, intellectualized minstrelsy. Published in 1934, Cunard's 854-page anthology presented black expression in what now would be an impermissibly patronizing context, together with white monkey-show perceptions of that new-minstrelsy olio that eventually would come to be called "the black experience." That her beneficent sentiments and intentions were, like Van Vechten's, sincere, proves only the sincerity of the condescension that was the bedrock underlying those sentiments and intentions.

Nancy Cunard was a shipping heiress who luxuriated amid the expatriates of Paris, where she took as her lover a black jazz pianist named Henry Crowder. As a publisher and patroness of the arts, she brought out through her Hours Press *A Draft of XXX Cantos,* lavishly printed under the direction of Ezra Pound himself, in 1930. "Nancy Cunard's 'coon,' he and I the only civilized creatures," Pound would recall of Henry Crowder years later to Charles Olson. "Says Henry: 'Ah been readin' Mr. Pound's Cantos. And Ah don't know why I read 'em, 'cause I don' understand 'em. Snobbism, I guess.'" It was also in 1930 that Cunard asked Samuel Beckett to write a poem for Henry to set to music. He complied with "From the Only Poet to a Shining Whore" — the "only poet" was Dante, the "shining whore" was Rahab, the harlot of Jericho — a poem that, even as he wrote it, Beckett dismissed as mere "tomfoolery." Soon after this, Cunard hired a scuffling Beckett to translate French poetry into English for her *Negro* anthology. (Among this poetry was "Armstrong" by Ernest Moerman, who was marginally better known as a banjo-player than as a poet.) "Did I tell you I was translating Surréalistes inédits for Nancy's nigger book?" he wrote to his friend Thomas MacGreevy. "Miserable trash."

I wonder what Beckett's response might have been to "For Samuel Beckett" (1987), the last work by the American composer Morton Feldman, which premièred in Holland in June 1987, three months before Feldman's death, two and a half before Beckett's death. Beckett had once written some lines of text for a piece by Feldman, and he was said to have expressed enjoyment of at least one of Feldman's works, which he heard on radio. But to the lugubriously cerebral orchestral composition that Feldman dedicated to him, I think he would have seen through the intellectual bullshit of Feldman's tribute as he had seen through the bullshit of *Negro* more than half a century before, and his response would have been an echo: "Miserable trash." For, while the music of Haydn and Beethoven was dear to opera-hating Beckett all his life, just as dear, and perhaps more so, were the low-brow songs of the music-hall variety shows, of which he remained a devotee from his youth until the end of his days (or, more precisely, the end of the music-halls' days). I think he would have much preferred Emmett Miller's "Lovesick Blues" to Morton Feldman's "For Samuel Beckett."

By the fall of 1935, when Bob Wills and His Texas Playboys recorded "I Ain't Got Nobody," hardly anyone remembered the man who had inspired that recording. The *Billboard* of January 4, 1936, reported that "Emmett Miller, the yodeling b.f. comedian, whose last minstrel engagement was with the Bradford-Redhill version of the Al G. Field Minstrels, is reported to be doing very well for himself in Atlanta. He is now working the night clubs in that city."

On September 1, 1936, in New York, Miller made his final commercial recordings, four sides for the Bluebird subsidiary of Victor: new versions of "Any Time," "I Ain't Got Nobody," and "Right or Wrong"; and a routine, "The Gypsy," with Gene Cobb.

It was the age of big-band swing, the season of sweet-voiced Astaire, of mellow-crooning Crosby. It was no time for Emmett Miller.

As in 1928 he opens "Any Time" and "I Ain't Got Nobody" with blackface-dialogue bits, here with Gene Cobb. Once again in "I Ain't Got Nobody" the comedy centers on a dead wife; there are echoes not only of the earlier prelude, but of "Sam and His Family" and "Sam's New Job" as well. Emmett is addressed in both bits as Emmett. In "I Ain't Got Nobody" of 1928, he had longed for a "sweet cracker mama"; here, foreshadowing the improvisatory flamboyance of Jerry Lee Lewis, he hankers for the object of his desire to be "that little old well-built thing of mine."

This was his third recording of "Any Time," his signature song, the song with which he had begun his recording career twelve years before. The song was a durable one. A dozen years hence, as recorded for RCA-Victor by the country-pop singer Eddy Arnold, it would become the biggest country hit of 1948. Foy Willing, a Western-pop singer from Texas who worked in radio in New York in 1933–35, had a modest country hit of his own that year with a cover version on Capitol. A 1951 RCA-Victor version by Eddie Fisher became a top-ten pop hit. Fisher, then twenty-three, had gotten his first national exposure on Eddie Cantor's radio show in 1949. Cantor, whose real name was Iskowitz, was a vaudeville contemporary of Miller. Eight years older than Miller, he had worked in blackface and become a star of the *Ziegfeld Follies* by 1917, the year of his first hit record. His Emerson recording of "Margie" was one of the biggest hits of 1921; his Columbia recording of "If You Knew Susie," one of the biggest of 1925. It and Gene Austin's "Yes Sir! That's My Baby" were the songs that had filled the air and infused the breezes in the late summer days of 1925, when Miller made his Asheville recordings.

"The Gypsy" was the last of Miller's dialogues to be issued on record. Echoing at its outset snatches of earlier routines, including the face-stomping bit from "Hungry Sam," it evolves into a bizarre and rhythmic, almost rap-like, patter about death and a spiritualist shakedown. It is the strangest of Miller's dialogues, and the only one in which Miller's partner is cast in a female role: a character who starts out as Emmett's wife and ends up, in uncanny dreamlike transformation, as the crooked spiritualist, the gypsy of the title. The role was played by Gene Cobb.

Born in Gordonsville, Tennesseee, on March 3, 1891, Cobb had been doing a female-impersonator act, known as Honey Gal, in vaudeville and minstrelsy since about 1912. He and Miller may have known one another since the early twenties, when both men had worked, albeit at different times, with the Neil O'Brien troupe.

It was during the 1921–22 season tour of the Neil O'Brien Super

Minstrels show — in which Cobb performed "I'm an Agitated Mama" in drag — that he had come to know Jack "Smoke" Gray, with whom he had gone on to perform for many years in a black-face act called Honey Gal and Smoke. The pair had made a record under that name for Gennett in the fall of 1928: a two-sided black-face routine with singing that was also released on the subsidiary Champion, Supertone, and Varsity labels. At this same Gennett session, Cobb and Gray had also recorded individually; but neither of these individual recordings, Cobb's "Sweet Lovin' Papa" nor Gray's "Alimony Blues," was released.

Though actual females in blackface were extremely rare, drag acts were a common feature since the early days of minstrelsy, as attested by E. P. Christy's son William Christy (1839–62), whose "greatest proficiency was in the delineament of the female character." It was through minstrelsy, and subsequently through vaudeville, that transvestite travesty became an element of popular American culture that flourishes until this day. Television's first star, Milton Berle, brought drag from vaudeville to the new medium, and its appeal for the masses has been without decline, from Berle in 1948 to *Some Like It Hot* in 1959 to RuPaul in the 1990s. This legacy of old-time blackface minstrelsy, this "delineament of the female character," has proven to hold a far greater, far more enduring, and far more pervasive attraction than old-time blackface minstrelsy itself. It is not men in blackface that have held sway over the mind and imagination of America, but rather men in dresses, beneath which those seeking sociopolitical meaning seem fearful to peek.

An intriguing and perhaps unique instance of female cross-dressing in minstrelsy is that of Dan Fitch's wife, who performed as a man with the Fitch troupe. Whiteface, blackface. Britches, skirts. The show goes on. From Rosalind unto Ganymede in Shakespeare's *As You Like It* — rather from the real-life Elizabethan male actor playing the part of the lady Rosalind disguised as the male

Ganymede in Shakespeare's *As You Like It* — to Mrs. Fitch in the Dan Fitch Minstrels; from Tiresias to the black former Atlanta used-car dealer called RuPaul: the show goes on. Back in the days before New York City became the biggest hick town in the world, the racketeer Vito Genovese (1897–1969) owned several celebrated nightclubs in Greenwich Village: the Club Savannah, at 68 West Third Street; the 82 Club, at 82 East Fourth Street; the Moroccan Village, the 181 Club, and others. He held them *sub rosa,* placing ownership in the names of others, such as his brother-in-law Tony Petillo or Steve Francis, the escort and confidant of his Lesbian wife, whom Genovese had widowed in order to marry, in 1932. Vito's joints presented entertainment in which the allure of real black female performers and that of transvestites effected a sexual blur whose draw proved mesmerizing. The Savannah featured a high-yellow chorus line of "14 Beautiful Savannah Peaches" and shows produced by Clarence Robinson, the black choreographer who had staged revues at the old Cotton Club in Harlem. The 82 featured transvestite acts. Vito, whose empire was built on dope, understood people and gave them what they wanted. His was a new minstrelsy, a transmutated minstrelsy, a sexual minstrelsy of flesh and fantasy, syncopation and Psyche, peaches and profits. As metaphor, the peach was a fruit of many meanings. In standard slang, a pretty girl was a peach. In the common vernacular of the blues, peaches alluded to the male genitalia: "If you don't like my peaches, don't shake my tree." In more obscure variations of that language, there were connotations of homosexuality, as in Guilford Payne's "Peach Tree Man Blues" of 1923. In Vito's joints, the orchard of ambiguity bloomed in full splendor in the neon night. The shadowland — the language, characters, and occurrences — of the Mobjoint milieu of which Vito's joints were a lingering part of Greenwich Village in the early sixties would imbue the lyrics and spirit of several of Bob Dylan's watershed songs: "Subterranean Homesick

Blues," "Like a Rolling Stone," "Highway 61 Revisited," and "Positively Fourth Street." There are more underworlds through which a poet-singer may pass than that to which Orpheus descended and from which he emerged.

Earlier in the year in which Gene Cobb recorded with Emmett Miller, he had traveled the South with his own show, *Toppin' Tops of 1936,* and was now doing his Honey Gal routine at WGY in Schenectady. Later, like other veterans of blackface, Cobb sought a living in country music, working for some years in the forties as a comedian and master of ceremonies with tent and theater road-show companies of the Renfro Valley Barn Dance program, out of Renfro Valley, Kentucky. He ended his days in St. Louis, where he died on September 18, 1970.

The Western-swing bandleader Milton Brown, a devotee of Miller's music, had sung "Right or Wrong" when he was in the Light Crust Doughboys with fellow Miller idolater Bob Wills. When Brown and Wills parted, both had kept the song in their repertoires. In New Orleans in March 1936, five weeks before the car crash that killed him, Milton Brown and His Musical Brownies recorded "Right or Wrong" for Decca. This recording, inspired by Miller's 1929 version, may in turn have inspired Miller to record the song anew.

Bob Wills and His Texas Playboys, with vocalist Tommy Duncan, recorded the song in Chicago on September 30, 1936, less than a month after Miller recorded it in New York. Wills's version was likely spurred by Brown's, or by news of Miller's new recording, or both. The song would have a revival of sorts the following year, in a low-budget James Cagney musical called *Something to Sing About* and a popular Vocalion recording by the jazz singer Mildred Bailey, featuring her husband, Red Norvo, on xylophone. Wanda Jackson would have a crossover pop-country hit with it in 1961; Merle Haggard, a devotee of Miller and Wills, would record it in 1970; and in 1984 it would be revived with commercial success by both George Strait and the Spinners.

Though Miller himself, at thirty-five, surely envisioned otherwise, the version of "Right or Wrong" that he sang that September day in 1936 was to be his last commercial recording.

On the surface, this new version was — like Milton Brown's recent recording — livelier than his old Okeh version, with something of a Dixieland feel; but there was, beneath that surface, something bleak and lifeless. He ended it exuberantly, though, with that trick of his voice that had brought him, however briefly, something of fame. The drummer struck the high-hat, and it was over.

Emmett's cousin Barbara Gore, the granddaughter of his aunt Emma Miller Simmone, was a teenager in the thirties. She recalled seeing Emmett perform in blackface at tent shows down at Broadway and Fifth.

"I've seen him pull up in limousines," she said many years later with fondness in her voice. "And I've seen him walking with all he owned wrapped in a bandanna."

Barbara's younger brother Emmett would retain little of his cousin Emmett but roguish, spectral images of a raccoon coat and a Cadillac.

He has been remembered as a heavyset man of short to medium height. He got heavier with age, and his hair fell away early, which was said to be a trait of the Millers. He dressed well and he smoked cigars and he smoked cigarettes and he was an alcoholic.

Did booze hurt Emmett Miller's career? Did it destroy his

chances to salvage himself as a singer, keep him from work in radio and pictures? Or did booze help him to go on, to persevere as the world he knew fell apart and faded, as the limousines pulled away forever and the whiskey got cheaper?

As the years pass, he certainly seems to have been willing to work. But there does not seem to have been much work. Did it revolve around cycles of drunkenness and drying-out, or was this all of it that he could wrench from fortune and adversity? According to Turk McBee, "Emmett, he got to drinking so bad that he started drinking essence of peppermint. It burned his vocal cords out."

You and I, dear mortal, will never know. Let us not pass judgment, lest the raccoon coat of karma shed upon our own fate.

Ultimately it is the words of Sallust that offer the most truth, the best explanation: "There can be no question that Fortune is supreme in all human affairs. It is a capricious power, which makes men's actions famous or leaves them in obscurity without regard to their true worth."

In 1937–38 Miller toured the South with a stage show he called the *All-Southern Revue,* booked by Thomas D. Kemp, Jr., of Southern Attractions. According to *Billboard,* the *Revue* was scheduled to hit the road from Charlotte on Labor Day 1937. Kemp (1902–96), originally from Alabama, was the brother of the bandleader Hal Kemp. Active in show business in New York since the early twenties, he had spent the early depression years abroad and returned to settle in Charlotte, where he wrote a column for the *Observer* and in 1934 began to build his own circuit under the auspices of the Paramount Wilby-Kincey chain of theaters. The Wilby-Kincey group, headquartered in Charlotte, comprised over two hundred theaters.

Both Bob Wilby, the founder of the chain, and H. P. Kincey were from Kemp's hometown of Selma.

As Kemp wrote in his self-published *People, Places and Perceptions: An Autobiography* (1995), the Wilby-Kincey chain exerted "almost a monopoly in the principal cities of the Southeast. All were primarily movie theaters but many had large stages. The era of building municipally-owned auditoriums and coliseums had not begun. Therefore, almost all stage entertainment in the South, from Richmond to Miami and west to Memphis, was played in our theaters. My job was to engage live performers, preferably the well-known ones, at the lowest cost.

"By February [1934] I had my 'circuit' ready. In larger cities we usually operated three theaters, dividing these into 'A', 'B' and 'C' houses. In 'A' houses I would use 'name' attractions and road shows. In 'B' houses I used 'tab shows' which were actually a couple of acts with a few girl dancers, a small orchestra, and Emcee to knit it together. These were usually packaged in New York or Chicago. We called them 'units.' The 'C' houses would play western and country acts. We sold popcorn in 'C' theaters, a nuisance we would not permit in the 'A' or 'B' houses. All attractions, except road shows, gave four performances daily at 2 p.m., 4 p.m., and 9 p.m. [*sic*] with movies shown between the stage shows. Within a year, I could give most attractions eight weeks of consecutive work which I would route geographically. The circuit became known in the theatrical industry as 'Kemp Time.'"

Of shows such as Miller's *All-Southern Revue:* "With few exceptions, the 'package' shows that played our 'B' theaters were put together by producers who usually traveled with their shows. They would package three or four shows a year, each show playing about eight weeks for us. The producers I learned to depend on were Lou Walters, Dan Fitch, Joe Karston, Charlie Mack, Harry Clark, Bernie Vici, Ross Russell and A. B. Marcus. Mike Todd did two shows for us and George White did one. There were a few performers who packaged and performed in their own shows. These included Sally Rand, an astute business woman; the O'Conner [*sic*] family, featuring Donald who, at age 14, was a fantastic dancer and later became a top movie star; and Ole Olson and Chick Johnson who called their show 'Helizapoppin' [*sic*]. They enlarged it after playing our circuit and it had a run of two years on Broadway."

Kemp worked with Miller from the thirties to the end. He may have known and worked with Miller earlier, and even may have played a part in Miller's relationship with Okeh. A look at Kemp's career certainly suggests this possibility: he became the manager of the Consolidated Orchestras Booking Office in New York in the fall of 1924, just weeks before Miller's first recording session; opened his own International Artists office at 1607 Broadway in the fall of 1926; worked extensively with the Keith organization, and with Cliff Edwards; was familiar with the Al G. Field Minstrels; was a friend of Irving Mills, the co-author of "Lovesick Blues"; knew the Dorsey brothers; was close to T. G. Rockwell, the Okeh recording manager who had brought Miller to record in 1928; and was no stranger to the Okeh studio on Fourteenth Street.

Yet Kemp does not mention Miller among the dependable producers with whom he worked, or among "the few performers who packaged and performed in their own shows." Elsewhere in his book, Kemp recalls that "One of the most popular entertainment events was the annual tour of the Al G. Fields [*sic*] Minstrel Show," and goes on to mention some of the "famous 'black-face' comedians such as Slim Williams, Cotton Watts, and Ned Waverly [*sic*]" who got their start in minstrel shows; and here again Miller's name is absent. In fact, nowhere in the more than five hundred pages of Kemp's book is Emmett Miller mentioned. Kemp does recall, however, that "the first performer I engaged [in 1934] was Gene Austin with a back-up duo called 'Candy and Cocoa' to back him up.

Austin's phonograph records were popular all over the western world. His second wife, Agnes, was then pregnant with their first child. I convinced them to move to Charlotte."

The evidence is that Miller did not perform in Charlotte that Labor Day season of 1937, though he and his troupe very well may have embarked from there.

Claude Casey (1912–99) was a young Carolina entertainer who turned twenty-five that September. Born in Enoree, South Carolina, Casey sang, played guitar, yodeled, worked in mills, hoboed through the Depression, had a radio show in Danville, Virginia, in the early thirties. He had hitchhiked to New York in April 1936 and performed on *Major Bowes' Amateur Hour,* the nationally broadcast NBC radio show; had been a member of the *Major Bowes' Amateurs on Tour* road show. In July of 1937 he recorded six songs for Art Satherly of the American Record Corporation. None of these recordings was released, but in January 1938 Claude and his new band, the Pine State Playboys, recorded in Charlotte for Bluebird, and there would be another session, in Rock Hill, in September. Casey's Playboys played a Southeastern-flavored sort of Western swing. They were a small group that included Willie Coates, a hot pianist from Danville, and the Carolina fiddler Jimmy Rouse, a brother of the more celebrated fiddler Ervin Rouse, widely known as the originator of "Orange Blossom Special." In 1939 Casey worked as a mill hand, played Florida with Ervin and Gordon Rouse, and toured the Ohio Valley with Fat Sanders' Country Cousins, a small troupe that featured a hillbilly strip-tease. With a new edition of the Pine State Playboys, he recorded in Atlanta in October 1940.

In 1941 Casey went to work at station WBT, the CBS station in Charlotte, where he remained for the next decade. Founded in April 1922, WBT was the first commercially licensed radio station in the Carolinas. Freeman Gosden and Charles Correll worked there in the twenties, Hal Kemp in the thirties. Casey performed on WBT as a solo act and as a member of two WBT groups, the Briarhoppers and the Tennessee Ramblers. With the latter he appeared in the 1943 Republic picture *Swing Your Partner.* After the war, with a new band, the Sagedusters, he recorded in Charlotte and Atlanta for Steve Sholes of RCA-Victor. In 1953 he made his final recordings, for MGM in Nashville, and later that year, he began appearing on WFBC-TV in Greenville, South Carolina. In 1961 he founded station WJES in Johnston, South Carolina, where he and his wife, Ruth, came to live.

Casey knew Emmett Miller. The photo of Miller published in the Country Music Foundation book was donated to the foundation by him and is signed by Miller with the words "Best Wishes to Boy Claude."

In the Country Music Foundation's 1982 oral-history interview with him, Casey said that it was in Charlotte that he first saw Miller perform, as part of a vaudeville program, which Casey described as essentially a "leg show." Later he recalled that this may have been a Kemp show in 1941. Casey married eighteen-year-old Ruth Derrick in 1942; and that was the year he came to know Miller, who visited him and Ruth often over the next several years, first at their apartment and later, after the war, at their house at 2236 Commonwealth Avenue.

I wrote to Casey in 1992, and he wrote back. In his letter he recalled that "Emmett used to visit my wife, Ruth and me when we lived in Charlotte, North Carolina where I worked at WBT and CBS radio. The last time I saw Emmett I spent a great deal of time with him. He was playing the Broadway Theater in Charlotte, and was being booked by T. D. Kemp of Southern Attractions. I used to catch every show when he played Charlotte. The last one back then he was playing without his black face."

As for T. D. Kemp, I was a day late and a dollar short in getting to him. He died in Charlotte on April 11, 1996, at the age of ninety-three. His memory was said to be lucid until the end.

"Let's put it this-a-way about T. D. Kemp," Casey said. "He helped a lot of people to keep from starvin' to death. I mean that sincerely."

Fading, fleeting images.

In October 1937 *Billboard* reported that "Emmett Miller's *All-Southern Revue of 1938,* after completing a number of dates in the Florida Sparks houses, is currently in Lucas & Jenkins theaters, to be followed by the Kincey & Wilby chain. Besides Miller, who is featured, company comprises Billy Henderson, Hager and Wiley, Buddy Mack, Bob and Phyllis Murphy, the Udell Triplets, Dave Workman and a five-piece ork, Lloyd Sullivan and his Southerners."

And in January 1938, another brief report: "Emmett Miller, yo-deling minstrel of a few years back, is working the Kemp houses in the South with his own unit show, *All-Southern Revue.* Emmett has been meeting up with a host of old-time minstrel lads down that way in recent weeks."

That phrase: "of a few years back." It was as if his existence had already been relegated to the past.

Dan Fitch was touring the South at the same time, as the owner, producer, and star of a forty-five-minute show called the *Big Apple Revue.* It featured Turk McBee, who performed some blues, played the xylophone, and joined Fitch in a blackface routine sans blackface. The show played the Capitol in Atlanta in December 1937. T. D. Kemp tells the story of the *Big Apple Revue* in his autobiography:

"Near Myrtle Beach, South Carolina was a pavilion then the 'in place' for dancing teenagers. These dancers developed a new routine which they called 'The Big Apple'. It was little more than a version of the square dance. News of the 'Big Apple' spread rapidly and there was much curiosity to see it performed. I suggested to Dan Fitch, one of our best stage show producers, that he put together a

'Big Apple Revue' featuring the dance. His choreographer went to the beach to study the 'Big Apple' routine. The choreographer learned the routine and engaged three of the young couples from the beach to work in the show.

"I named it 'The Big Apple Show' and it packed our theaters. I received a call from Sam Rothafel, better known as 'Roxy', saying he wanted his dance director to stage a 'Big Apple' show at his Roxy Theater in New York. I had him fly his choreographer down and I met her at the airport. We drove to Columbia, South Carolina, where our 'Big Apple' show was then playing. With my approval, she engaged our show (which she would enlarge) to play at the New York Roxy Theater when the tour of our theaters ended three weeks later. My brother Hal also engaged three couples from the show to demonstrate the dance at eleven o'clock each night at the Astor Hotel Roof where his orchestra was then playing. Thus, by late 1937, the 'Big Apple' had become as famous in New York City as in the Carolinas. The dance caught on quickly in New York and received so much publicity that people began calling the city 'The Big Apple'."

Actually, New York was referred to as "the big apple" at least as early as 1909, in a book called *The Wayfarer in New York,* edited by Edward S. Martin; and Walter Winchell wrote in 1927 that "Broadway is the Big Apple, the Main Stem, the goal of all ambition, the pot of gold at the end of a drab and somewhat colorless rainbow."

In February of 1938, Miller was "spotted in front of the Oliver Hotel, Atlanta," with a group of other former minstrels, including Bill Henderson of the *All-Southern Revue,* Cotton Watts, and Homer Meachum, the old-timer who said, "They'll always come back for the cork."

In April it was reported that "Emmett Miller and Bill Henderson are still sojourning in Atlanta."

Later that spring Miller set out on another tour of the South, this time as a featured performer in the show *Swing Parade.* The show played the James Theater, Newport News, Virginia, in early June.

A year later, in June 1939, *Billboard* published its final "Minstrelsy" column. Emmett Miller's name virtually vanished from sight.

In April 1940 Miller toured the South as a player in Billroy's Comedians, a traveling tent show owned by Billy Wehle and comedian Jimmy Heffner.

A decade earlier, there had been a great deal of resistance by small-town theater-owners to shows such as Billroy's. In Bainbridge, Georgia, in the fall of 1930, local movie houses had conducted an advertising campaign against Billroy's. Headed "Tented Parasites vs. Legitimate Theater Entertainment," one ad asked: "Are the modern carpetbaggers that come South in the winter with the geese worthy of family patronage or should the lovers of clean amusement support legally operated theaters in the community?" The ad spoke of attractions that were "half-dressed or nude" as opposed to the "high-class, moral and refined entertainment" of the theaters. Another ad bewailed "the great amount of money taken out of the community by the tented aggregation," and the threat to "home-owned, home-operated and home-financed" providers of "high-class, moral and refined programs of talking-singing pictures."

Most tent shows had folded during the depression, but Billroy's had survived. The 1940 Billroy's itinerary was not a glamorous one: Rome, Calhoun, and Dalton, Georgia; Cleveland, Tennessee; Bristol, Virginia. The show, featuring a six-piece band and a six-girl line, was structured as a three-act farce with vaudeville bits between the acts. Miller, singing and yodeling in blackface, was joined onstage by Lue Wanna and her Savage Dancers. (*Billboard* renders madame's name and act as such; an advertisement in the Calhoun *Times* tells of "'LUANA' in Her Sensation 'Danse Savage.' A Heat Wave From the Old Argentine!")

Billed as "America's Greatest Blackface Entertainer," Miller was the show's "1940 Singing Star"; Jimmy Heffner, "Our 1940 Comic Star." The show itself was advertised as "The Greatest Show on Earth for the Money" (children, fifteen cents; adults, two bits; ladies free if accompanied by one paying adult). "PRESENTED WITH THE BRILLIANCE OF BROADWAY AND HOLLY-WOOD IN THE WORLD'S LARGEST AND MOST BEAUTIFUL WATERPROOF TENT THEATRE," Billroy's boasted of a cast of "80 People 80 (Mostly Girls)."

The Billroy's tent show played John P. King Park in Calhoun on the night of April 16. A plug in the weekly *Calhoun Times* featured a photograph of Lue Wanna (one assumes) surrounded by her savage dancers — seven, count 'em, seven — arms akimbo, in ornate head-dress, flowing robes, G-strings, and bandeau halters. Though the Copacabana of New York would not come to be until later this year, these ladies nonetheless look very Copa. Emmett Miller is not mentioned, only "Girls, girls, girls, blondes, red-heads and brunettes, alluring and captivating."

From Calhoun, the show made its way to Dalton, then on to Cleveland, Tennessee, and through Tennessee to enter Virginia at Bristol on April 26.

Posed the way ya like 'em. Lay your black kinky head in a bed on a pillow of white. Guy here, old timer, he does the trick voice. Stopped this one, 'cause I cut it off up to his neck.

In June of 1996, pursuing the trail of Emmett Miller in the Carolinas, Sally Hinson of Charlotte visited with Claude and Ruth Casey at their home in Johnston. Sally found them to be a lovely couple. It turned out that they had friends, and Charlotte, in common. Claude Casey told me it was "a delightful visit."

Sally's tape-recorded visit turned into quite a morning. Claude, soft-spoken and sharp at eighty-four, took out his guitar, accompanied himself as he sang "Any Time" and "Right or Wrong," a snatch of this and a snatch of that, a bit of Jolson and a bit of Bob Wills, some of his own and a taste of a risqué old thing about mutual yo-yoing that decorum forbade him to finish. Serenade and reminiscence flowed as Claude and Ruth recalled what they could of Emmett Miller's sporadic visits throughout the years 1942–49.

Claude and Emmett would sit around and play one another's records.

"I can remember him sittin' in a chair there, y'know, and we were playin' one of his records, and this is what he said. He said, 'That's Emmett Miller singin'.' Talkin' just like a black, y'know: 'That's Emmett Miller.'"

"And he'd tell you to be quiet," Ruth said of his comical displays of deference for his own recordings.

Her memory stirred Claude, who tried to approximate Miller's blackface voice: "'Be quiet now, Emmett Miller's singin'.'"

The Caseys bore witness to Emmett's love of Eddie Lang, his pride of having recorded with him. He never spoke, they said, of Jimmie Rodgers, of Bob Wills, or of Hank Williams's "Lovesick Blues."

Claude and Ruth thought that Emmett may have been a guest on the WBT Briarhoppers show, but they were not sure. They said they never knew him to drink around them; and they never saw him with a woman.

On September 24, 1943, Emmett Miller married Bernice Valentine Calhoun, the forty-five-year-old daughter of Stonewall Jackson Calhoun and Emma Tharpe Calhoun. Remembered as a wonderful woman by those who knew her, she had other attributes as well that might have recommended her to Emmett as a bride: she had a job, and her brother ran a liquor store.

Emmett, by most accounts, was an alcoholic. He ran with his first cousin Jesse Simmone, the son of his father's sister Emma. Jesse was a housepainter. The both of them, Emmett and Jesse, were good-natured fellows, according to Barbara Gore Hardwick, a niece to Jesse, a cousin to Emmett. The only trouble was that the two of them together "tried to drink all the whiskey in Macon."

Buck Calhoun's liquor store, the Black Cat, was located in the Lanier Hotel building, on Mulberry between Second and Third. Emmett and Jesse frequented the many joints down on Second Street; and it may have been through Buck Calhoun's Black Cat that Emmett met Bernice Calhoun.

Emmett's parents had been living for some years at 2023 Second Street, in the block below Second Street Methodist Church, which they joined in 1936. Emmett and Bernice, however, were married in a civil ceremony, performed in Macon by Judge Walter C. Stevens. After the wedding, Emmett and his new bride lived together at the Second Street home of Emmett's mother and father.

John Pink Miller, known in his later years as Uncle Pink, had retired from the fire department, then worked a bit at the C. H. Yates Motor Company. He remained active as a member of the Second Street Methodist Church, and of the Franklin Lodge of the Independent Order of Odd Fellows. He died on March 14, 1944, after an illness of several weeks.

Following her husband's death, Lena Miller moved to 193 Magnolia Street. In early September of 1948, she suffered a stroke, brought on by arteriosclerosis and hypertension. Two weeks later at her home, on the afternoon of September 20, she passed away, and on the following afternoon was buried at her husband's side. (Though her death certificate would correctly give her year of birth as 1873, both her obituary and her tombstone would mysteriously and wrongly alter that year to 1863, making of her, fancifully, a child of the Confederate twilight.)

Emmett's sister, Nora Belle, had been married since March of 1921 to a man named William Sanford Carlos. Before her marriage, she had lived at home and worked as a cashier at Union Dry Goods; after, she moved in with her husband and his widowed mother at their place on Ross Street. Carlos then was a clerk at the Sparks Motor Co. on Broadway; later he rose to parts manager. Eventually, both of them became workers out at Robbins Air Force Base, Nora as a stock tracer at the logistics center. They had one child, a daughter named Marguerite, who married a man named Edgar J. Parent and made a great-grandmother and great-grandfather of Lena and Uncle Pink in the few years before their death.

In 1949 — the year Hank Williams's "Lovesick Blues" hit Number One; the year Wesley Rose referred to Miller as "Emmett something or other" — the Macon directory listed Emmett and Bernice living at 1079 Magnolia. Emmett's occupation was listed as "traveling showman"; and it was indeed in 1949 that Emmett Miller made his final tour, working with Turk McBee in a show called *Dixiana*.

The title was that of a 1930 RKO picture set in the antebellum South. The movie had featured a tap-dance finale by Bill "Bojangles" Robinson (1878–1949) and a title song that gained some popularity. A small show in Hoosick Falls, New York, had operated as the Dixie Anna Minstrels in the summer of 1931. Dan Fitch had toured twice with a Kemp-circuit *Dixiana Revue:* in 1936, when Turk McBee received second billing in the program, as "the Dancing

Xylophonist," after "Models on Parade"; and again in 1941. The latter, opening the stage-show season at the Broadway in Charlotte on Labor Day weekend of 1941, played with *Thieves Fall Out,* an Eddie Albert drama about rival mattress-factory families ("Not just a picture"). Fitch's cast of thirty was advertised as "featuring the most beautiful girls in the Southland." One advertisement bore the legend "A Dan Fitch Show Means a Dan Good Show!" Fitch was back at the Broadway in September of 1942 with another girlie show, *Beauty on Parade.*

Miller described his own, Kemp-circuit *Dixiana* of 1949 as "the last great minstrel show." Preparing for publicity that never came, Miller or McBee, or the two of them together, drafted a three-page typewritten "Rough outline — Radio interview with Miller and McBee":

Announcer: As you may have heard, the stage presentation at the ———— theatre ———— on ———— is aptly called "DIXIANA"

The feature of this southern revue is one of the few remaining Black Crow type act, Miller and McBee.

These two comedians are with us in the studio, and I am going to introduce them and ask a few questions about back-stage life. First Mr. Emmett Miller. Good afternoon, Emmett.

Emmett: Good afternoon.

Ann: And Turk McBee. — Hello, Turk.

Turk: Hello ————

Ann: Emmett and Turk, this afternoon, with your permission, I'd like to ask a few questions about the theatre.

Turk: Make them easy.

Emmett: Yes, Turk means, keep away from the Drahma. We are just a couple of eleven forty fivers.

Ann: Very well, question, number one — What is an eleven forty fiver?

Turk: He means minstrel man. You see, the minstrel shows always held a parade every day at exactly eleven forty five. That was to catch the Noon crowd.

Emmett: That's right. It was eleven forty five ob all shows.

Ann: Did you parade in cold weather?

Emmett: They sure did.

Turk: The musicians would cut out holes in a sack and slip it over the clarinet, or trumpet, and play right along.

Ann: That must have been "way back." How long have you been in show business, Emmett?

Emmett: Thirty years.

Ann: And how long doing blackface?

Emmett: Thirty years.

Ann: Of all the minstrel shows you have been with, which remains in your memory?

Emmett: Well, there have been many wonderful shows, and it depends upon which period you have in mind, when you ask which is the best? In my time, I believe Al.G.Fields had the finest show.

Ann: Where you ever on that one?

Emmett: Yes twice.

Ann: And what did you do on the show?

Emmett: Oh, like everyone else, I did a little of everything.

Turk: His second time on the show, he was the comedy star.

Ann:	The star of the Al.G.Fields show. — That was your one ambition, I presume.
Emmett:	Yes, every blackface looks forward to be on that one.
Ann:	But, Turk here looks a little young to be a minstrel man. There have been no minstrel shows in years.
Emmett:	Turk started young, too.
Ann:	At what age, Turk?
Turk:	Eleven.
Ann:	Eleven years of age? With what shows?
Turk:	With Mr. Coburn. That was all arranged when I was born. My daddy had been a minstrel drummer, and was with Mr. Coburn for years. He taught me drums, then next came Xylophines, and dancing — After that the minstrel show.
Ann:	Minstrel shows, see, to be part of the entertainment of every community, even tho there are no professional productions. — Just when did they start.
Turk:	Well, the word Minstrel, goes back for centuries, but in this country, it means negro characterization.
Ann:	And when did they start this "blackface comedy" as we now call it.
Emmett:	I can answer that one — according to records, blackface comedy started in 1799 in Boston.
Ann:	In the North?
Turk:	Yes, a fellow named Graupner, blackened his face and sang, "The Negro Boy". That is generally considered the first blackface in history.
Ann:	And when did they start the Minstrel show itself?

Emmett: I know that one too? Will I get a prize? — That was in 1843

Ann: I suppose in the deep south?

Turk: You see, by that time, there were many actors appearing in blackface, but no full show. Then four men got together and called themselves "The Virginia Minstrels" One of them was Dan Emmett —

Emmett: He wrote a song called "DIXIE" to use in the show, and I guess bu now everyone has heard "Dixie"

Ann: Well, it sure got around. I suppose was from the south?

Emmett: Nope, he was from Mount Vernon Ohio.

Ann: Well, before we go any further, are you boys from the south?

Emmett: What do you think?

Ann: I have the slightest doubt about it. — but I cannot figure out what part.

Emmett: I'm from Macon Georgia.

Ann: And you Turk?

Turk: Greenville, South Caroline.

Ann: Well, I finally found two southern minstrel men.

Emmett: Oh most of them are from the south, but it seems odd that it started in the North.

Ann: Do you think Minstrel shows will start up again.

Emmett: I don't think you will ever see them as numerous as they one were, but if someone would produce a good big show, I think it would go over big.

Ann: And what old Title, do you think they should revive.

Emmett: The Al.G.Fields Minstrels, — No other.

Ann:	By the way — was Mr. Fields a southerner?
Emmett:	No, he was from Ohio, too.
Ann:	Another Yankee minstrel. — Well, thank you Emmett Miller and Turk McBee, and may your visit to ———— be a happy ~~and prosperous~~ one.

The author of this document — or its primary author — may have been McBee rather than Miller, as the pages issued from the same typewriter, and adhered to the same style, that McBee used in drawing up several blackout dialogue routines — "Women Bit," "Cigarette Bit," and others — that he proposed to Miller. These sheets, like the three-page "radio interview," were among the belongings of Turk McBee, who also kept a "cash book," seven and a half inches wide by twelve inches high, of other routines, one-liners, ideas for potential material, and lists of "slow" and "fast" xylophone pieces. This book likely dates to the early fifties, or later, as one of the jokes in it centers on Marilyn Monroe, who until then was relatively unknown.

Booked through Kemp's Southern Attractions, the show played the Capitol Theatre in Ashland, Kentucky, in early February of that year. Dick Martin, the manager of the Capitol, wrote in what appears to be a solicited letter of commendation addressed to "Emmette [sic] Miller and 'Turk' McBee," dated February 12:

"Just a note to thank you boys for a very successful engagement. Our audiences liked your show and we did, too.

"You have a bunch of good, clean and talented people that work hard and have been especially co-operative in every way.

"It has been a pleasure to have you here and we hope you will come back."

The troupe played the Shea Theatre in New Philadelphia, Ohio, on February 20. William Gillam, the theater's manager, wrote to Kemp the following day — again apparently at the request of

Miller and/or McBee; copies of these letters were kept by McBee until his death — reporting that "Jack Burke's unit" of *Dixiana* "as presented here consisted of eight people one of which was Emmett Miller. The entire group gave a versatile and pleasing program consisting of various musical instrumentations, dancing and comedy."

Another letter to Kemp, from Fred Fisher, manager of Mid-State Theatres, Inc., in Bellefonte, Pennsylvania, dated March 9: "We played the musical revue Dixiana with a pack house. The show is very good and any manager or theatre operator who would like a good stage presentation here is a show you don't have to be afraid of. The people in the show are clean type and very nice to work with. Don't be afraid to spend a little money on advertising and your box office will give you a darn good return. Our gross was the biggest yet for this type of show. Also our patrons liked the show and I will give them a return date later on in the year."

A theater-manager in Crisfield, Maryland, wrote to Kemp in a letter dated April 14 that the Burke show was one of "the cleanest shows this theatre has presented."

Miller was in Charlotte for two nights, April 14–15, at the Armory Auditorium as part of a show called the Five Star Revue. Of the five acts, he was billed fourth — "Emmett Miller: Black Face Comedian" — beneath an acrobat named Betty Lou Drake, the "famous leaning fiddler" Herb Camp, and Mickey Rhodes, "wizard on the accordion." Adults, fifty cents. Kids, a dime. Tax included.

The Armory shows were sponsored by the *Charlotte Observer,* and LeGette Blythe, a staff reporter for that paper, interviewed Miller on Friday, April 15, in the lobby of the Hotel Clayton, where he was staying.

"Emmett Miller," the piece began, "wouldn't be at all surprised if the American public right now wouldn't go for the old-time minstrel shows, the sort he starred in as one of the topflight performers in the old Al G. Fields Minstrels."

It was here that he envisioned his great comeback:

"You know," he said, "I just might start me up a minstrel company pretty soon. I've got four rich guys, a banker, a big contractor, and a couple others with plenty of dough, who have already approached me. They want me to get a show together and start out this fall. And I just might do it."

There was a photograph of him — the last known of the few photographs of him — sitting in a chair: heavyset, grinning, whiskey-faced; sharp hat, sharp suit, white shirt, sharp tie, cigarette betwixt well-scrubbed whiskey fingers.

To the best of the Caseys' recollection, Miller gave Claude the autographed photo in 1948 or 1949. It was likely at this time. The Caseys would never see him again.

"He seemed in very good spirits," Ruth recalled.

"Yes, he did," Claude agreed.

They remember that he was with a new manager of sorts, a man who said little.

"They were on their way somewhere," Ruth said.

Four rich guys. Plenty of dough.

There exists, in an old box of tattered memories in Turk McBee's hometown of Greenville, South Carolina, an old and tattered handbill, crudely lettered and crudely printed, announcing that "Jack W. Burke brings you" the "vodvil revue" *Dixiana,* "featuring Miller & McBee," the "best in blackface — in person!" After the Burke show disbanded, Miller and McBee tried to keep it going, as "Gags and Girls," under the aegis of a new producer, Jerry Clayton.

And that was that.

At this time, another Macon showman, an audacious singer of a different sort, was coming up. Richard Penniman, at eighteen, would make his first records, as Little Richard, for RCA-Victor in Atlanta in October 1951, twenty-four years to the month after Emmett Miller's triumphant entry into that city. One of Richard's songs, "Miss Ann," would covertly celebrate the proprietress of Ann's Tic-Toc Club, a gay bar at 434 Cotton Avenue in Macon. I think of them, old Emmett and young Richard, passing one another in the street, barely seeing one another, in the hushed late-summer afternoon.

Steve Sholes (1911–68), the Victor A&R executive who signed Richard, had a few years before recorded Claude Casey and gotten Seger Ellis to make some country-pop records under the name of Harry Houston; a few years hence, in 1955, he would sign Elvis Presley to Victor, and would arrange for Presley's appearances in 1956 on the Dorsey Brothers' CBS television program, *Stage Show.* And Elvis would sing Little Richard's "Tutti Frutti" on the Dorseys' show, just as Emmett twenty-eight years before, with the Dorseys behind him, had sung the songs of other black men. For the Dorseys, it soon would end. Tommy would die a few months later, in November of 1956. Jimmy would follow in 1957. But the strange and endless song whose waves they had sailed went on, from "Shake, Rattle and Roll" of 1919 to "Shake, Rattle and Roll" of 1954, as before and as beyond.

It went on, the strange and gaudy medicine show of American culture: the secrets of its history, its revelations, lost beneath its sound and fury, like the secrets and revelations of an ancient mystery cult, lost to the dust of time, that endure, untelling, where dead voices gather, beneath the endless veils of passing.

It went on, and on it goes. To follow "Lovesick Blues" from Tin Pan Alley to Emmett Miller to Hank Williams is to saunter along some forgotten shore of history. To follow the path of minstrelsy to rap is to go on a journey, the nuances and essential truth of whose cultural meaning we are just now beginning to understand. When television networks offer as entertainment comedy shows in which refined suburban blacks play at artful caricatures and white-scripted concepts of ghetto-culture speech and mannerisms, is it really different from the coon shows, the blacking up by black men, of the past, except that today's black minstrels are perhaps even more a product of white America than their forebears, and thus more akin to the blacked-up white men of yesterday than to the black?

From the plantation to the 'hood, the painted backdrops change, but the nature of the racket remains the same. The smiling entertainer is outré; the mask of seriousness and profundity is now the vogue. Showmen have become artists, spielers have become spokesmen. Does Spike Lee differ from turn-of-the-century coon-show hustlers, except that he pretends to substance and importance? Does he differ, except in the arrogance of this pretense and the gravity of demeanor, from Louis Vasnier, the Creole of a hundred years ago and more who advertised his ability to play a black man without benefit of makeup? Indeed, to his credibility as minstrel, there are times when Mr. Lee's delineations of negritude are quite convincing to the rubes of Hollywood and other suburbs of reality.

Does "Cop Killer," fine and wonderful an entertainment as it is, differ from "All Coons Look Alike to Me," except that it traffics in another stereotype, sells a different and more modish candy? There is, in fact, in all of late-twentieth-century rap music, no pose more bloodthirsty, razor-slashing, swaggering, and deadly, no performance more nastily and vehemently free with and full of the word "nigger" as epithet, nor with and of menace as ethos, than that of "The Bully," a coon-song hit of 1907 by the coon-song shouter May Irwin (1862–1938), but a coon song that, as the eminent blues scholar Paul Oliver convincingly suggests, derived from an authentic black songster source, perhaps originally performed late in the nineteenth century by the St. Louis brothel singer Mama Lou. Ah, but to hear "The Bully" done up anew today, in full technological violence of rhythm, by, say, the Wu-Tang Clan — now that would be something: the wielded blade of a century past brought down across the throat of the here and now, the throat not of that bully of the town in that song of yore, but of the true and greater Bully, which is the bully of mediocrity, of this world.

Is the pose of many contemporary rap groups dissimilar in essence to that of the black coon acts of the past? Is an exaggerated pretense of being bad, dangerous, and lawless anything more than a variation on the exaggerated pretense of being benign, comical, and docile, the pretense to which "The Bully" was a notable exception? Are they not in essence both theatrical coon acts, built on stereotype? *Hollywood Shuffle,* Robert Townsend's perceptive film comedy of 1987, was a rare attempt at illumination.

Examining the polar temperaments of minstrelsy and rap, it is clear that the latter has grown inevitably from the former; that, polar as they are, it is the shared umbilicus of fantasy that sustains and unites them. From the evolution of these polar temperaments — from the popular images, invented and self-invented, of the happy darky of minstrelsy, the bellicose gangsta of rap — unsaid, unsayable cultural equations emerge: slavery is good; freedom is bad. Not merely slavery and freedom as it relates to blacks, but as it relates to a self deeper than color: to other unsaid, unsayable things, deeper ambivalences and deeper conundrums, myriad fears and falsehoods that compel conformity, sublimation, and repression to cling to delusions and shibboleths of individuality. And in that evolution from amiable darky to threatening gangsta, the black entertainer has filled and defined his role well; but ultimately, today as a hundred years ago, the business of stereotypes, and the greater share of its profits, remain the domain of the noble white man.

No one alive today in America knows what slavery was. The black who professes to be the heir of its suffering, the white who professes to be the heir of its shame: these are the stock characters of a minstrel show gone berserk, and they are made for one another, loving slaves to a delusion that protects them from looking beneath their own skin, slaves to a fear that keeps them from loving except through hate. And that makes for damn good business, a culture where the customer and the product are one in the great mall of mass-produced individualism. As it is writ: all consumers look alike to me.

We perceive the coon show of yesterday as gross folly, regard the coon show of today in purblind innocence. Louis Armstrong singing "Shine" with a smile on his face is one thing. But what is to be made, in a supposedly more enlightened age, of a whitened Michael Jackson declaiming in rhythm, ascowl with dramatic sincerity, that he is "Bad"? They are, these theatrical posings — of our culture, and of our psyche — like a mirror held at different angles to our self, that self which is both white and black: the reflection changes, but that which is reflected remains the same. And that which is reflected, no matter how radically its reflection changes, remains as deeply enigmatic today as it was in the days of minstrelsy. It goes on. Beneath the singer, beneath the song. It goes on.

In the summer of 1951 — the summer of the first television broadcast of *Amos 'n' Andy* — Miller appeared with other old minstrel acts in *Yes Sir, Mr. Bones,* a low-budget, two-reel, sixteen-millimeter black-and-white film produced by director Ron Ormond and his wife, June.

Ron's real name was Vic Narro. He had taken the name of his

friend and mentor, Ormond McGill, a stage magician. June was the daughter of entertainer Cliff Bragdon, top banana in the team of Cliff and Cuckoo Morrison; she had been a showgirl in her teens under the name of June Carr.

The Ormonds were friends of Miller's buddy Claude Casey, who appeared with Spade Cooley and others in the Ormonds' first musical, *Square Dance Jubilee* of 1949. That picture had been followed in 1950 with *Hollywood Varieties,* produced at a cost of ten thousand dollars. Casey recalled that many of the acts in *Yes Sir, Mr. Bones* were booked by T. D. Kemp of Charlotte.

The forty "C" theaters in the Kemp circuit were known as "grind houses." As Kemp recalled in his autobiography, these theaters presented "primarily cowboy movies, often along with the personal appearance of one of its stars." Two of the cowboy-picture stars that Kemp booked into the grind houses were Lash LaRue and his comic sidekick, Al "Fuzzy" St. John. They "became so popular in the South that both spent more time making personal appearances in our theaters than in making pictures. Ron Ormond, who managed both of them, discussed with me the possibility of organizing a movie production company to produce LaRue–St. John pictures. As a result, we formed Western Adventure Pictures Corporation. Ron Ormond and his talented wife, June, would manage production. Francis White, a North Carolina theater operator with offices in Charlotte, became president. For a few years, before the rise of television and the dwindling interest in cowboy pictures, our little company was quite successful, turning out about 10 westerns. I later sold my interest at a nice profit."

June Ormond told me in 1996 that her father had taken her to the summer-season minstrel shows at the Steel Pier in Atlantic City, New Jersey, and it was there that she had first seen Emmett Miller, when she was "nine or ten." She was born in 1912; this would have been in 1921 or '22. She went on to say that, "If memory serves,

Emmett had a song in the show about 'Get Out of the Kitchen, I'll Do the Cooking.' It was a great song."

According to June, the idea for a minstrel-nostalgia exploitation film had been brought to the Ormonds by their associate Bob Lippert, who became the film's distributor. As she recounted to me in a letter, the Ormonds at the time of Lippert's idea had recently seen Miller "in Hollywood when he had written and appeared in a show at a little theater on Las Palmas Ave. Sorry, I don't recall the name of the show. I do remember it as very entertaining." She said that the black entertainer Sherman "Scatman" Crothers (1910–86) offered to introduce the Ormonds to Miller, who eagerly agreed, along with Crothers, to appear in their minstrel picture.

Crothers's first big movie role lay ahead in the 1953 musical *Meet Me at the Fair,* but his career by this time already had begun to flourish, on stage, radio, television, and recordings, as well as in movies. Coming west from Indiana as a musician and comedian, Crothers had made his first film in 1945, when he was featured with Bulee "Slim" Gaillard in Astor Pictures' *Ovoutie O'Rooney.* Nineteen fifty had been his busiest year thus far: he had appeared with Nat "King" Cole in a Universal musical featurette; performed on Phil Harris's RCA-Victor hit of "Chattanoogie Shoe Shine Boy"; recorded his own comic songs for London and Capitol; sung on records by the Red Callender Sextet; filmed a song-and-dance bit with Marie Bryant for British Lion's Technicolor production of *The Story of Gilbert and Sullivan;* been a regular on the CBS radio show *Beulah* and the KTLA television show *Dixie Showboat;* and been considered for the role of Lightnin', the janitor at the lodge of the Mystic Knights of the Sea, in the developing *Amos 'n' Andy* television series. His success and growing fame notwithstanding, his surname appeared as Caruthers in the credits of the Ormond film.

June remembered Miller as "very gentle, very talented." Regarding the film, she stated in her letter: "Emmett does a great routine with Scat Man Caruthers."

But there are two Millers in the film, and the one that performs with Crothers is a black man. Appearing here as F. E. Miller, he is none other than Flournoy Miller of the old team of Miller and Lyles. Flournoy had been making pictures since the late thirties, when he collaborated with Herb Jeffries and Spencer Williams, Jr., in a series of black Westerns. He had made three movies in 1948 alone. Except for *Stormy Weather* of 1947, they were all low-budget, all-black films.

June evidently has confused Flournoy and Emmett. And the song, "Get Out of the Kitchen," that she remembered Emmett Miller singing: it is sung by Flournoy E. Miller in the film. So whom had she really seen long ago in Atlantic City, and at that little theater in Hollywood? To whom did Scatman introduce her? As far as is known, Emmett Miller never performed west of the Mississippi.

In the end June said that she had, after all, not known Emmett Miller all that well. She suggested that I talk to Bob Harrison, a man who went back to the days of the Dan Fitch Minstrels. Harrison, whom I found in Chicago, turned out to be an exuberant and lucid gentleman of eighty-seven. Born into a show-business family on the Lower East Side of New York, Harrison had indeed been a member of the Fitch troupe, and his memory seemed quite reliable. He told me that Fitch was from Savannah, when in fact Fitch was from Augusta; but he also told me that Fitch settled in Miami, and I later found out that by 1938 Fitch was indeed living at 1418 Collier Avenue in Miami Beach. He told me that Fitch's wife, Myrtle, was from Hattiesburg, Mississippi; that the legendary theatrical agent and producer Pat Casey (1874–1962), who handled them, was also their partner, and that his Pat Casey Agency office in the Mayfair Theater Building in Times Square served as the headquarters of the

Fitch troupe; that rehearsals were held across the Hudson River in New Jersey. At the mention of Emmett Miller, he responded with great familiarity and enthusiasm. But Harrison had joined the Dan Fitch Minstrels in 1926 — he was a boy of fifteen then, and he still remembered the exact date, June 20. By then Emmett Miller had left the troupe. Harrison remained with Fitch, he said, until 1931. Miller, we know, rejoined Fitch in the spring of 1928. Yet Harrison could not remember having ever actually met Miller.

And so it went. Like Seger Ellis, who barely and unclearly remembered him and did not recall performing with him, and like Joe Tarto, the surviving Georgia Cracker who told me, "The only Miller that I knew was Eddie Miller," the rare and dwindling few living others who shared the breezes of Emmett Miller's life could not seem to summon him from the shadows of memory, as if he had moved among them like a ghost, remembered as someone he was not, or remembered not at all.

Emmett Miller's role in *Yes Sir, Mr. Bones* was a small one: two brief blackface routines with fellow old-timer Ches Davis, whose *Cavalcade of Stars* had toured the South during the same lean and fading days as Miller's *All-Southern Revue* and Dan Fitch's *Big Apple Revue*. (One of Davis's troupers, Hoskins L. "Dud" Deterly, had left the *Cavalcade* to join Miller's revue in Charlotte.) Davis also worked in the thirties with Gene "Honey Gal" Cobb, who recorded "The Gypsy" with Miller in 1936.

The first routine recalled part of "Thousand Frogs on a Log." In it Miller performed the swirling yodel that was his bygone signature, here to evoke the howl of the bothersome alley cat. The second was "Hungry Sam," which Miller had recorded with Roy Cowan back in 1928. It here is expanded to include a blackboard-arithmetic bit that is similar to one associated with Abbott and Costello. Miller's cousin Barbara Hardwick recalled him performing this bit in Macon.

Another act in the film, Cotton and Chick Watts — Cotton bug-eyed, blackfaced, and resplendent in a faux-leopard-skin suit; Chick, his lily-white straight-lady — did "The Lion Tamers," the routine that Miller had done as a Sam-and-Bill bit with Dan Fitch.

In the film's opening credits, Miller received fourth billing, while posters for the film ("Sixty Minutes of Mirth and Melody! Gals! Gags! Giggles Galore!"), did not even mention his name. (A lobby card, however, did picture Emmett standing with Ches Davis, Cotton Watts, Slim Williams, and others.)

"Ormond has done an acceptable budget job," said *Variety* in its review of August 1, 1951. Its prognosis was terse: "Turned out as a programmer for supporting booking in the smaller situations, it will get by in that bracket."

In the early fifties Miller reportedly scuffled the Nashville nightclub circuit. In Nashville he may have performed with a piano-player named Mack McWhorter, or Mac McWhirter, or a combination thereof. The tale of Miller and McWhorter, or McWhirter, which has since achieved some circulation, has its origin in a recollection by the musician and writer Doug Green, also known as Ranger Doug of the Western group Riders in the Sky. Some time after *Country* was first published, Doug wrote me a long letter addressing many aspects of the book, among them Emmett Miller, in which context he mentioned his encounter with McWhirter — Doug's spelling — and McWhirter's memories of Miller, matters which Doug later shared with others, and which became a part of Miller lore. In the summer of 1996, I asked Doug to put forth his account in writing for me, which he graciously did in the form of a letter.

"Regarding Mac's recollections of Emmett Miller," Doug said in his letter, "this is the best I can do, and I sure wish it was more:

"Back when Riders in the Sky was just beginning, in the late 1970s — I was just Deputy Doug in those days — I supplemented my meager income by playing in a Dixieland band at Shakey's. The longtime leader of the outfit was a true character, an ex-vaudeville musician, actor, arranger, etc named Mac McWhirter, who had worked tent shows and in all manner of 'the show business.' A longtime trumpeter and singer, he had taken up the piano actively only after literally losing his chops: he couldn't play trumpet with his false teeth. On the plus side, he knew, I think, every song ever written in English before 1955, and he could usually sing a verse or two as well in a tuneful and exuberant, but not particularly mellow, tenor. On the minus side, he rushed tempos with abandon, and many a song resembled a runaway stage. Golf and music were his passions — he was long retired from the accounting profession he'd taken up after his active performing years were done — although he continued to perform to greater or lesser degrees throughout his life. I asked Mac offhandedly about Emmett Miller one night — curious because of your earlier investigations into this shadowy character — and it turns out he not only was quite aware of who Miller was, but that he had met him, perhaps several times, in Nashville, in the heyday (I'm assuming 1940s) of Printer's Alley, the legendary area of the town where refreshment and female flesh could be had in the days before liquor by the drink, strip bars, and massage parlors. My guess is that Miller did some music and/or comedy routine between exotic dances, but that is my own inference; if Mac made it more clear, I've forgotten. In the passage of very nearly two decades I've forgotten anything more specific Mac might have said, and Mac himself has been dead for a decade or more (he died on the golf course, a happy man). The other steady musician on the job, Louis Brown, remembers no such conversation at all, so I'm sorry to report that all I remember is this brief recollection of Miller performing in Nashville, apparently quite unheralded."

Even Doug, it appears, has to some extent become a victim of the Miller memory virus, the mysterious engram-affecting phenomenon that erases or scrambles all remembrance of Miller by those who have crossed his path, or in this case, one who has crossed the path of one who has crossed his path. Ellis, Tarto, Ormond, Harrison — not to mention Bill Callahan, T. D. Kemp — and now, alas, young Doug. I wonder if here the effect is compound: that is, can McWhirter, like Claude Casey, have been one of the rare individuals to have escaped the Miller memory virus? Or was he himself already a viral host at the time of the Shakey's encounter?

On the eve of my departure for Macon, I summoned to my computer monitor a file from a diskette on which I had stored much Miller data. I found that entire Miller files had been eaten away, had in whole or in part been spontaneously obliterated or reduced to ASCII gibberish. I had never known something like this to happen. Furthermore the destruction was ongoing, viral; upon my return from Macon, I found it to have worsened, to have inexplicably spread to other diskettes. I have for some time now feared, and as I write these words I continue to fear, that the hard-disk memory itself will succumb at any time, that all of this will sputter and vanish; that such will be the horrible, and yet somehow devastatingly perfect, end of this ghostly hunt, this mad labor for which no audience exists, this accrescence of consciousness that has grown now into a book — a book so bereft of commercial potential that not even I, who can skin a snake without its knowing it, can hope to con the most benighted and gullible of publishers into paying a decent dollar for it. Then again . . .

I think Emmett Miller is evil," my buddy Carol said to me not long ago. I asked her what she meant, and she told me that she thought Emmett Miller was devouring my life.

Maybe she's right. As I write this, it's a beautiful summer day, with a beautiful blue sky. There's a gym a few blocks away with an outdoor pool on the roof. I'm a member; I spent all last summer lying by that pool, but I haven't been there yet this year. I've got a contract for a magazine story that will pay me thirty grand, and I haven't done a stitch of work on it. I've got an unfinished novel that's the best thing I've ever written, and I haven't looked at it for months. I've got a beautiful and brilliant girlfriend that I haven't talked to in five weeks. I could be on a deserted beach somewhere. And yet here I am, every day, with Emmett. Whatever this disease is, it must end soon. He is wherever I look. As one sees the passing figure of a lost lover in glancing at every stranger of remotest resemblance in the street, so I can hear no song, read no line without perceiving the ghostly presence of Emmett therein, nexus *ad infinitum,* nexus *ad insaniam.*

[A note — clinical observation, if you will — upon reading the above two years later: I haven't talked to the woman named Carol in over a year. Perhaps she truly did come to feel that Emmett Miller, and therefore I, were of the Devil, or that I, independently of Emmett, strode side by side with the Dark One. It's summer again. I still haven't been to the gym, but I now no longer have any interest in the pool on its roof. I did hear mention, however, of a fine swimming-pool at a fine remote hotel in old Morocco, and I did go there with an inexplicable sense of urgency to lie in the lush gardens nearby it. I've got a contract for a different magazine story, one that will this time pay me fifty grand, and I haven't done a stitch of work on it. I've still got the unfinished novel that's the best thing I've ever written, and at which I now haven't looked for years. And now there's also another, envisioned novel, far more beguiling and greater a work, that lies before me, awaiting me. I've no longer got a beautiful and brilliant girlfriend that I haven't talked to in five weeks. I lied, anyway: there were two, for a while there were three, of them. Whatever: they're gone. If one of them should return before these words go irrevocably to press — as I must believe I will allow them someday, soon, to do, I can re-singularize the matter, which matters not. I could still be on a deserted beach somewhere, but I've been on several since that musing, have sought my escape herefrom through flight to distant shores, from the isles of Egadi to Bora Bora to the sacred Akamas peninsula of Cyprus, and the only one, the only deserted beach, left for me, for now, is that of penury. Yes, much has changed, and yet the last lines of the above paragraph remain steadfast and true. The end is near. After twenty years and more, at 3:13 in the dark of a morning whose date I do not know, I swear it: the end is near. There will be no more rewriting, no more tooling of obsessive detail. (It is now 4:03 as I reread these few rewritten and retooled, and ultimately likely destined for deletion, *della mia mano destra,* words.) Yes, now, at last, no more. I shall be free. I shall again know love, or at least masturbation. And I take this opportunity to warn you, and to beseech you to warn yours in turn: bang that babania, drink that booze, shovel down those pills; but stay away from that spook called Emmett. It is going on twenty-three years now as I write this. Others have raised families. I, like the saburra of a discarded Borges tale, have raised an obelisk to the back-alley gods and windblown garbage of meaninglessness.]

"Some recalled his 1952 appearances at the Rainbow Room in the Printer's Alley district of Nashville," I wrote regarding Emmett Miller in my 1994 Emmett Miller article in the *Journal of Country Music,* in a passage that also alluded to "a piano-player named Mack McWhorter." I may have based this statement in part on my memory of Doug Green's earlier letter, in part on statements in a one-page article that Charles Wolfe wrote for the British publication *Old Time Music* in 1978, where Miller is said to have surfaced "in the Rainbow Room in Nashville's Printer's Alley." Wolfe's following sentence refers to "Mack McWhorter, who knew Miller quite well." When Wolfe recycled this information for a new one-page article in an American publication in 1994, Miller in 1952 is "back on the club circuit, working with a pianist named Mack McWhorter." In his liner notes to the 1996 Sony CD, Wolfe tempers his statement: "Some say he was working in Nashville's club district, Printer's alley, with a piano player named Mack McWhorter in 1952." Wolfe in the past has not responded to inquiries concerning his Miller research; and, as Doug Green has told us, McWhorter, or McWhirter, has long since departed for the putting green of eternity.

By the year of Miller's reputed spell in Nashville, a new alchemy was brewing. They called it rock 'n' roll. New, yes, and without burnt cork, but neither stranger nor so deeply different from Miller's own alchemy. By the time it took hold of America, Emmett Miller was forgotten.

Though no one knew for sure, it seemed not unreasonable to think that he may have lived through the sixties, perhaps into the seventies; and for a long time I wondered if he may have been alive when I started this search. But that wondering is done.

Emmett Miller ended up where he began: in Macon. He didn't stay married long. Bernice was the sister of a liquor-seller, but she had little tolerance for her husband's drunkenness, and he seemed none too interested in getting right. As far as is known, Miller never sought help for his alcoholism. Men with trick voices rarely do.

When his short-lived and childless marriage to Bernice fell apart, he took to staying for spells at the home of his sister and her husband. He also took a second-story room over a storefront down on Poplar Street near Broadway. He remained a known character in

Macon. Del Ward Napier, who began working as a local television personality in the late fifties, interviewed him twice on WMAC-TV. There are no records of the broadcasts, and Del has no memories of them, other than that Emmett was "a delightful guest." He got by on the kindness of family and friends and barroom strangers. In time there was nothing left but whisky and smoke and the verdigris of memory.

The last address he had was his sister's: 3854 Brownley Drive. It was the address given when he entered Macon Hospital on February 28, 1962, a few weeks after his sixty-second birthday.

He died there, a month later, on the Thursday afternoon of March 29, 1962. The cause of death was stated to be carcinoma of the upper third of the esophagus and recurrent carcinoma of puriform sinus, with malnutrition and dehydration cited as contributing conditions. On his certificate of death, in the space indicating the usual occupation of the deceased, it said simply: Entertainer.

"I can't give you anything but love, baby . . ."

William Faulkner, Emmett Miller. They both died in 1962, the one venerated, the other forgotten. The end, perhaps, of something. It was the year of Dee Dee Sharp and "Mashed Potato Time," of Little Eva and "The Loco-Motion." Bob Dylan was recording in New York, the Rolling Stones were coming into being in London.

"Mashed Potatoes started long time ago." In the beginning was the Word. Λόγος — a word, the Word, translated, rendered, merely as such, and as such making no sense; a word, the Word, which encompasses all that is ineffable and that is mystery. From Heraclitus to Heidegger, that word, that Word, whose merest meaning is "word," has remained unfathomed, has been all there is of light and dark, a word of more meanings than there have been breath and

breeze since that beginning whose own breath and breeze were λόγος itself, which we, throughout all time, for all our eloquence, can call only *word,* or, in primitive exaltation, the Word, as if the need to express ourselves were the one almighty and preternatural power, which preceded beginning and will endure beyond end, un-created and everlasting. And, from the pre-Socratics to the lesser and more cerebral attempts throughout the ages of unlocking the source, the Word, Dee Dee Sharp's explication bears as much fine wisdom as any: "Mashed Potatoes started long time ago" — the endless rhythm and wail: the sound and fury of Shakespeare be-come, with a common definite article raised from the dirt to re-splend in brilliance as a maker of meter anew, the sound and the fury of Faulkner; an old song made new, to shake souls, then as now, now as then. "The thing that hath been, it is that which shall be; and that which is done is that which shall be done: and there is no new thing under the sun." Lovesick never changes, but "Lovesick Blues" sure can make it new, as Uncle Ez said. "The influence," said Bob Dylan in 1965, the year he forsook fraud for that ancient soul-shaking thing made new; "the influence," he said, "is all sort of mashed up, you know, like the influence isn't in its given form anymore." The influence was the mist from the wave. "I mean," he said twenty years later, "I don't copy from guys who are under fifty years old." Jimmie Rodgers — his ghost, his spirit, the lost winding echo of his fine blue yodel — rides in that god-wrought, demon-fendered, rhythm-borne Buick 6 that Dylan drove; and forgotten Emmett Miller — his ghost, his spirit, the lost winding echo of that an-cienter, weirder fine blue yodel that startled the sparrows in the Asheville trees so long ago — is the lovesick groom still waiting at that altar. There ain't no use of me working so hard; got me a debu-tante with a mama in a fancy graveyard. Elvis, with his candy-ass ways, could not kill rock 'n' roll. Men such as Emmett Miller and the even more forgotten men they stole from, and those in turn who stole from him — holy thieves all — ensured with their long-ago howls — howls you can hear among those in "Sympathy for the Devil" — that, under whatever name, or namelessly, it would endure. As it is writ: to kill a cop is a beautiful thing, but to do the police in different voices is far more blessed and far more potent magic still.

"History" descends ultimately from the root ιστορ, which connotes inquiry. True history seeks, it does not answer; for the deeper we seek, the deeper we descend from knowledge to mystery, which is the only place where wisdom abides. Yes, Mashed Potatoes started long time ago. But it came not *ex nihilo.* And in the end, it doesn't mean a damn. Just turn the volume up, and if whoever's making the noise knows that so-called creativity ain't got shit to do with power or beauty, you'll feel that gust from that unknown place; and that gust, as Deacon Jones said, shall set you free.

There was an obituary in the Macon papers. It was as plain and brief as the obituaries of the others who had died thereabouts in the last few days. The funeral service was held on that Saturday morning, March 31, at Memorial Chapel on Cherry Street. Presiding were Rev. Allen Evans and Dr. Ernest Saloom, pastor of the Tabernacle Baptist Church on Second Street.

Miller's background was Methodist. I wondered how a Baptist pastor had come to preside at his funeral. I found my way to Rev. Saloom, who kindly took the trouble to answer to my inquiry. But his response was like that of so many others whose memories Miller had eluded. Apologizing for his inability to help, he stated: "I frankly do not recall any information about Mr. Miller, or how I came to preside at his funeral."

The undertaker's file lists the songs that were played at the service: "The Old Rugged Cross," "Precious Lord, Hold My Hand," "Moonlight and Roses."

He was buried beside his mother and father in the family plot at Fort Hill Cemetery.

I thought back to November 1977, the month that *Country* was originally published. I was in Macon with my friend Delbert McClinton, who was recording an album there. If only I had then known that I was walking the streets that harbored the solution to the mystery that had so provocatively beguiled me in *Country*. Miller's sister then was still alive, and Miller's ex-wife, Bernice, and his niece, Marguerite, as well.

But by the time I returned to Macon in May 1996, they were gone: Bernice had died, of a ruptured aneurysm of the aorta, at the Medical Center of Central Georgia on January 25, 1984; the widowed Nora Belle — arteriosclerotic and hypertense, like her mother — of a sudden heart attack, on January 24, 1987; her daughter, Emmett's niece, not long after.

Even Fort Hill Cemetery in East Macon had been given over to the ghosts: abandoned, with no caretaker, no sexton, it was now the only city cemetery without even a map to indicate the locations of its plots, or a record of who was buried there. We were warned repeatedly and ominously that it was in a bad part of town: "You don't want to go there." But we went there anyway, Bret and I; and somehow, amid the dense, desolate acres of graves and weed, Bret came upon the stone that seemed to mark the end of that mystery, that obsession, that had beguiled for twenty years and more. I'll never forget his voice in the dusk: "Hey, Nick, over here."

It was a crude prone slab upon the ground, chiseled with his name, the date of his birth, and the date of his death. I cannot recall ever having looked with such wonderment and such satisfaction on an object so lackluster and so plain.

One of the few left who seemed to remember Emmett Miller was his nephew through marriage, Edgar J. Parent, the widower of his niece. Now in his eightieth year, E.J. kindly told me what he could.

"He was a rounder," he said. "All he knew was vaudeville. All he knew was the stage." He said that Emmett drank a lot: "If that man hadn't drunk so much, he would've been a millionaire." He told me about Emmett and Hank Williams getting drunk together, like that time they wrote "Lovesick Blues" and Emmett ended up giving it over to Hank. I did not feel it right, somehow, to disabuse him of this tale, to tell him that "Lovesick Blues" was written before Williams was born, and certainly not by the uncle of his late wife. Ironically, a week later I would read an unpublished short story by John Fahey in which Emmett Miller writes "Lovesick Blues," Hank Williams makes it famous, and in the end Miller turns out to be Hank's true father. This would get me to pondering the possible occult kinship between Fahey and the curiously named Parent.

E.J. told me that Emmett's brother-in-law wouldn't tolerate Emmett's drinking; Emmett would go down and stay with the railroad people, down where they stayed, down the railroad yards. He told me about Emmett having been married, before Bernice, to a gal up in Canada, or so they said.

Right, right. But what was he like? Was he a nice guy, or what? It was hard to remember. "You might say he was a nice guy. When he was sober, he was a nice guy."

There was one thing he clearly remembered: "He always had a good press on his trousers, and his shoes were shined."

I began then to feel that all that I had written regarding him of the trick voice and creasèd trousers might be brought to fuller form and harmony in, well, perhaps, a book. A small book, of course; but a book nonetheless. Yes. All I have to do, maybe, is get Emmett Miller's name out of the fucking title. I remember, some years ago, Greil Marcus told me he was writing a book that was ostensibly about Bob Dylan's Basement Tapes but was really about Dock Boggs. The book he was talking about came to be published as *Invisible Republic.* Yeah, maybe that was the way to go. Trick voices, trick titles. Yeah. *Empire of Evil: William Faulkner's Karaoke Tapes.* No, no. But not to worry; it would come to me. Surely thus should I make my fortune, and in the service of knowledge most pure. And surely then no man should say of me when ghost I be: he *could have been* a millionaire. Then, truly, Bret Wood, like unto me, should know the rewards justly due him. Then, truly, Bret Wood, and indeed all those along the way who heartened rather than scorned me in the course of these many-yeared studies; then should they share the bounty of my table. Yes. Then. I swore it. Thus the illness in full of this labor came to be.

I have fancied these words a culmination, a bringing to an end. But now I begin to feel that questions remain. What of the five years between 1919, when Miller's career seems to have begun, and 1924, when we have our first glimpse of that career? Who were his inspirers — from whom, so to speak, did he steal? Who was Walter Rothrock? Did Bernice have nice legs? Should I entrust these matters to lesser men, or delve on, deeper into the dark?

But, no, enough is enough. I entrust the younger generation of Miller scholars to pursue all that lies unanswered.

Youth, I salute you. I place upon your shoulders the mantle of this mission, in your hands its fate. May your journey to Fort Hill Cemetery be golden-bowered and fruitful; may Lue Wanna and her Savage Dancers love you as they have loved no other; and may the ghost of Joe Tarto smile down upon you. Go now, and seek closure. Selah.

INDEX

Unless otherwise indicated, titles in quotations marks are of songs.

Index

Index

Beck, Martin, 175

Beckett, Samuel, 220, 253–254

"beer dance," 10

Behn, Aphra, 10

Beiderbecke, Bix, 153

Bell, Alexander Graham, 40

Bell, Chichester, 40

Ben Harney's Rag-Time Instructor, 187

Ben-Hur (film), 68

Bennett, John, 197. *See also* Bernard, Alfred "Al"

Bentley, Gladys, 149

Benton, Brook, 99

Berkeley, Busby, 179

Berle, Milton, 256

Berlin, Irving, 13, 44, 221–223, 225

Berliner Records, 103–104

Bernard, Alfred "Al," 33, 191, 197–198, 206, 217, 220, 225–227

Bernard, Rhoda, 221

Berrigan, Bunny, 153

Berry, Leslie, 72, 76, 83, 170, 172, 245–246; as interlocutor, 71, 79, 82

Bert, Flo, 162

Betty Boop, 31

Beulah (radio show), 284

Bevacqua, James, 243

Beyond Good and Evil (Nietzsche), 27

Bible, the, vii, 119, 138, 190, 192–193, 215–216

Biese, Paul, 98, 155

Big Apple Revue, 265–266, 286

"Big Bad Bill Is Sweet William Now," 58, 60, 62–63, 161

Big Boy (Broadway show), 49

Big Broadcast, The (film), 153, 179

"Big Footed Nigger in the Sandy Lot," 181

Bigger than Barnum's (film), 71

Biggs, Bunny "Jamup," 182

Big Parade, The (film), 94

Bijou Theatre (Boston), 174

Billboard magazine, 61, 66–67, 182, 249; "Minstrelsy" columns, 6, 42, 51, 76, 173, 178, 241, 242, 246, (final

column) 267, (quoted on Miller) 77, 78, 170, 241–250 *passim,* 254, 260

Bill Boyd and His Cowboy Ramblers, 122

Billroy's Comedians, 267–268

Billy Kersands' Minstrels. *See* Kersands, Billy

Bingham, Ralph, 131

Birch and Birch, 59, 60

"Birth of the Blues, The," 161

Black Bottom (dance), 67, 130

Black Brothers, Jim and Joe, 229, 230

Blackface, White Noise: Jewish Immigrants in the Hollywood Melting Pot (Rogin), 12, 178

blackface acts: beginning of, 10–11, 15, 20, 274, (demise of) 228, 251; blacks in, 20–24, 72, 179, 183, 190, 250, 280, (blacking-up abandoned) 228; black v. white, argued, 13–14; comedy routines (recorded), 30, 34, 100–109, 147, 182, 190, 197, 220, 230, 234, (dialect songs) 33, 102–104, 241 (*see also* coon songs); females in, 143, 228, 243, 256–257; Jews in, 12–13, 29, 35, 255; minstrelsy without, 123, 265; in talking pictures, 178, 179; transvestite acts, 255–257; white routines, 24, 168, 174, 179, (Miller and) *see* Miller, Emmett Dewey; (two-man white teams) 104–107; yodeling as aspect of, 65

Black Manhattan (Johnson), 184, 195

black Westerns, 285

Blake, Blind, 66

Blake, Eubie, 189

Blake (Delany), 26

Bland, Bobby, 125

Bland, James A., 20, 23, 25, 194, 230

"Blind Willie McTell," 135

Blonde on Blonde (album), 133, 215

Blood of Jesus (film), 106

Bloom, Rube, 165, 243

303

Index

Index

Index

Dylan, Bob (Robert Zimmerman), 99, 135, 136, 138, 162, 206, 216, 219, 257, 298; influences on, 132–134, 151, 294; and "railroad men," 57, 204; recordings, 113–114, 211, 212, 215, 293, (notes to) 217; and rock 'n' roll, 214; and talking blues, 108, 116

Earle, Gene, 63
"Early Bird Catches the Worm, The," 107
Early History of Negro Minstrelsy (Brown), 11
Economist, The (periodical), 28
Eddie and Oscar (guitarists), 207
Edison, Thomas A., 40
Edison Kinetoscope, 178
Edison Records, 33, 149, 155, 197, 220–228 *passim*; cylinders, 101, 122, 226
Edmonds, Shepherd, 23
Edwards, Cliff "Ukulele Ike," 43, 44, 143, 149, 154, 157–158, 262
Edwards, Dave, 151
Edwards, Harry Stillwell, 40–41
Egyptology, 138, 202
Ehrich, Sam, 45, 162
Eliot, T. S., 40, 163, 213
Ellington, Duke, 60, 190
Ellis, Seger, 145, 149, 154, 229–232, 279, 286, 289
Elwood, Ola, 64, 85
Embassy Dance Orchestra, 231
Emerson Records, 197, 255
Emmett, Daniel Decatur, 7, 14–15, 72, 275
Emmett, Joseph Kline "Fritz," 227–228
Emmett Miller: The Minstrel Man from Georgia (CD), 4, 50, 62
Emmet Miller Acc. by His Georgia Crackers (album), 4, 132
Emmett Miller and His Varieties of 1932 (act), 249
"Emmett's Lullaby," 228
Empedocles, 213–214

Encylopaedia Britannica, 237
Encyclopedia of African-American Culture and History, 23
Eneas Africanus (Edwards), 40–41, 48, 235
England, American minstrelsy spreads to, 11, 12, 15
English, Peggy, 155
E. Payson Re and His University Five, 129
Erlanger Theatre (Atlanta), 91
Ernst, Max, 136
Essence (dance), 22
Essex Dialect Dictionary (Gepp), 238
Estes, Sleepy John, 112, 212
Estlow, Bert, 149
Ethiopian Serenaders, 15, 16; Gavitt's Original, 19
Etting, Ruth, 155
Étude music magazine, 186
Europe, James Reese, 33
Evans, Rev. Allen, 295
Evans, Sir Arthur, 203
Evans, George "Honey Boy," 32, 86, 247
Evans, Roy, 164–168
"Evening with the Minstrels, An," 101
Everett, Billy, 43, 170, 172
"Everybody's Smiling Down in Dixie," 84
"Every Race Has a Flag but the Coons," 101
Eviston, Jim, 234
"Evolution" (dialogue recording), 241
Evolution of Ragtime, The: A Musical Suite of Six Songs Tracing and Illustrating Negro Music (Johnson), 186
Excelsior Quartette, 117, 120–121, 124, 125, 226
Exile on Main St. (album), 22

Fahey, John, 297
"Faking Blues, The," 199
Farmer's Register (Virginia), 10, 19
Fashion Plate Minstrels, 173
Father of the Blues (Handy), 31

309

Index

Index

Index

Index

Index

Maximum Poems, The (Olson), 206
"Mayor of Dixie" (blackface routine), 105, 196
Mazziotta, Frank, 243
Meachum, Homer, 38, 266
"Me and the Devil Blues," 151
"Mean Old Bedbug Blues," 141
"Medicine Show, The," 229–231, 233
medicine shows, 26–27, 97, 168
Meet Me at the Fair (film), 284
Megansett Tea Room (Cape Cod), 129
"Melancholy Mood," 158
Mellencamp, John, 133
Mellnotte, Roy and Hughie, 77, 78, 79, 82, 87, 89
"Memphis Blues, The," 31–33, 57, 189
Memphis Jug Band, 112, 211
Mencken, H. L., 227
"Me No Speaka Good English," 220
Meredith, O. A., 77, 78, 95
Metropolitan Orchestra, 103–104, 186
Metropolitan Theatre (Atlanta), 233, 234
MGM (Metro-Goldwyn-Mayer), 264; MGM Movietone Act (film), 167
Miami Daily News, 69
Miami Herald, 68, 69
Michaelson, Nick, 222
Midnight Airedales, 162
"Midnight Call," 150
"Midnight Cannonball," 205
Midnighters, 209
Miff Mole's Molers, 143, 196
Miles, Lizzie, 117
"Milk Cow Blues," 112
Miller, Eddie, 168, 286
Miller, Emmett Dewey
    PERSONAL LIFE: alcoholism, 259–260, 270, 292, 297; birth and death, 5–8, 36–37, 202, 293, 295–296; childhood, 37–39; marriage, 270, 271, 292, 297
    PROFESSIONAL LIFE: and blackface, 3, 67, 77, 87, 91–94, 115, 259, 267–268, 277, (begins) 38, 273, (blackface dialogue) 100, 107–108,

129–131, 144–146, 229–230, 234, (minstrel movie) 282, 284–285, 286–287, (out of blackface) 43, 264 (*see also* photographs of, *below*); early career, 41–48, (first stage appearance) 38, (performs in Asheville) 49–52, 58–60, 61, 81–82, 97, 255; with Field, *see* Al G. Field Minstrels; with Fitch, *see* Dan Fitch Minstrels; influence of, 5, 35, 53, 63, 66, 96–97, 114, 115, 144; influences on, 227–228; minstrelsy tradition and, 9, 14, 35; organizes or joins shows, 248–250, 260–268 *passim*, 277–278, 286; photographs of, 278, (in blackface) 4–5, 59, 67, 69, 83, 94, 264; popularity of, 49, 213, 228, 236, (decline in sales) 99–100, 156, 176, 229, 232–233, (forgotten) 132, 168–169, 265, 267, 271, 272, 286–296 *passim*; recordings by, 46–49, 61–66, 125–126, 127, 132, 144, 156, 161, 176, 190, 197, 226, 231, (British and international) 142, 143, 160, 162, (CD collection, 1996) 4, 47, 62, 292, (dialogues) 100, 128, 254, 255, (first and last commercial) 44–45, 258–259, (with Georgia Crackers) *see* Georgia Crackers, (with revived Field troupe) 242–243 (*see also* Okeh Records); singing and speaking style, 63–65, 124, 155–158, 163, 166, 259, 269, ("clarinet voice") 87–89, 93–94, 245, (and "cracker papa") 147, 160, (stammer) 90, 115, 127–128, 145, (yodeling) 64–65, 68–71, 99–100, 128, 132, 286; song written by, 60; in vaudeville, 77, 177, 183, 255
Miller, Mrs. Emmett Dewey (Bernice Calhoun), 270, 271, 292, 296, 297
Miller, Flournoy E., 105, 106, 196, 285
Miller, Frank, 76, 79
Miller, Glenn, 169
Miller, John Pink, 36–39 *passim*, 73, 94, 95, 96, 270, 271

Index

Index

Index

Index

Index

Index